THE CITY

ANDREW SAVULICH

THE CITY

NEW YORK SPOT NEWS AND STREET PHOTOGRAPHY 1980 – 1995

With an essay by Brendan Bernhard

STEIDL

To Mary Jo, Nick and Will

“If there’s one thing you can say about my work, it’s that it is compulsive, repetitive … obsessive.”

Andrew Savulich

Social and cultural transition is usually hard to gauge. New York in the 1980s and the first half of the 1990s was clearly a different place than it is now. The city was more violent and more street weird. Times Square was still wonderfully sleazy. Andrew Savulich is a photographer living and working in New York City. His work is a unique mix of spot news and street photography – capturing scenes of crime as well as everyday life. The startling immediacy of the moment prevails in his black-and-white images on which he provides handwritten captions. What at first seems like objective commentary soon reveals the photographer’s dry ironic tone, at times bordering on black humour.

THE CITY

IN A SEPARATE PLACE

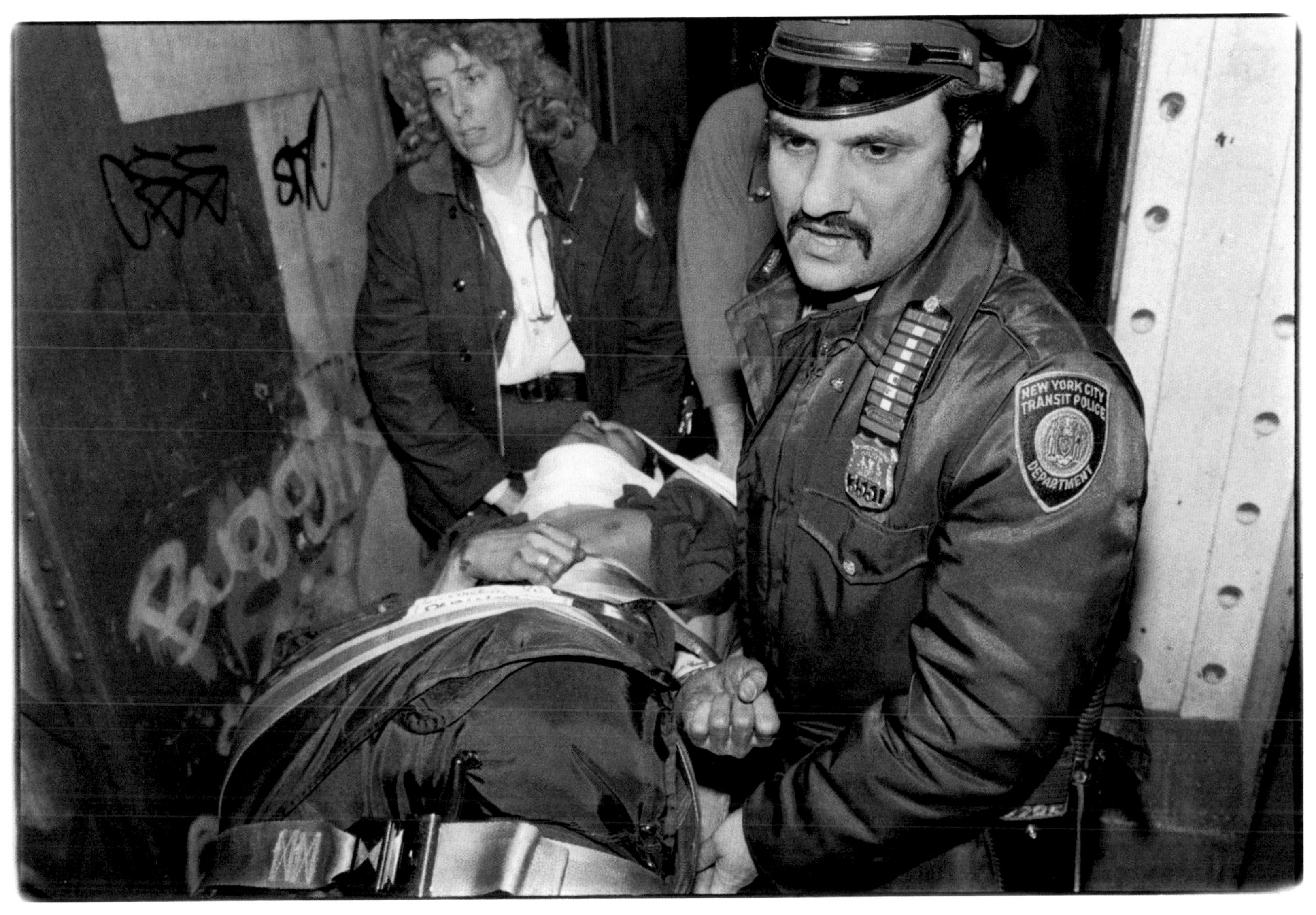

MAN FALLS BETWEEN SUBWAY CARS.

1984

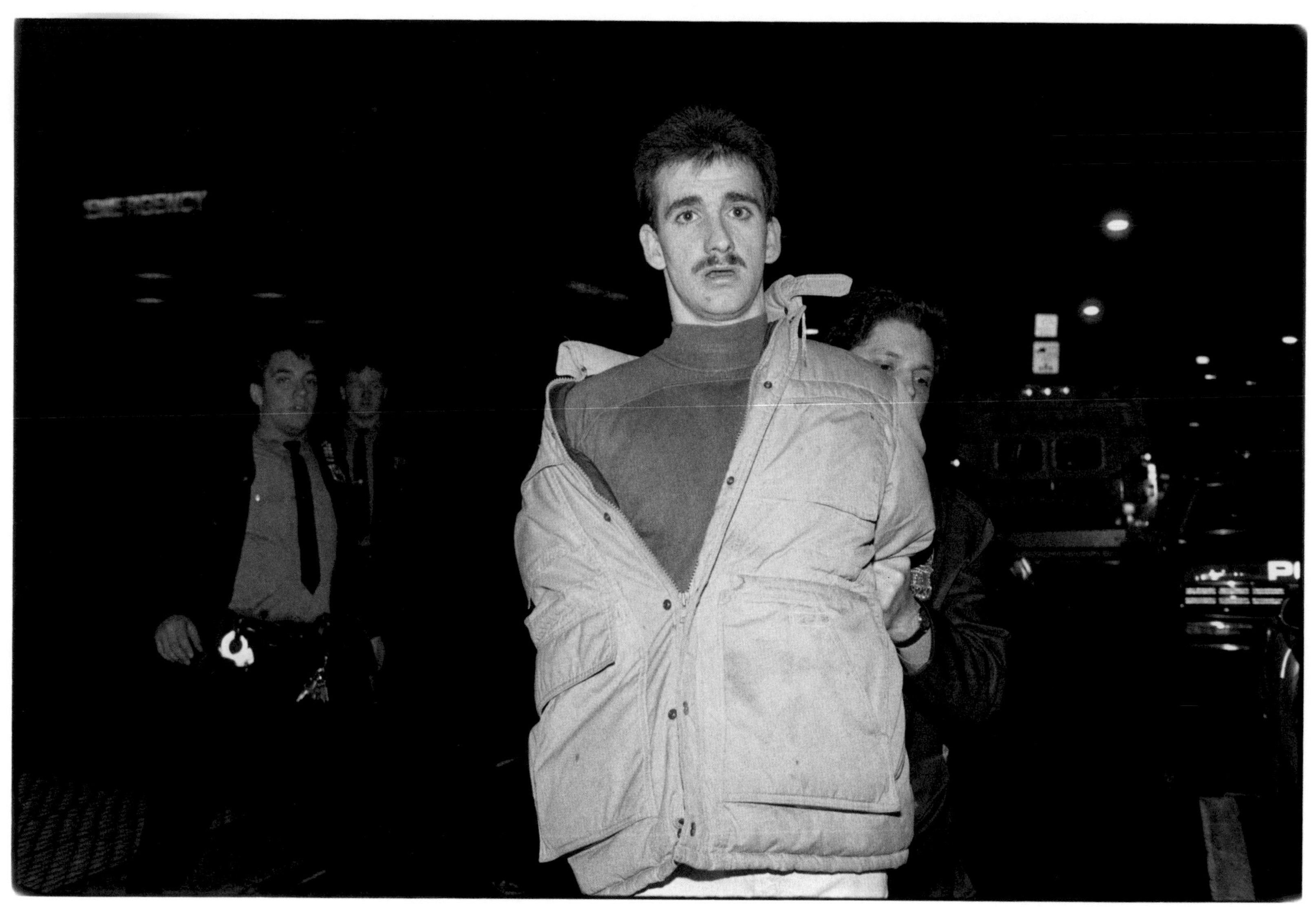

STABBING SUSPECT LEAVING HOSPITAL AFTER BEING IDENTIFIED BY STABBING VICTIM.

1989

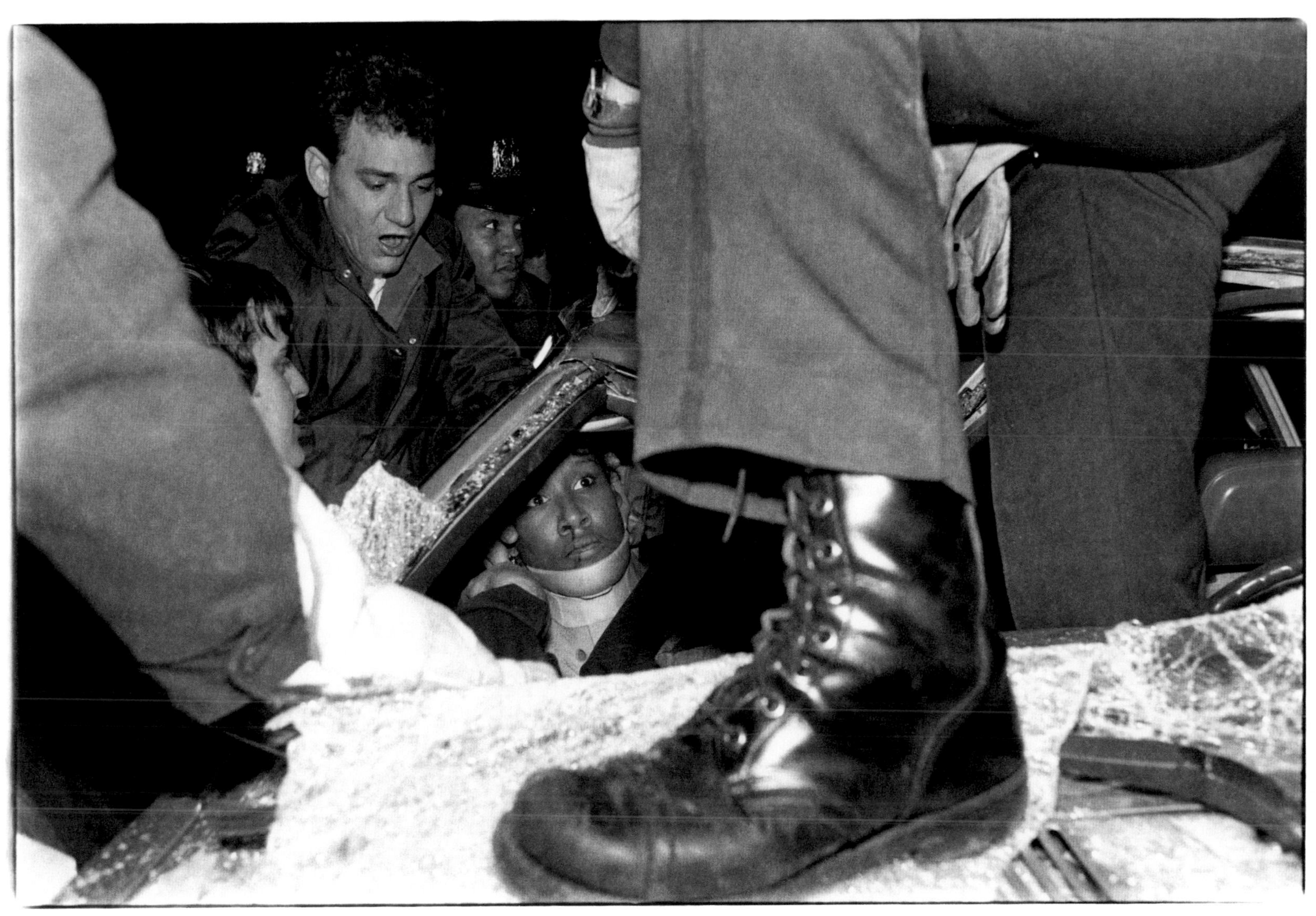

WOMAN IN SHOCK TRAPPED IN CAR WRECK.

1984

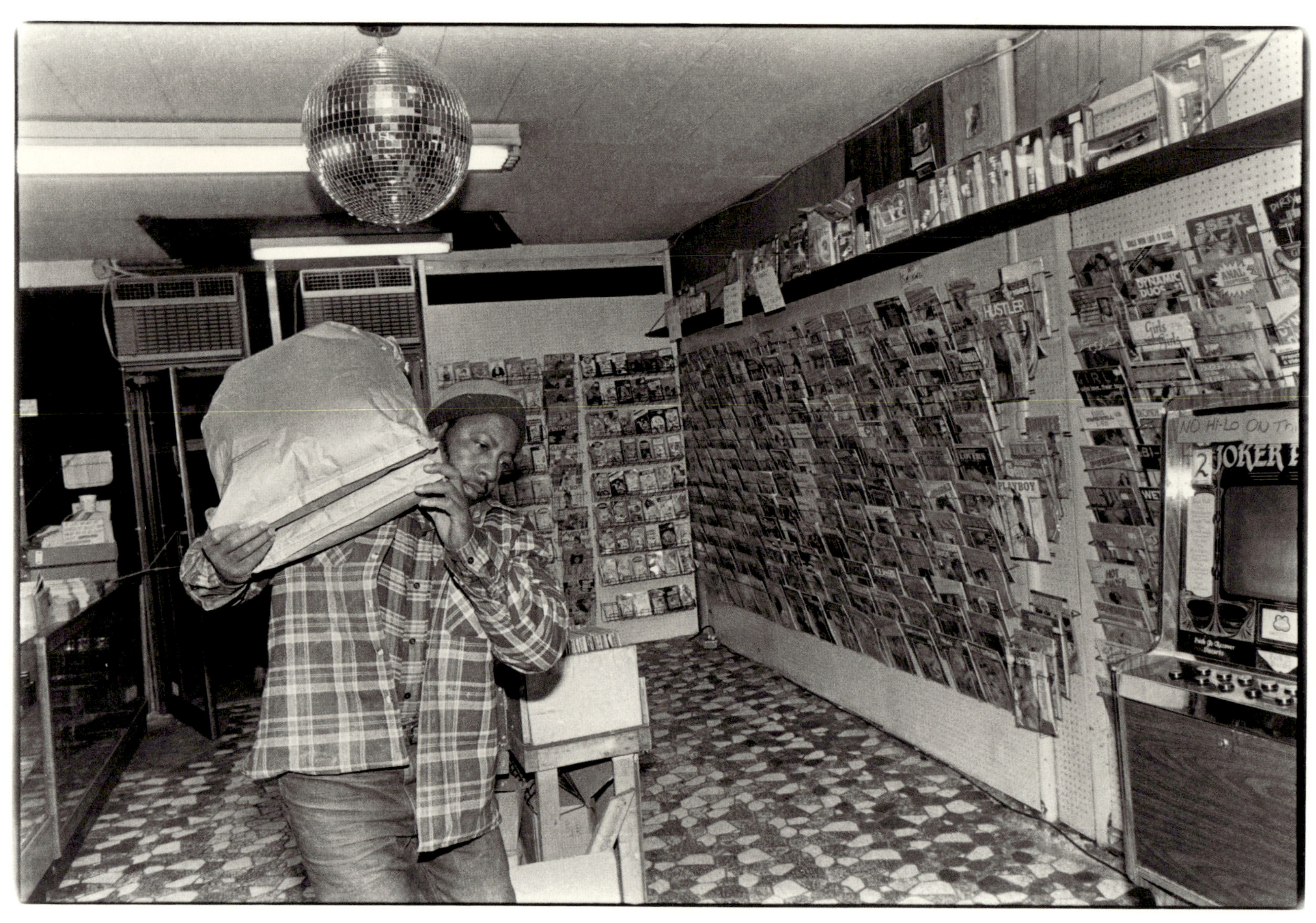

MAN DELIVERING BIRDSEED TO SEX SHOP.

1985

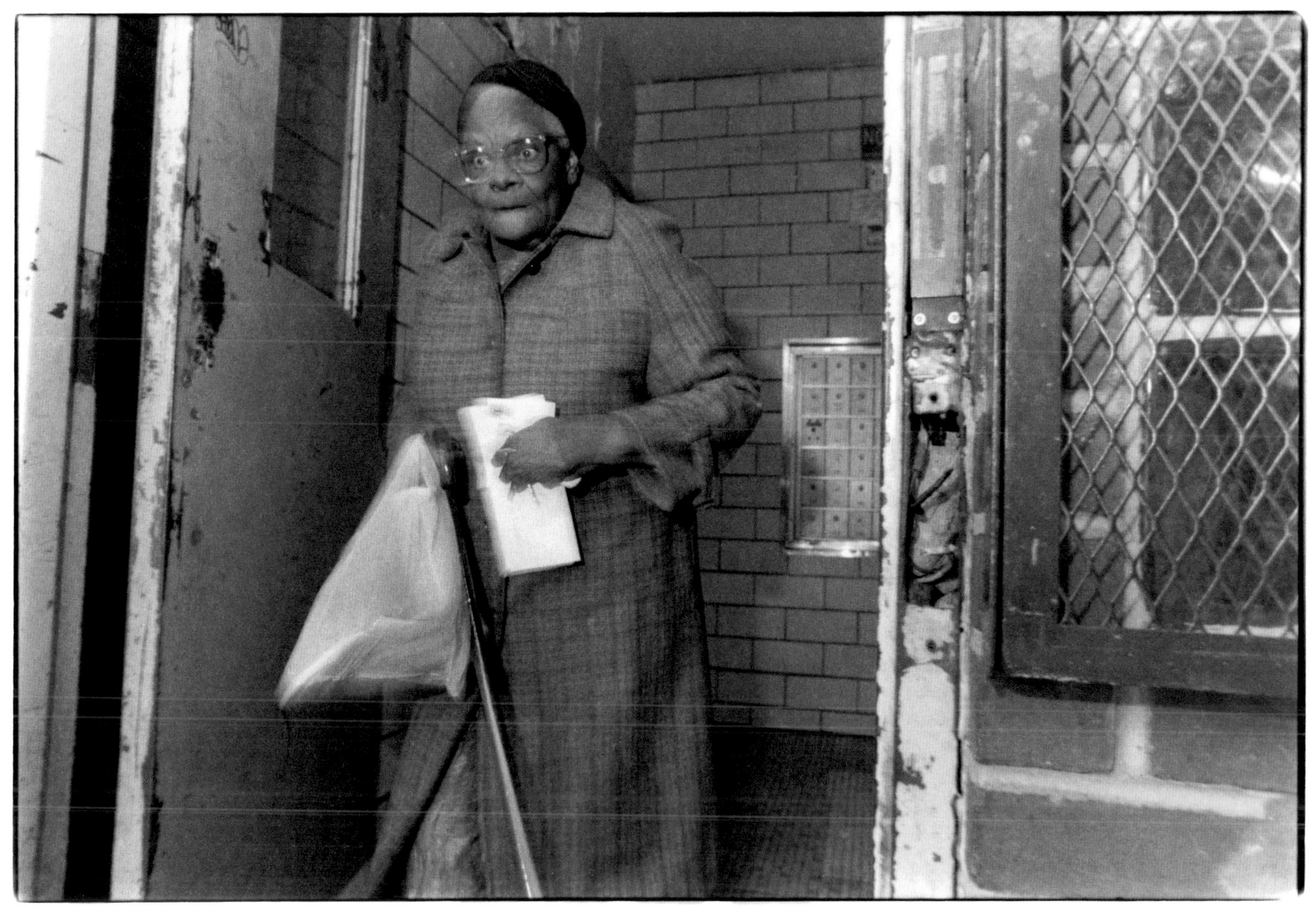

WOMAN — WHO HAS LIVED IN THE SAME HOUSING PROJECT FOR THE PAST 36 YRS. — GOES OUTSIDE FOR ERRANDS.

1994

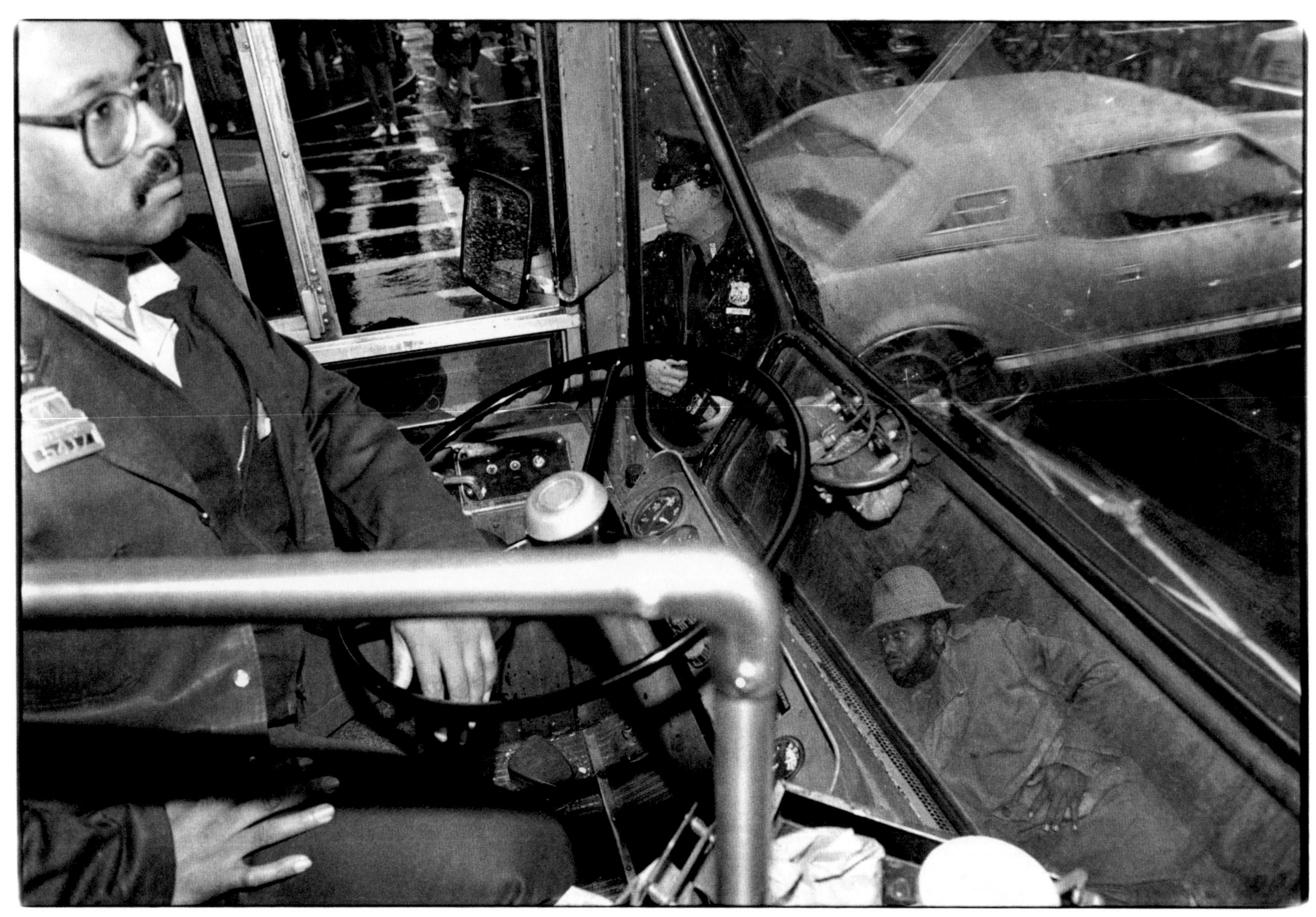

BUS DRIVER WAITING FOR AMBULANCE.

1987

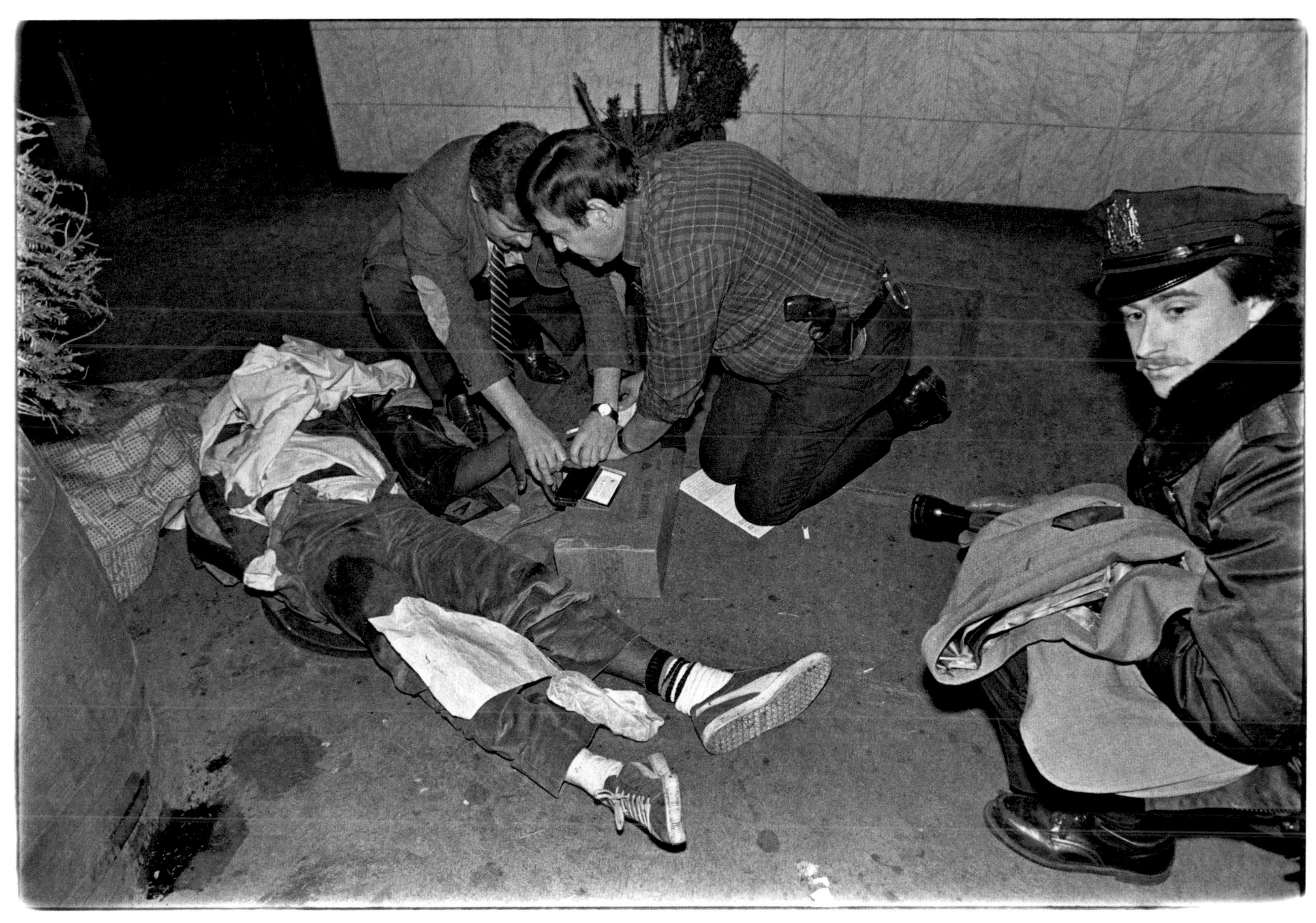

DETECTIVES FINGER PRINT DEAD ROBBERY/MURDER SUSPECT.

1984

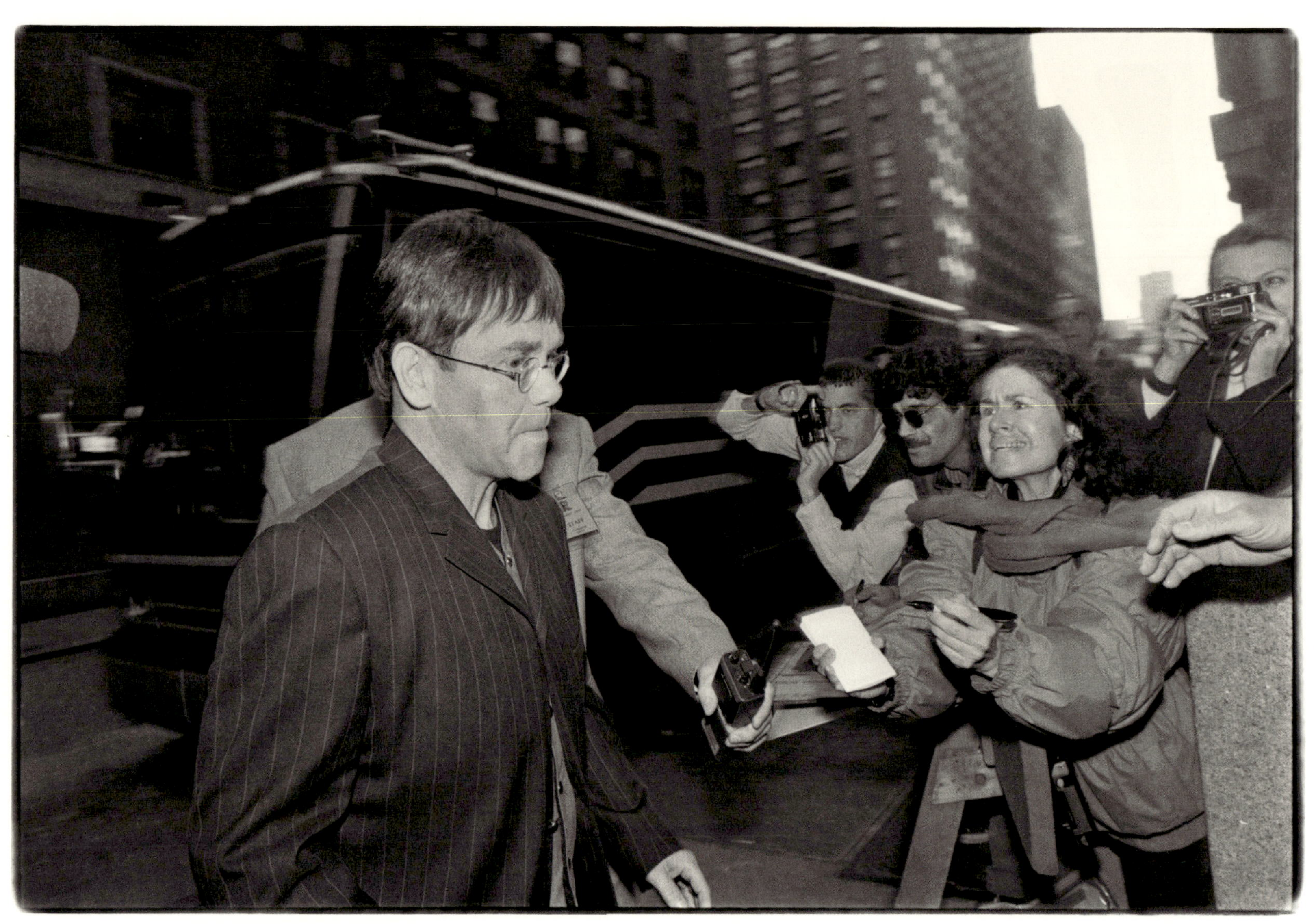

ROCK STAR IGNORING FANS AT STAGE DOOR.

1994

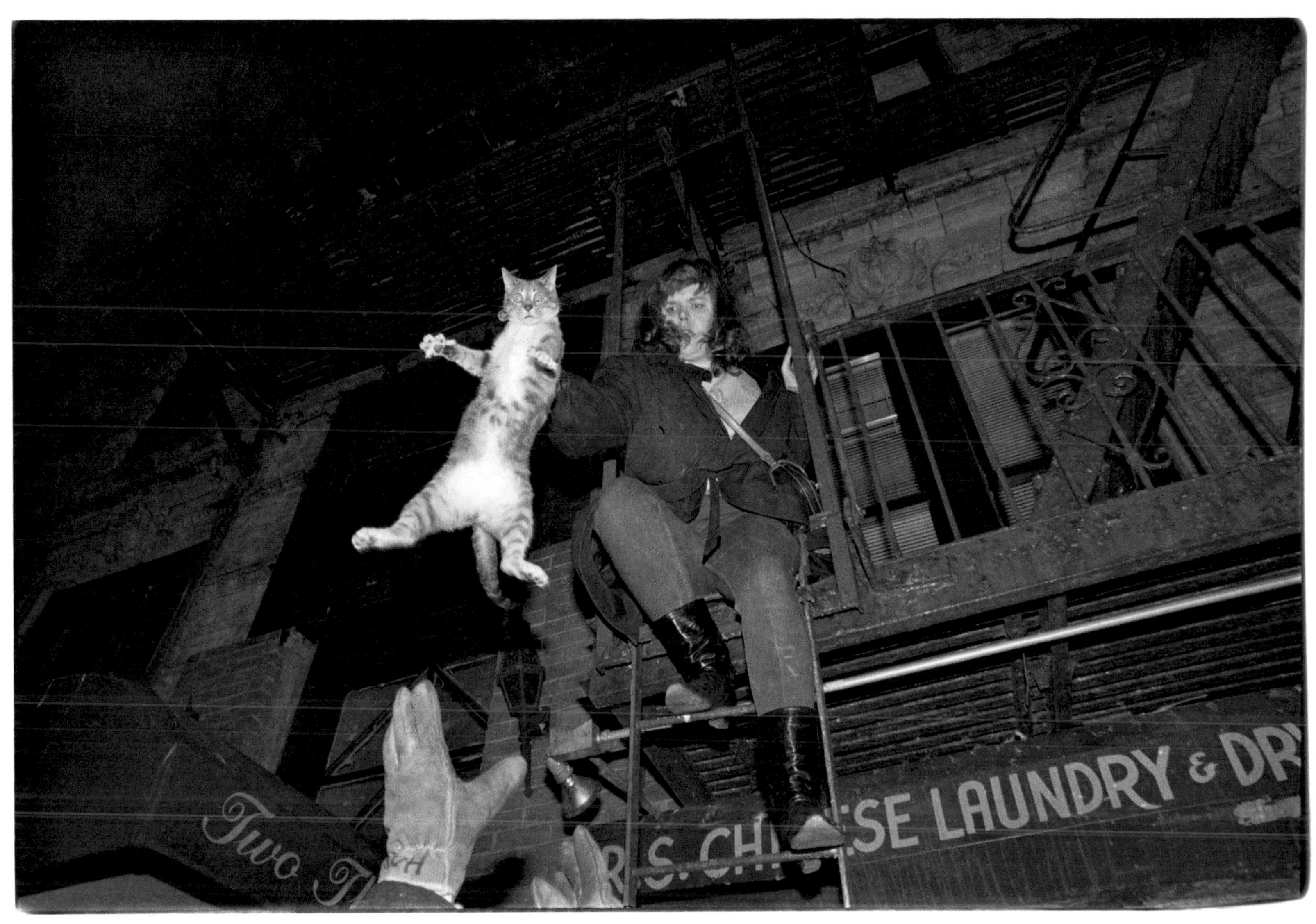

WOMAN WITH CAT ESCAPING 4 ALARM FIRE.

1994

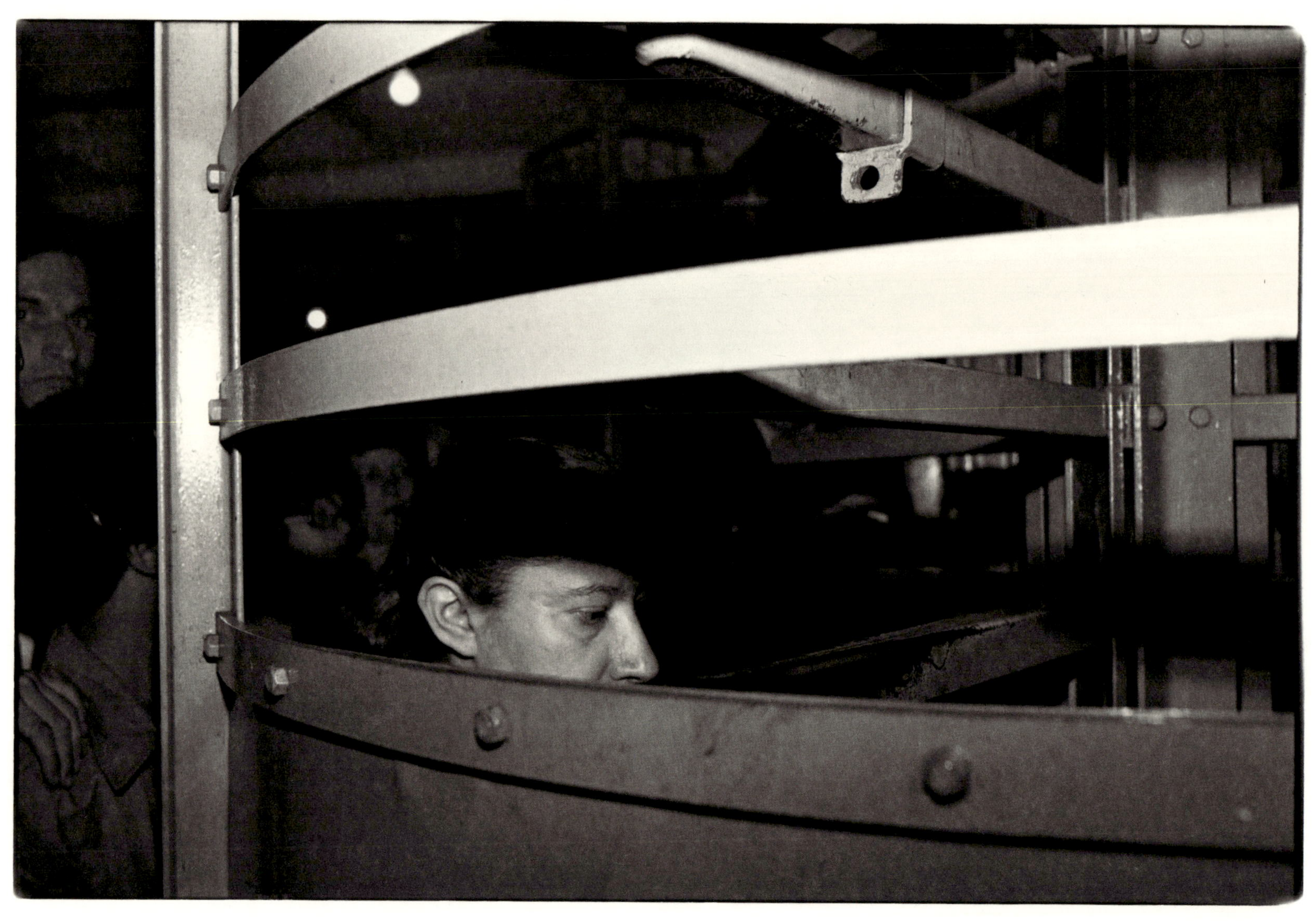

WOMAN GOING INTO SUBWAY.

1981

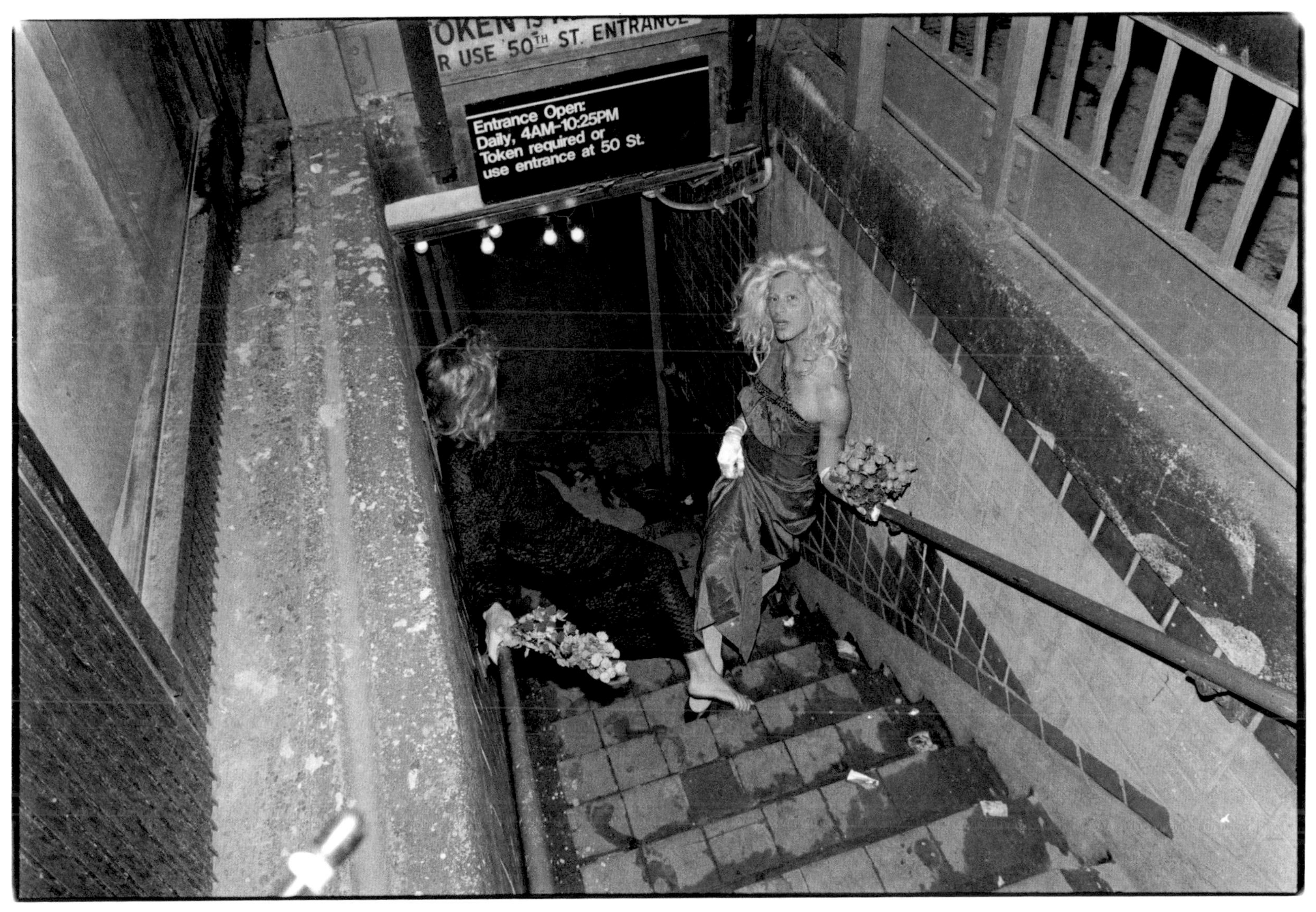

IATE NIGHT WATER MAIN BREAK AFTERMATH.

1989

WITNESS

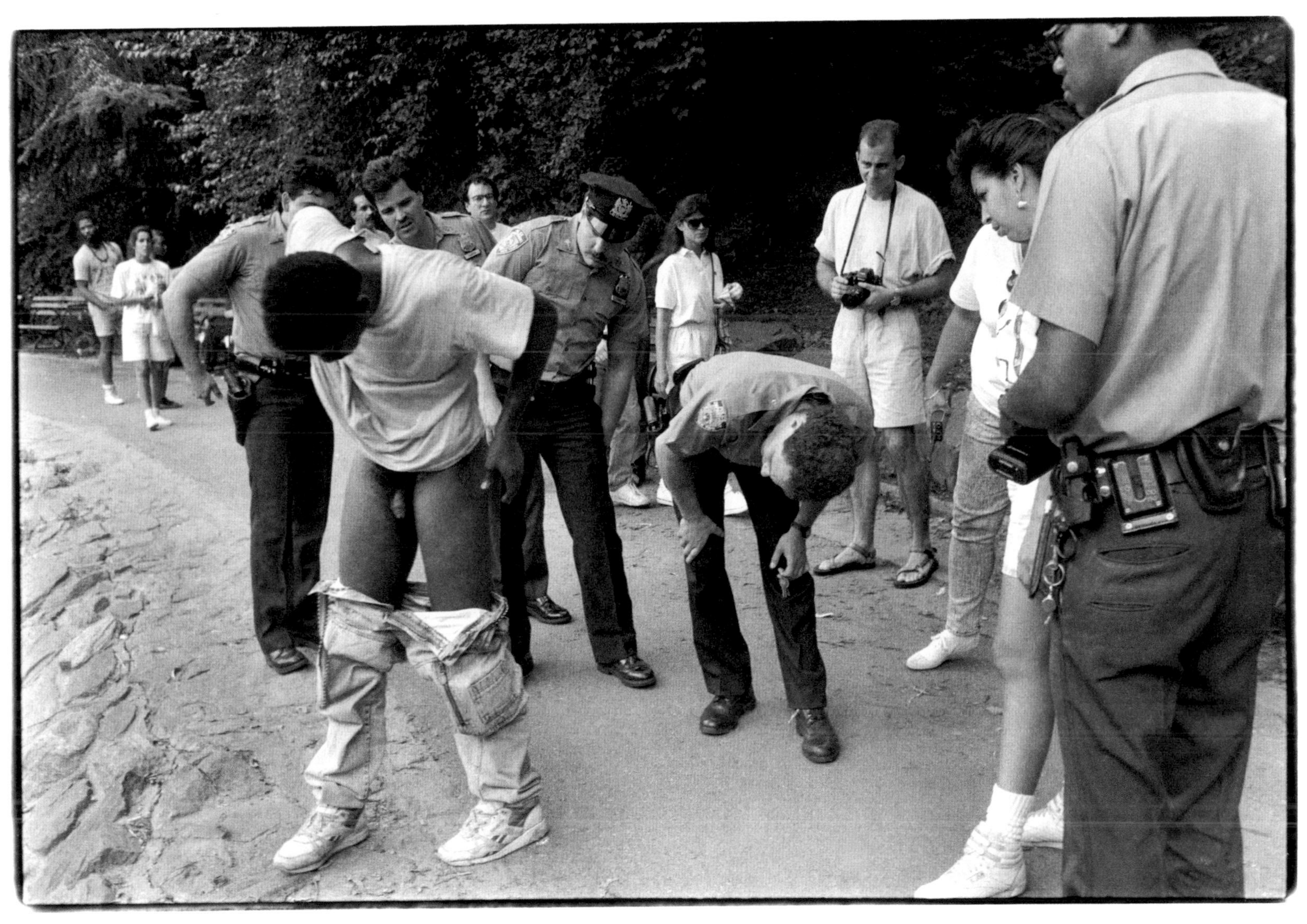

MAN SHOT IN THE REAR END WHILE SLEEPING ON PARK BENCH.

1990

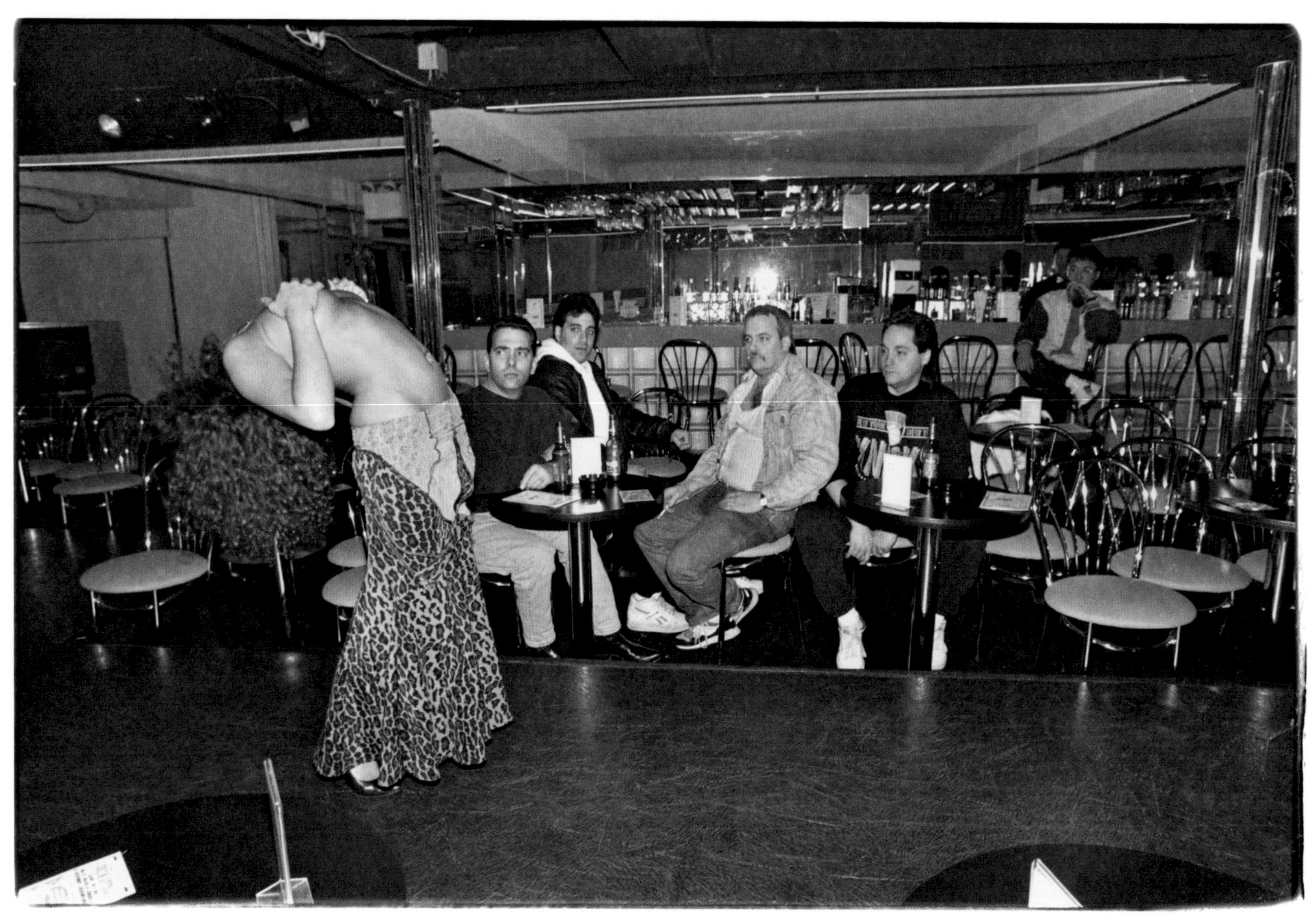

WOMAN PERFORMING IN STRIP CLUB.

1993

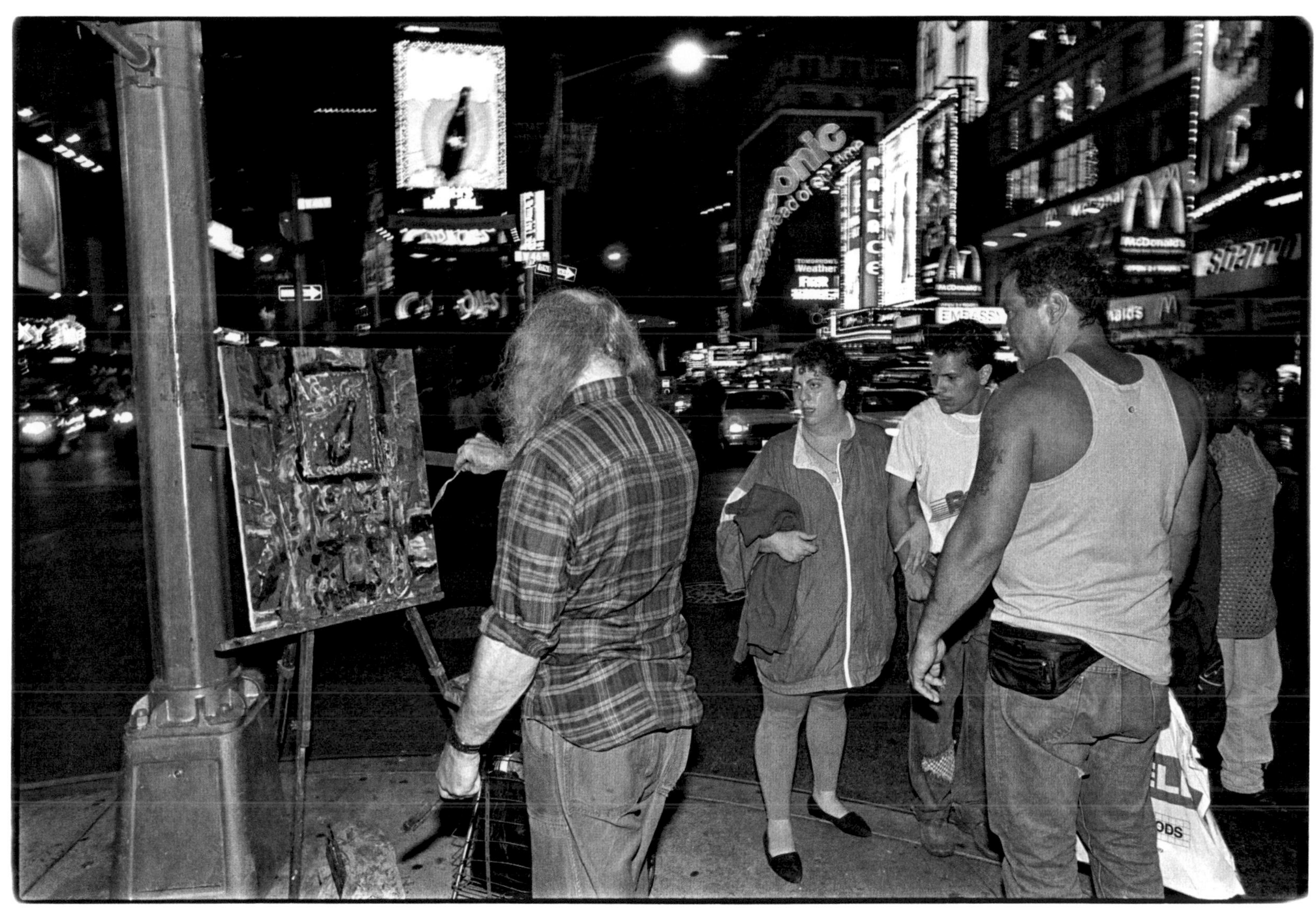

TIMES SQUARE — PEDESTRIANS ENCOUNTER ARTIST.

1992

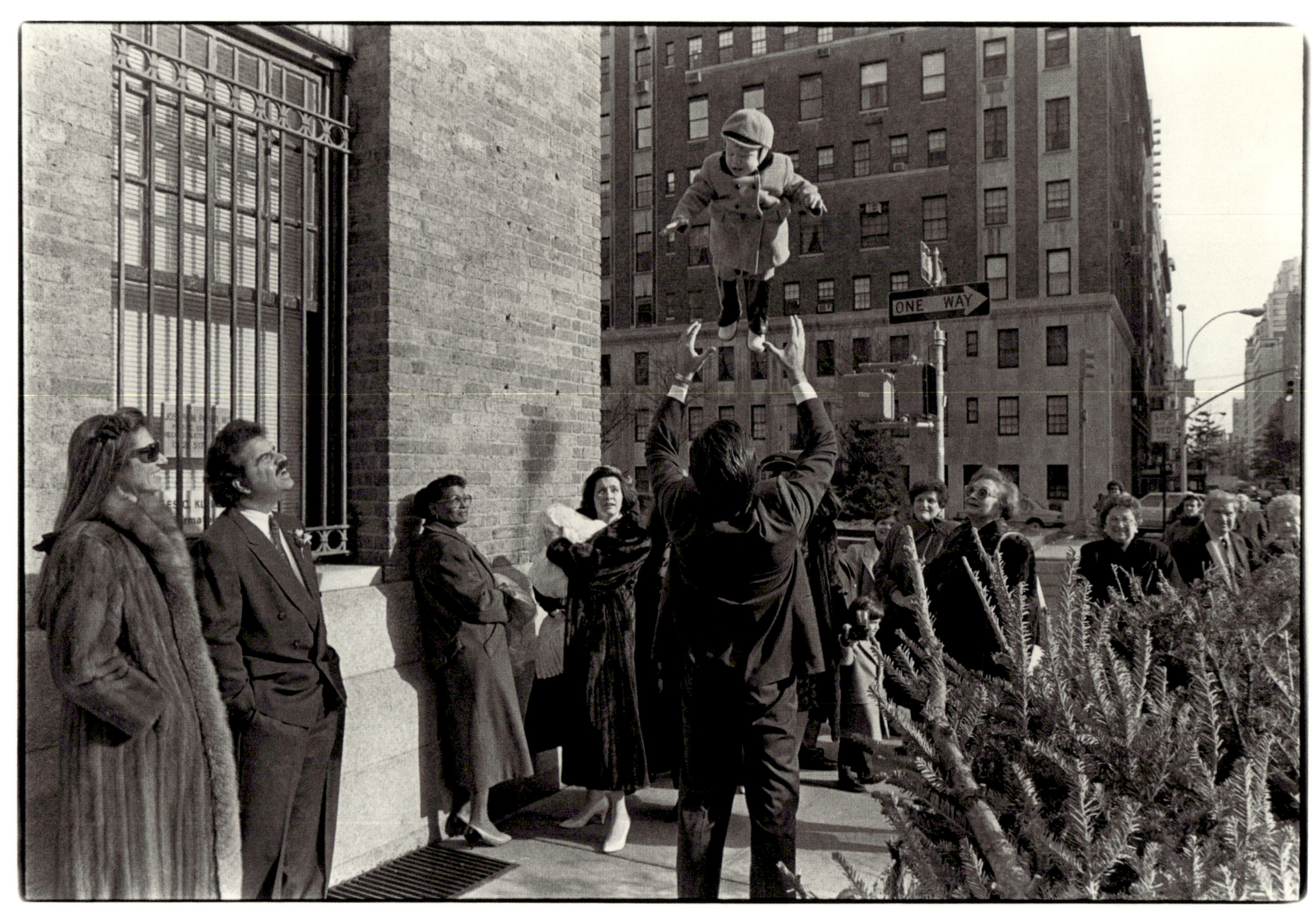

CROWD WATCHING MAN THROW BABY.

1992

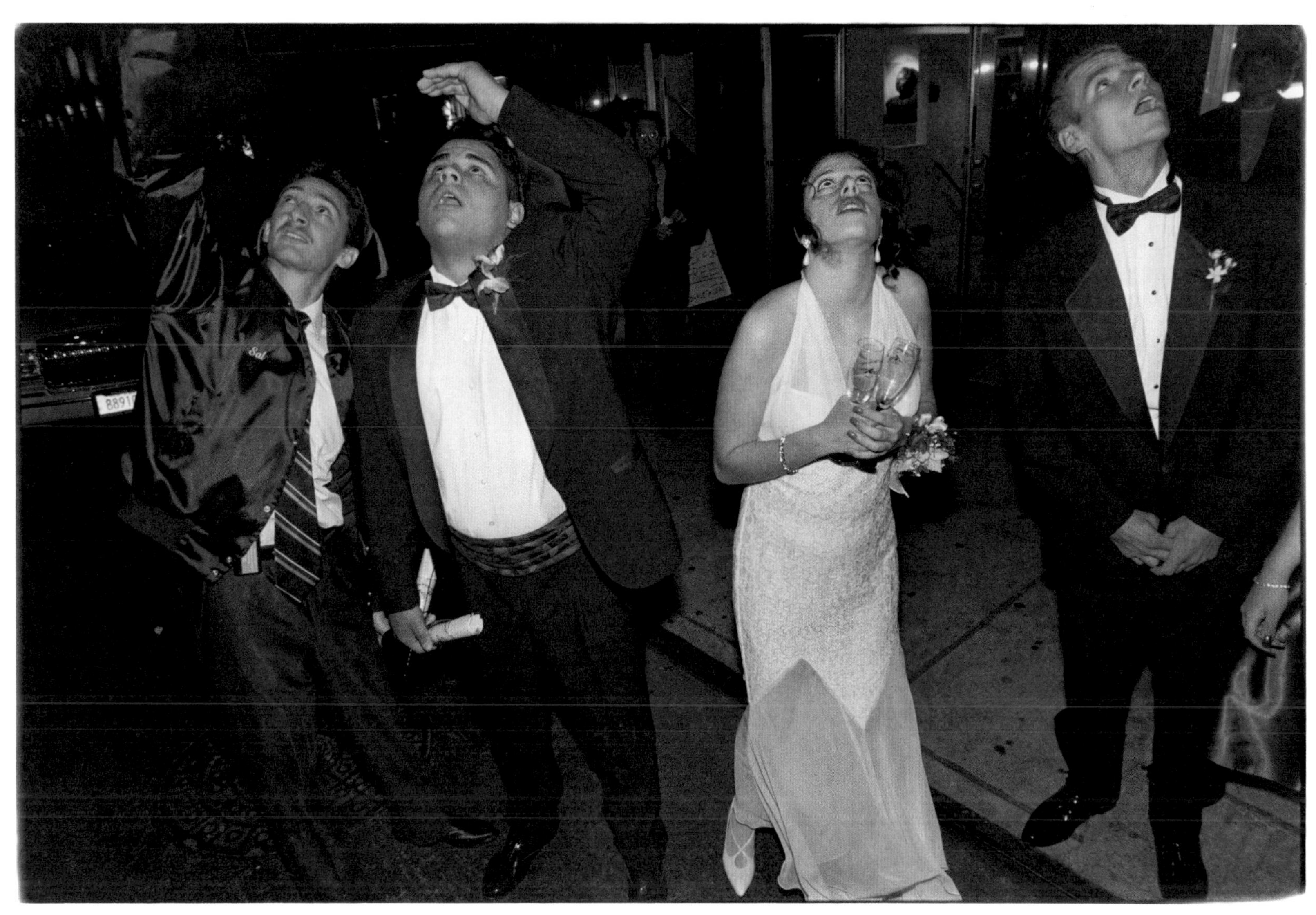

PEOPLE WATCHING JUMPER ON HOTEL ROOF.

1993

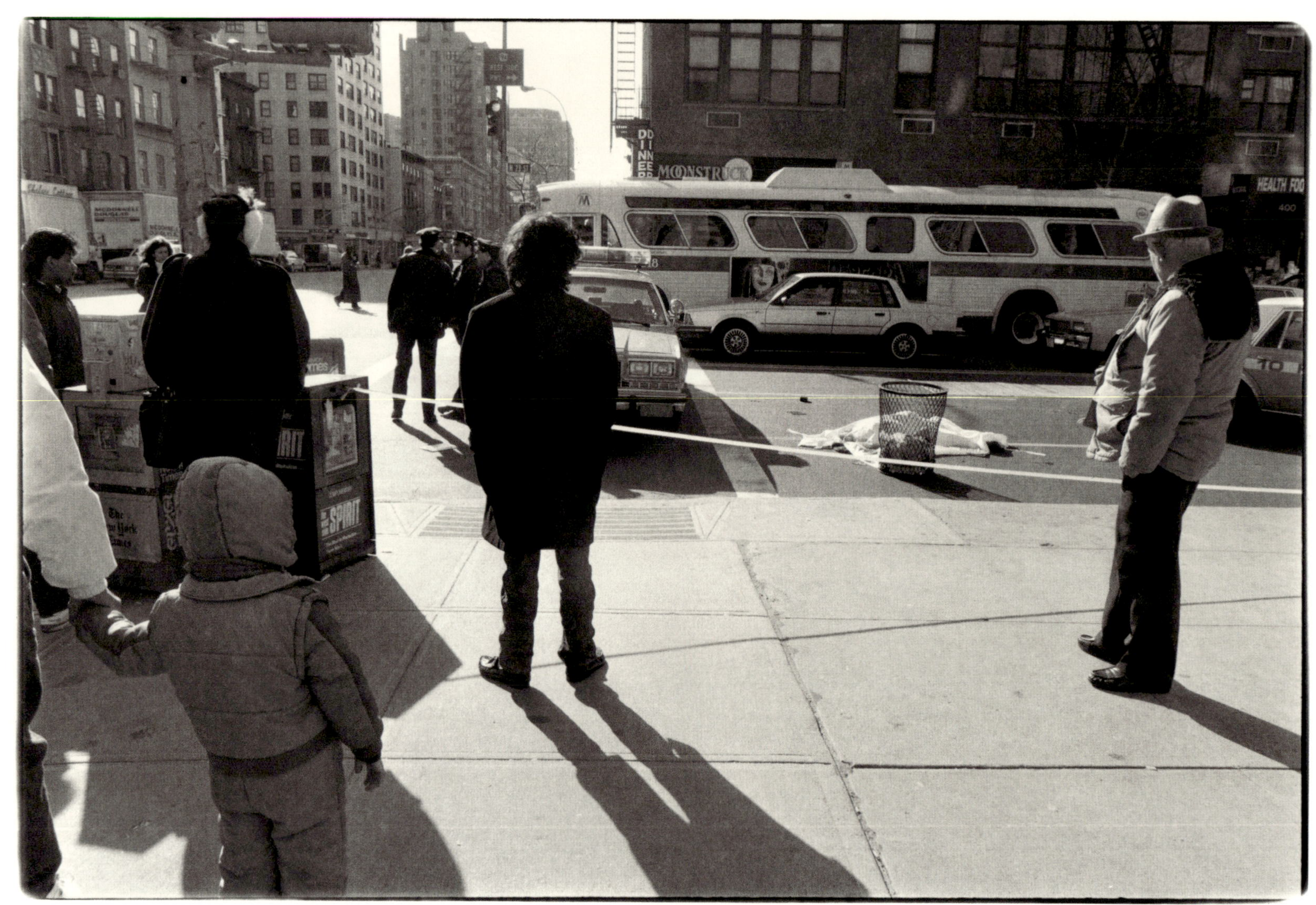

HIT AND RUN VICTIM — W 23 ST.

1990

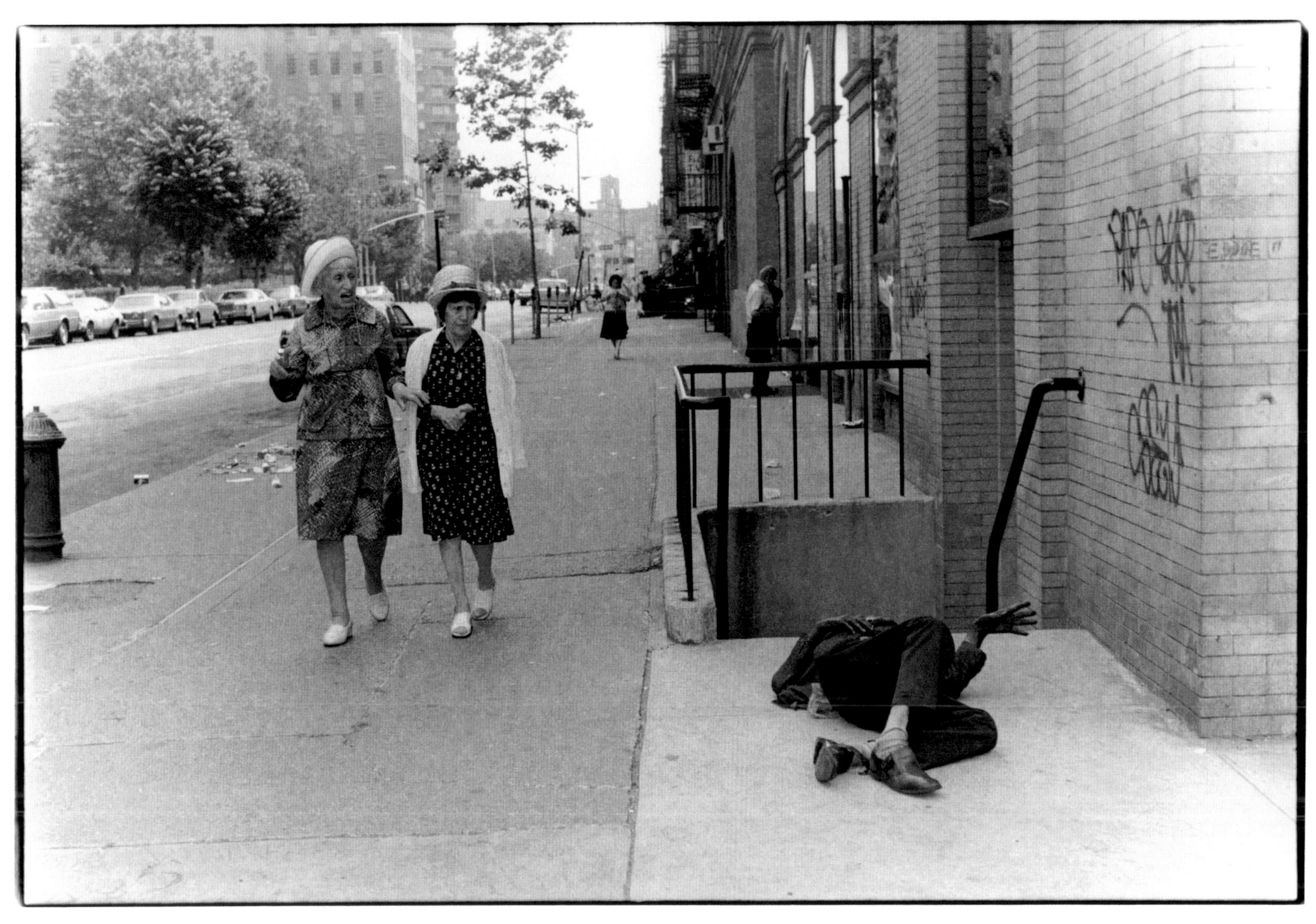

WOMEN STARTLED BY MAN LAYING ON SIDEWALK.

1980

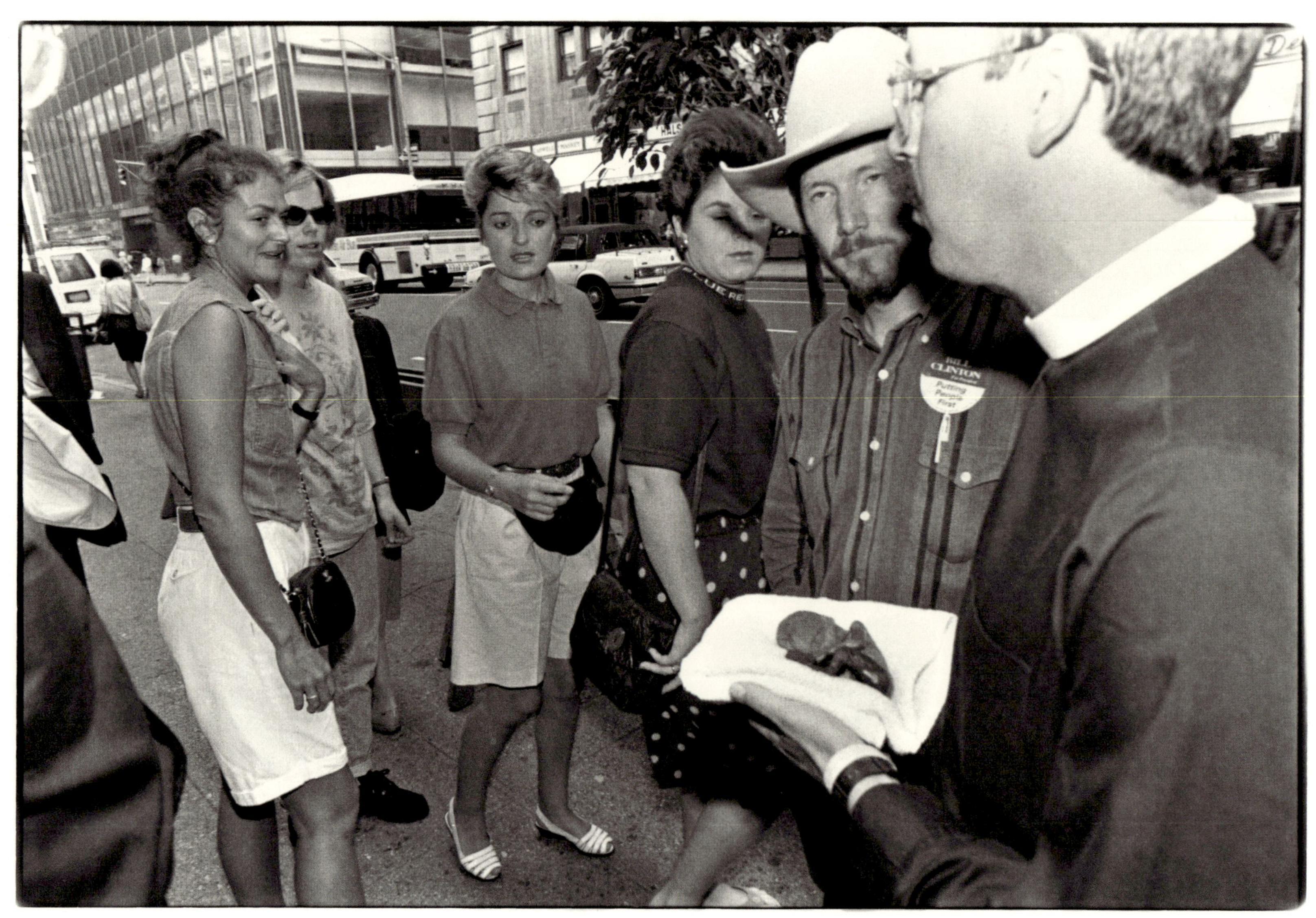

WOMEN WALKING PAST MAN HOLDING FETUS.

1992

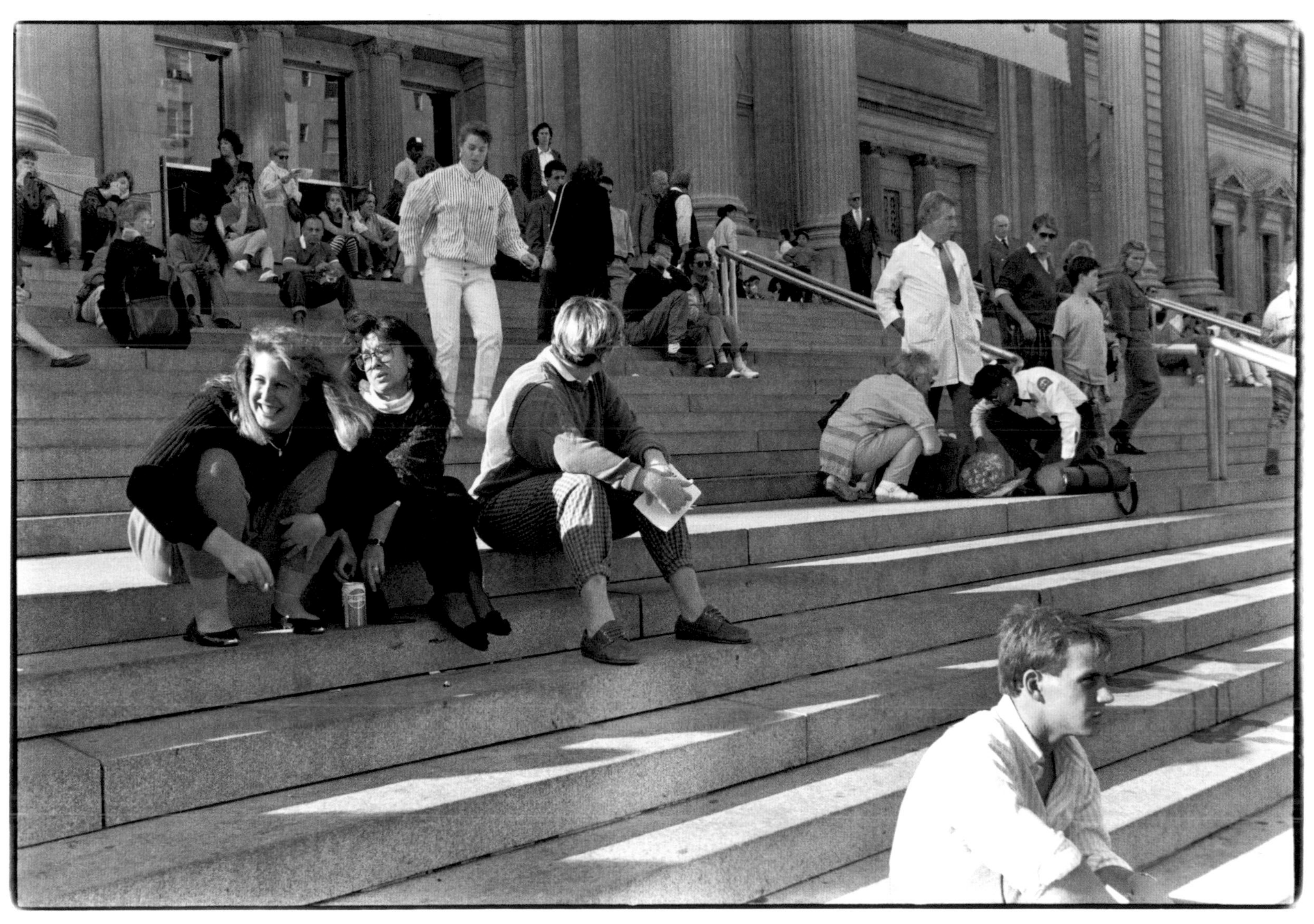

ELDERLY WOMAN FALLS DOWN MUSEUM STEPS.

1988

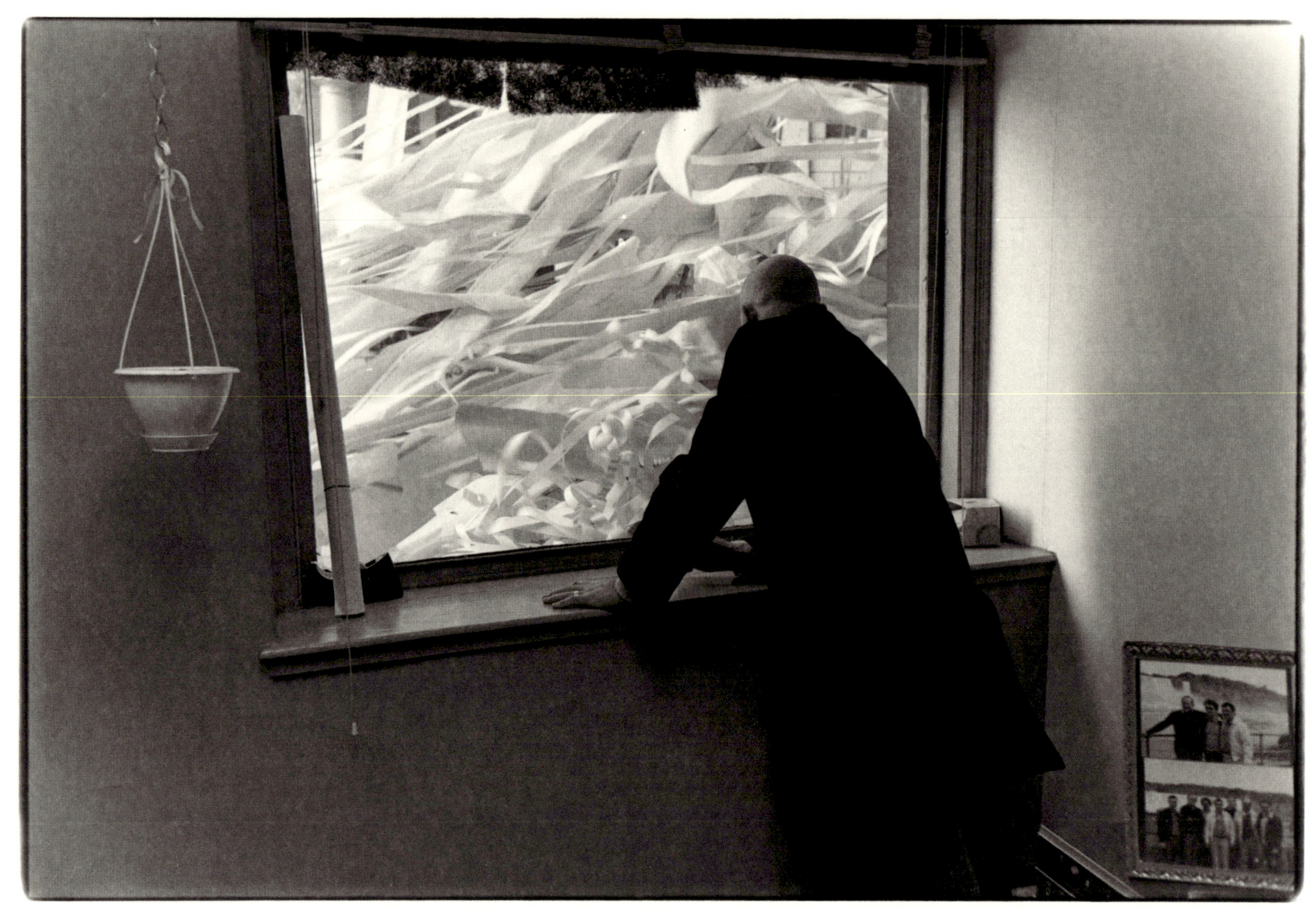

MAN WATCHING TICKER TAPE PARADE FOR AMERICAN HOSTAGES RELEASED FROM IRAN.

1980

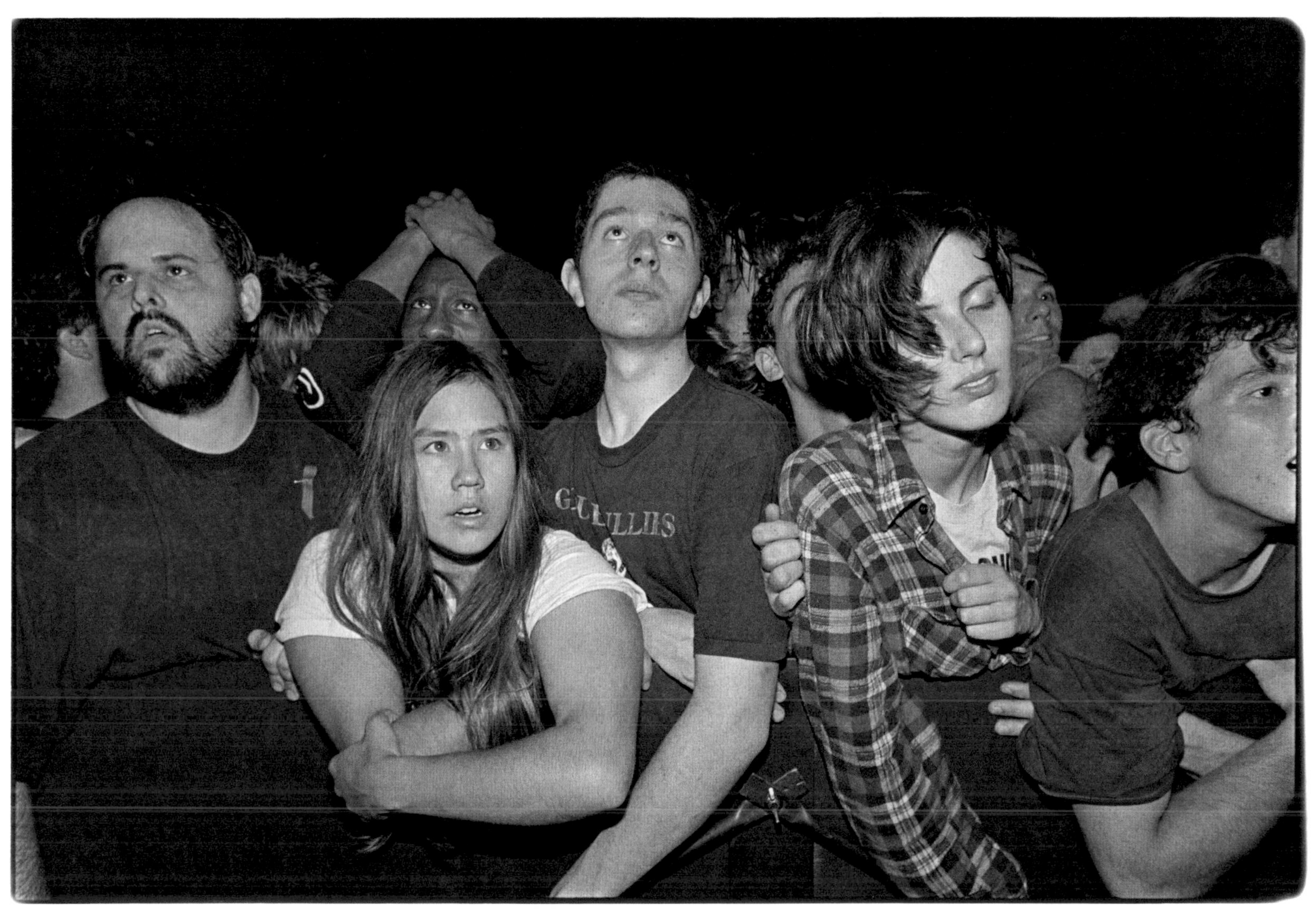

AUDIENCE DURING BUTTHOLE SURFERS BENEFIT CONCERT.

1992

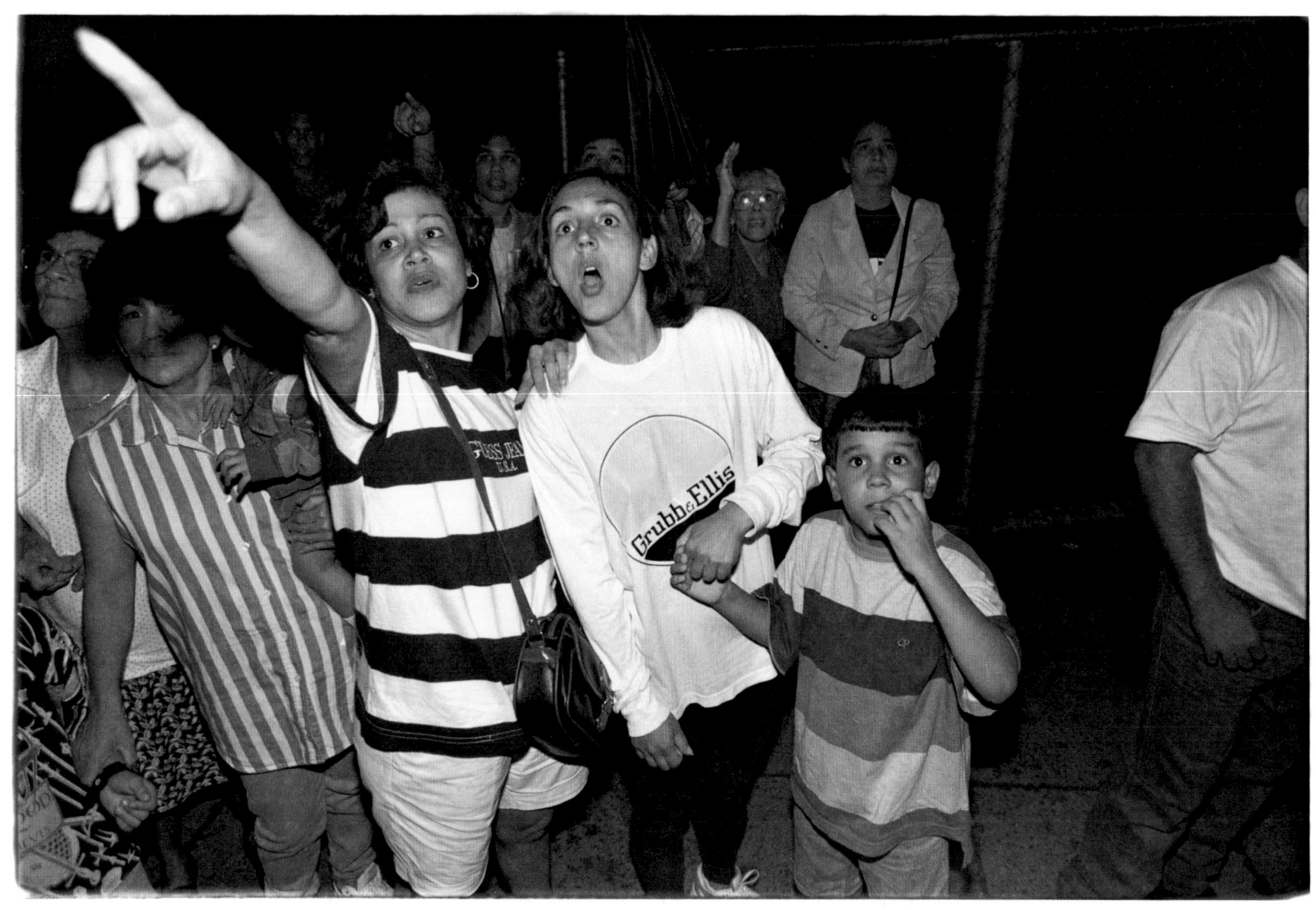

PEOPLE THINK THEY SEE APPARITION OF JESUS IN BATHROOM WINDOW OF TENEMENT.

1993

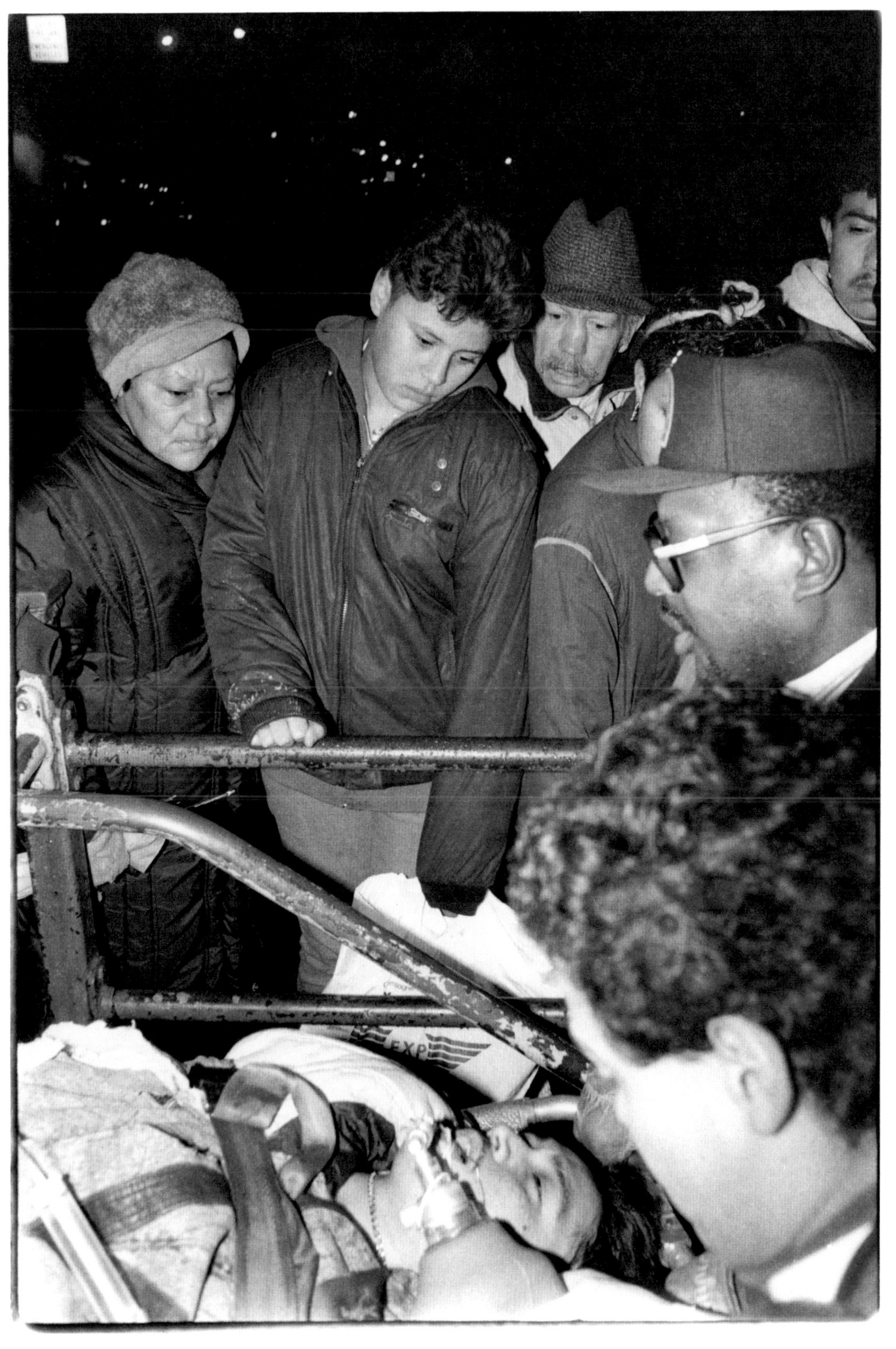

YOUTH SHOT IN SUBWAY FOR DISSING — STARING TOO LONG.

1994

VICTIMS

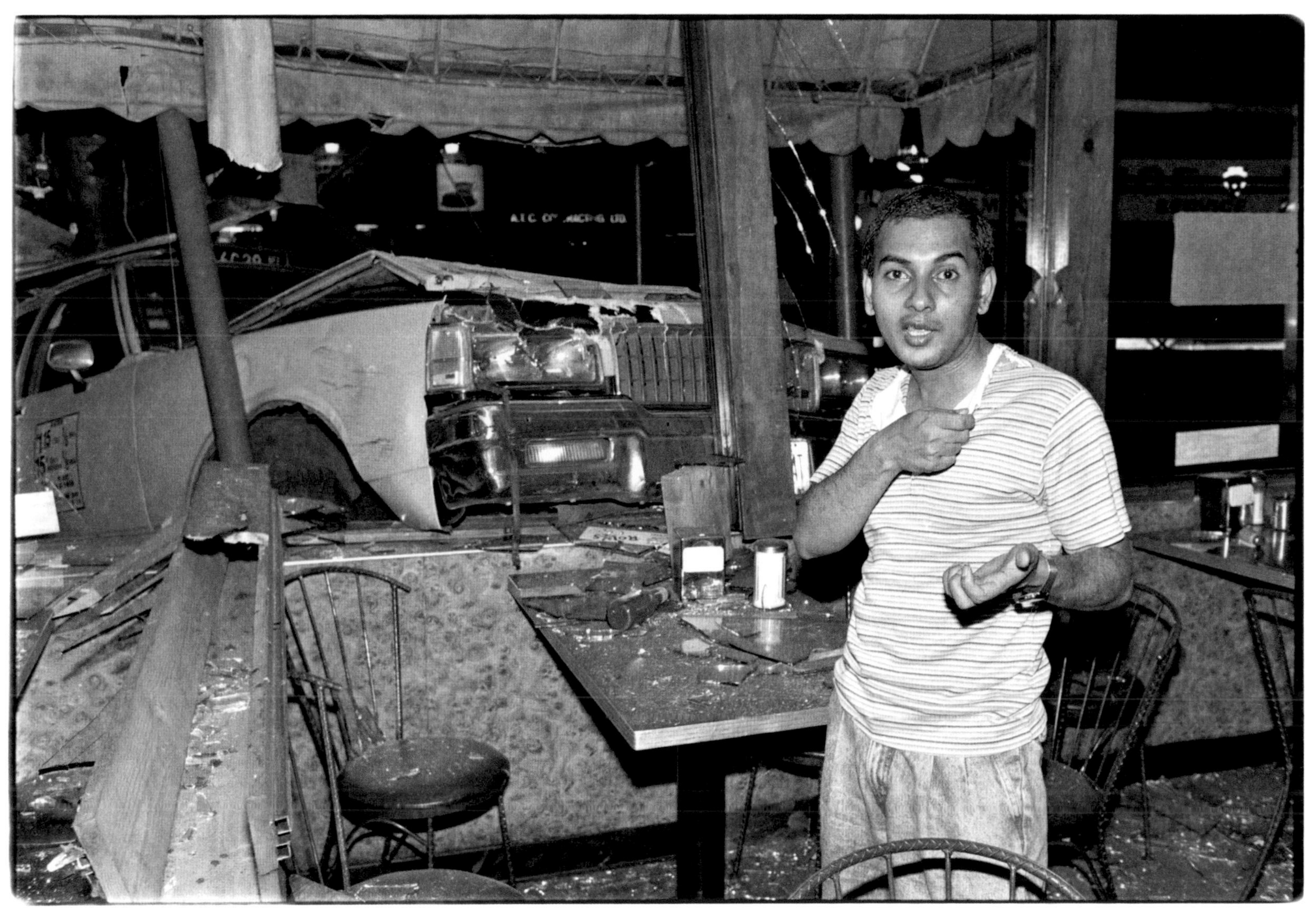

TAXI DRIVER EXPLAINING HOW AN ARGUMENT WITH A PASSENGER CAUSED HIM TO DRIVE INTO RESTAURANT.

1989

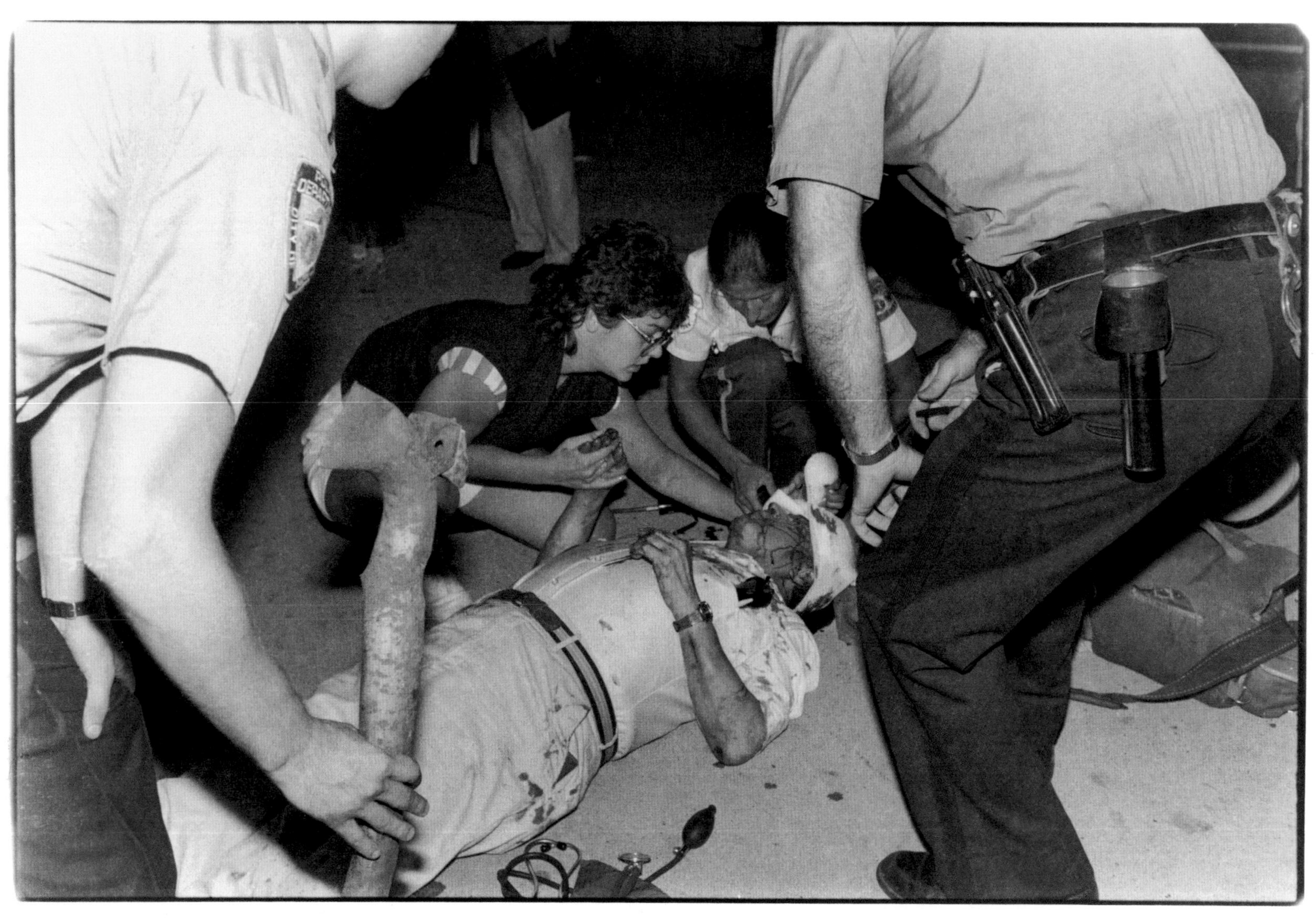

PEDESTRIAN ATTACKED BY MAN WITH JAGGED TAILPIPE FOR NO APPARENT REASON.

1983

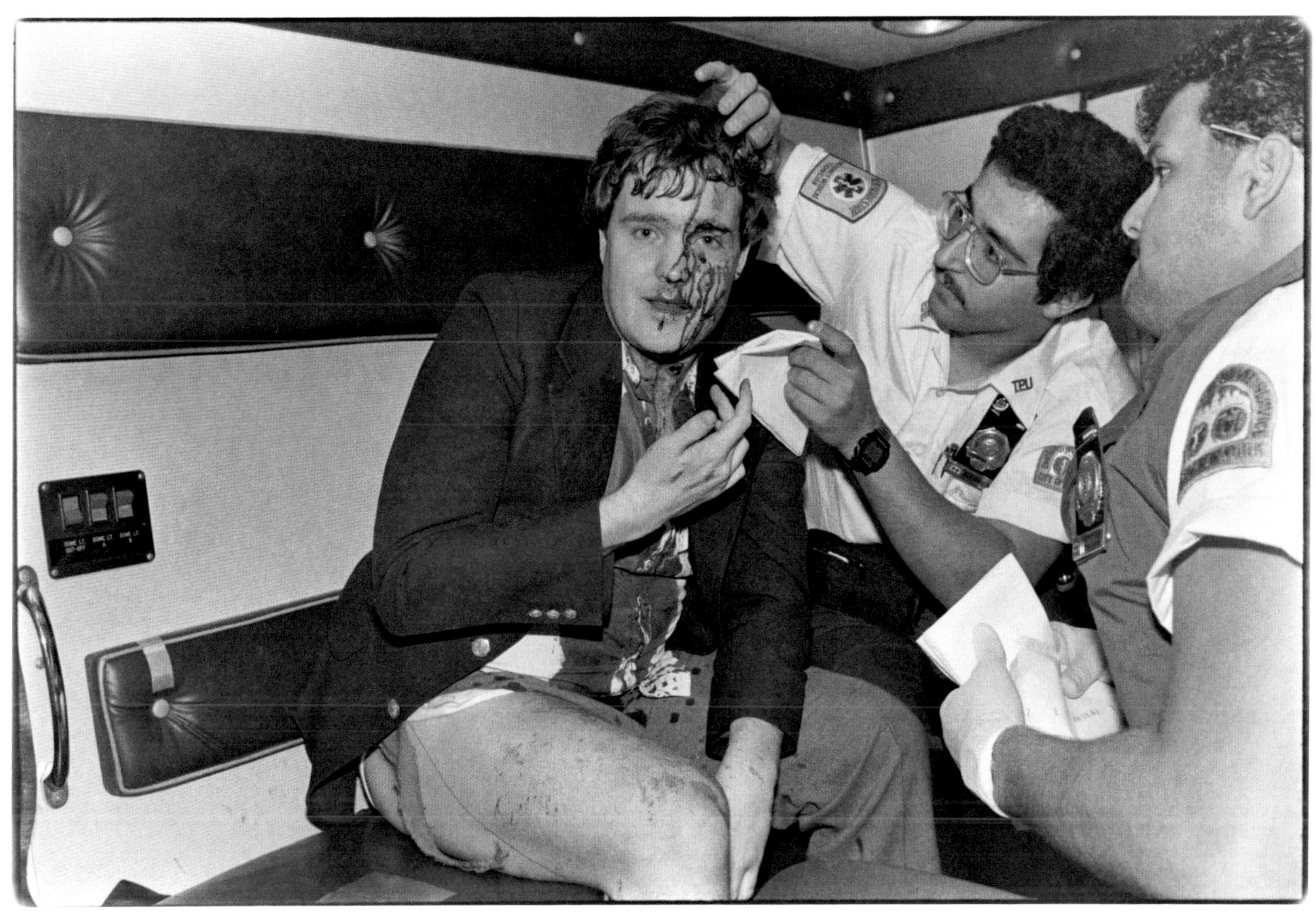

MAN COMPLAINING HE WAS ATTACKED AFTER HE GAVE HIS MONEY TO ROBBERS.

1992

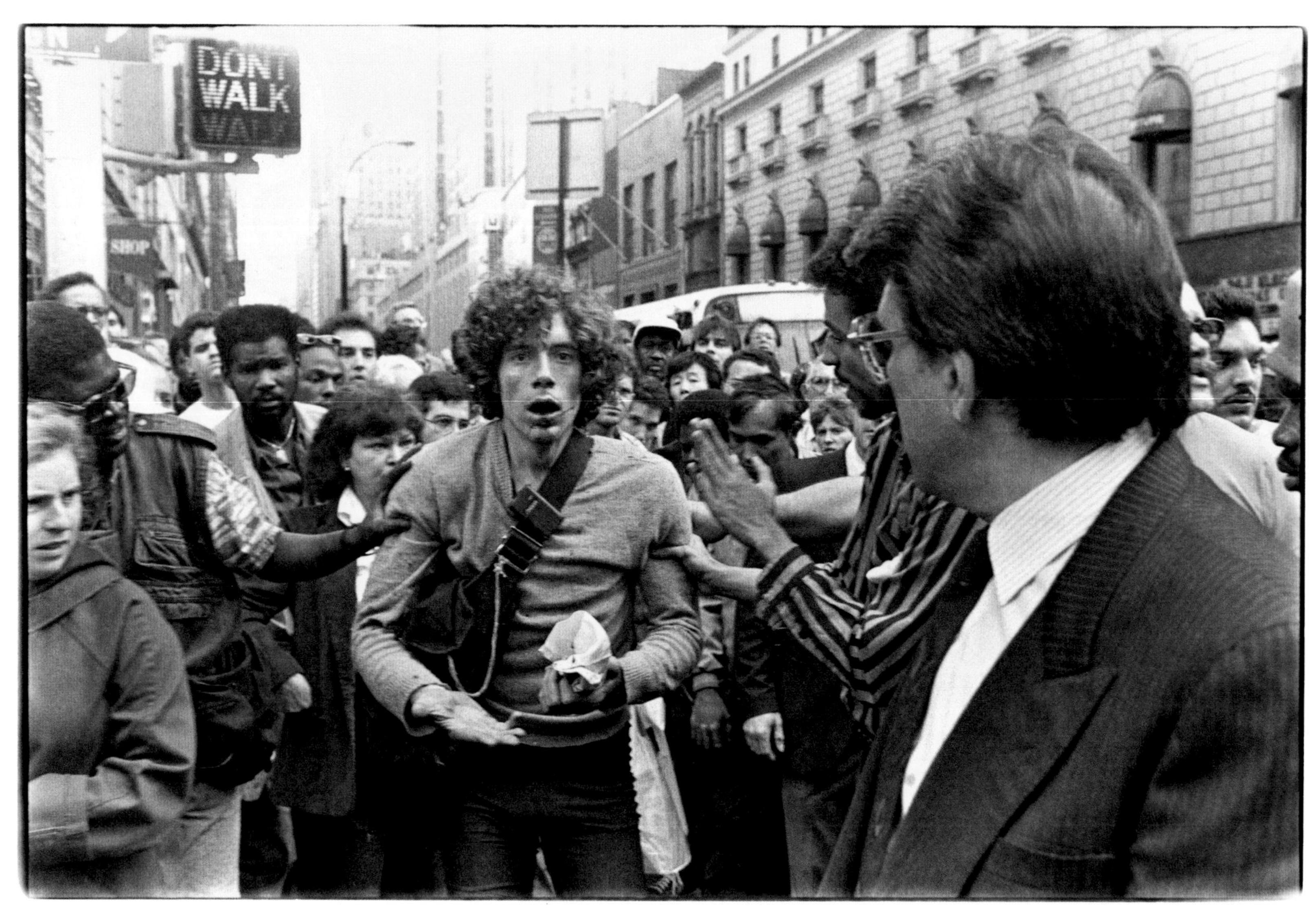

BICYCLE MESSENGER AFTER BEING ATTACKED BY ANGRY MOTORISTS.

1988

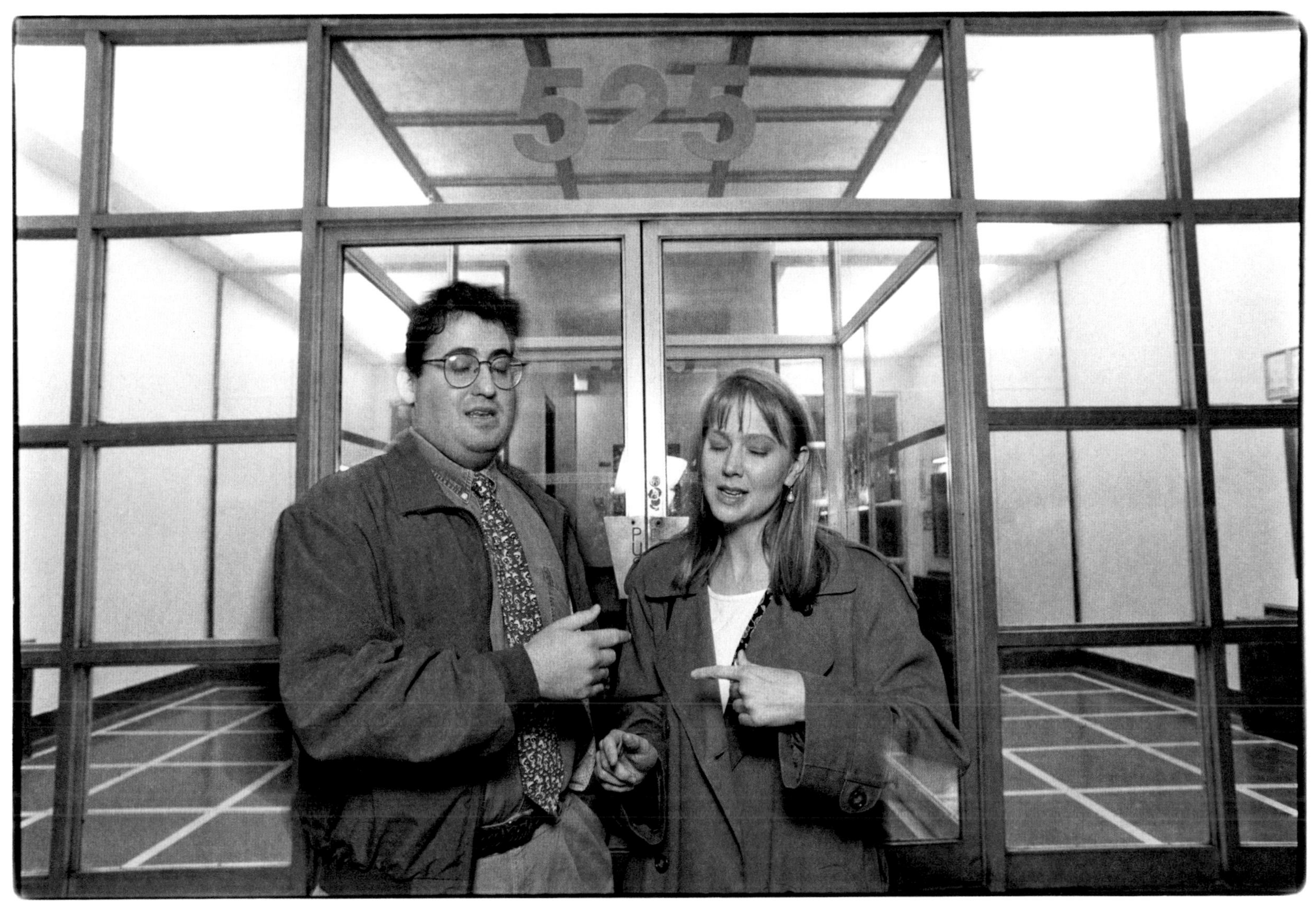

COUPLE DESCRIBE RETURNING HOME TO FIND THAT THEIR APARTMENT HAD BEEN ROBBED.

1989

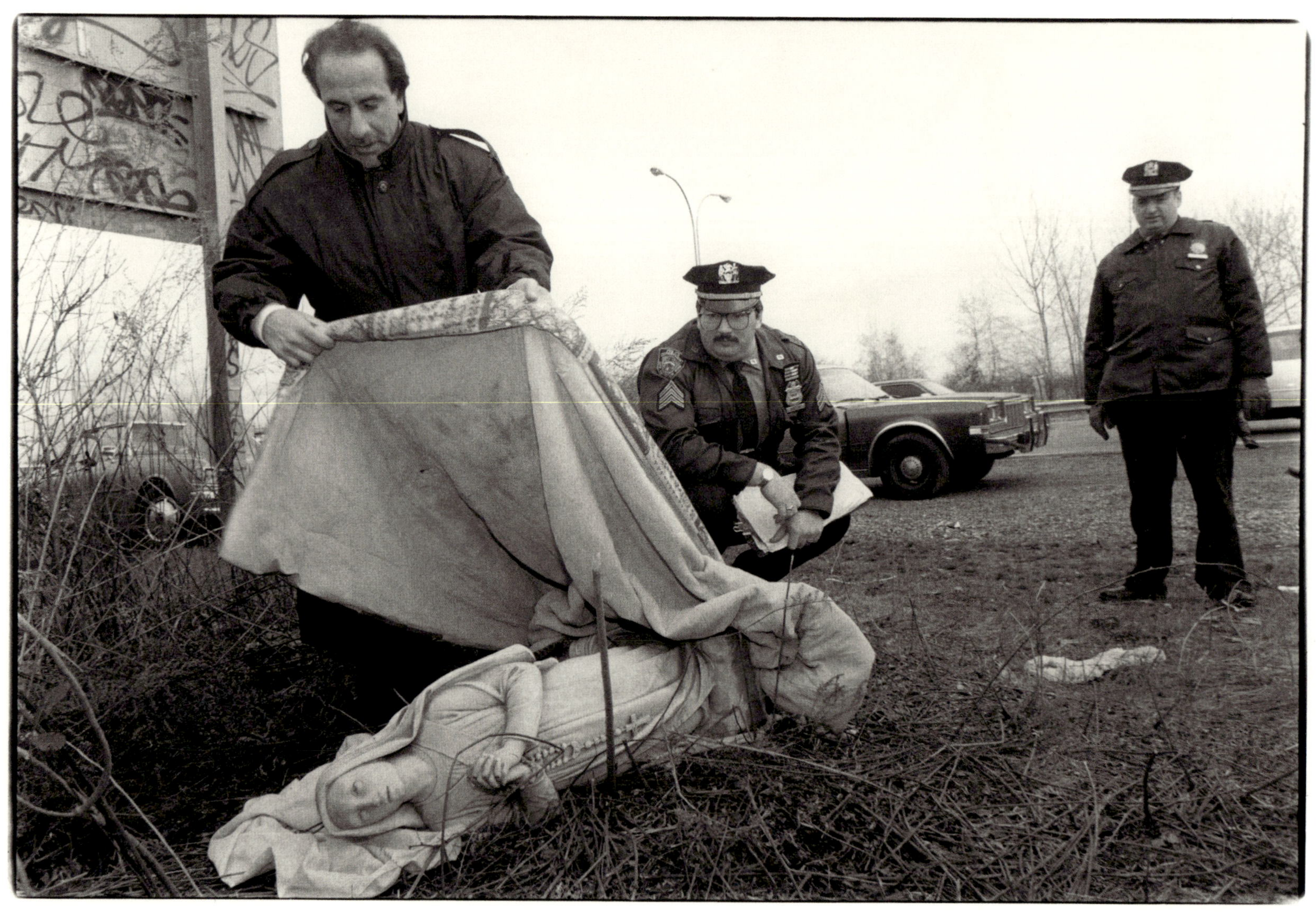

STOLEN FROM A BROOKLYN CHURCH ON CHRISTMAS — ST. BERNADETTE WAS FOUND DUMPED NEAR THE BELT PARKWAY.

1992

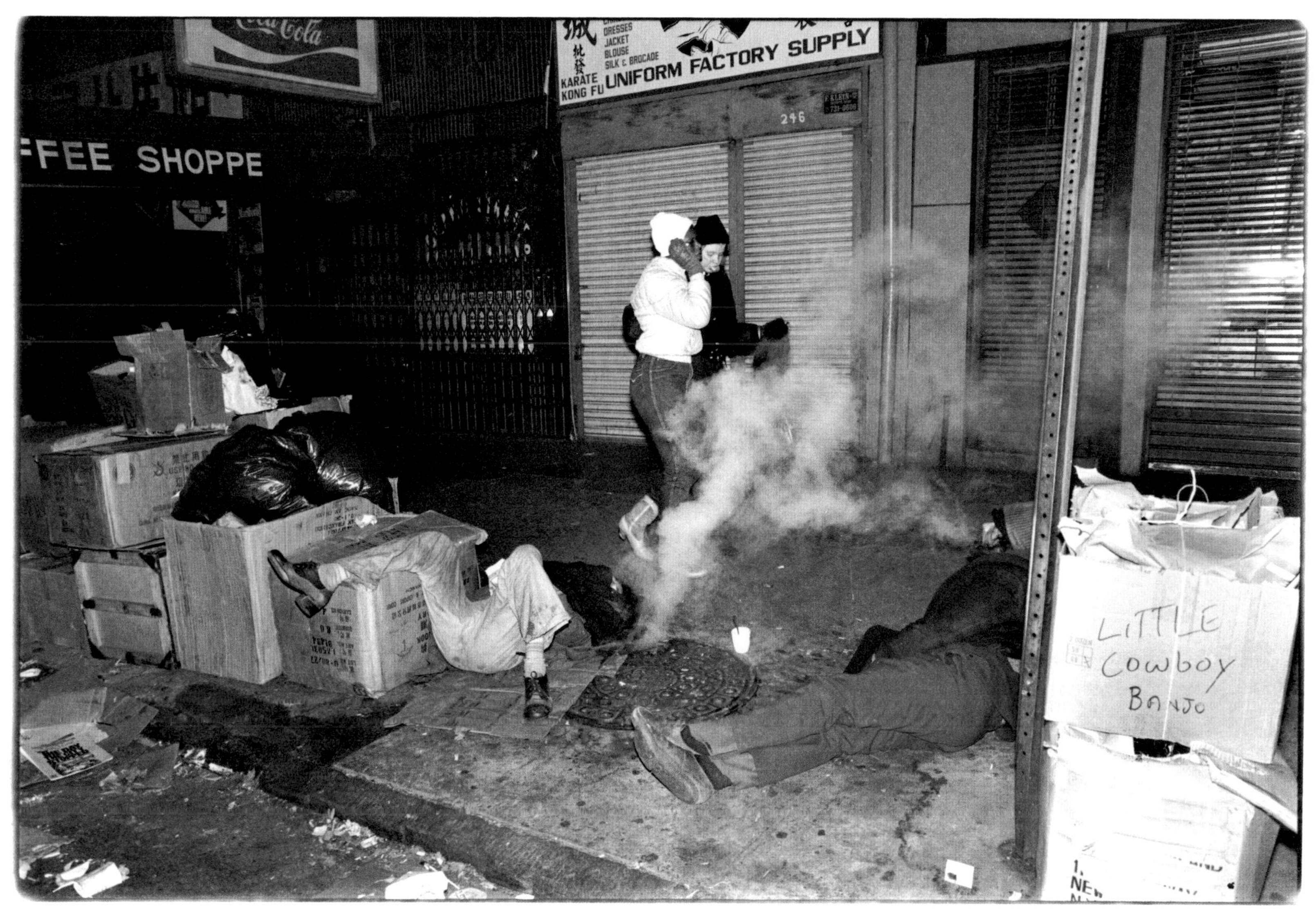

WOMAN BEING HELPED HOME AFTER BEING ATTACKED IN NEARBY RESTAURANT.

1981

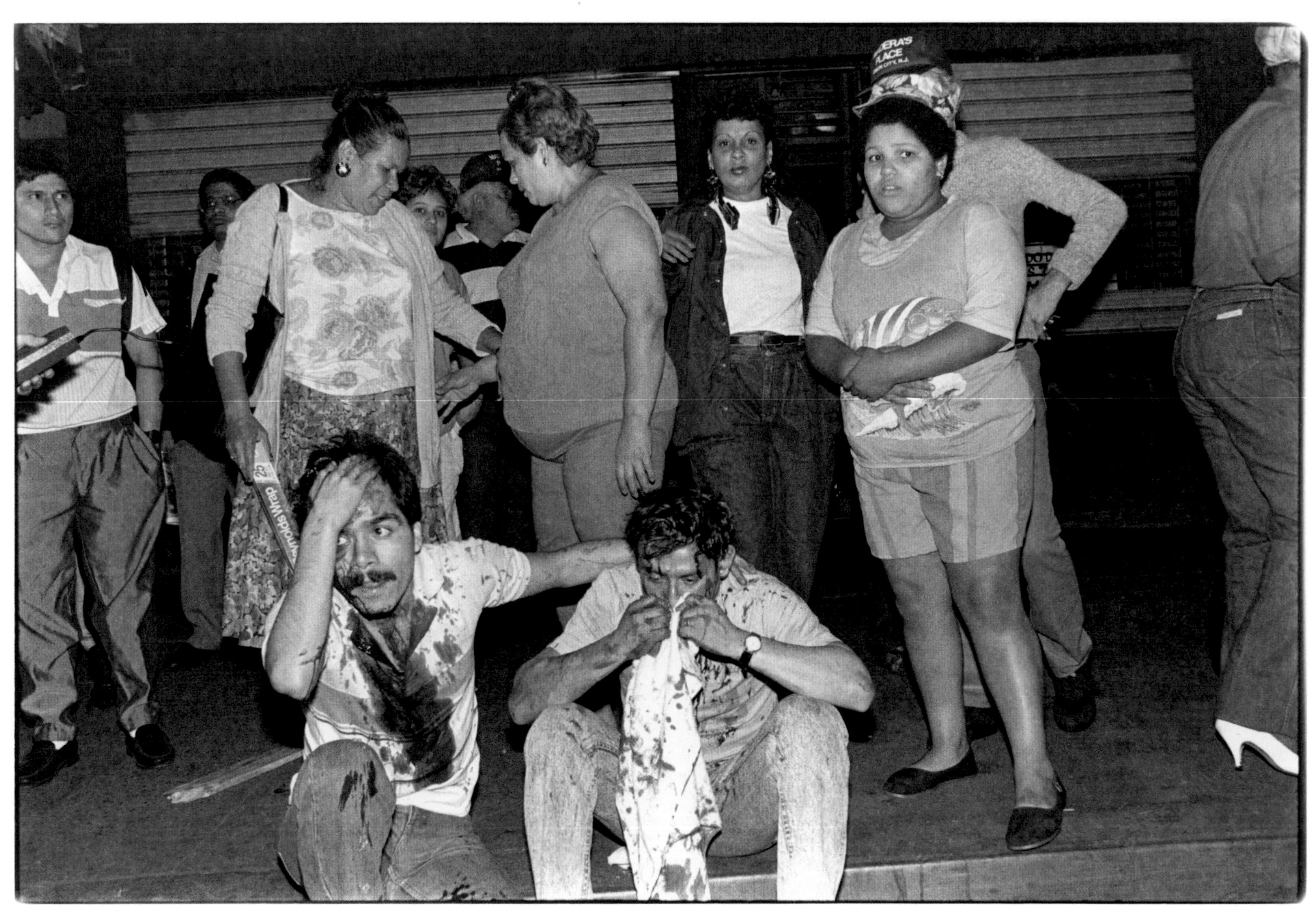

AFTER A FIGHT — HELL'S KITCHEN.

1985

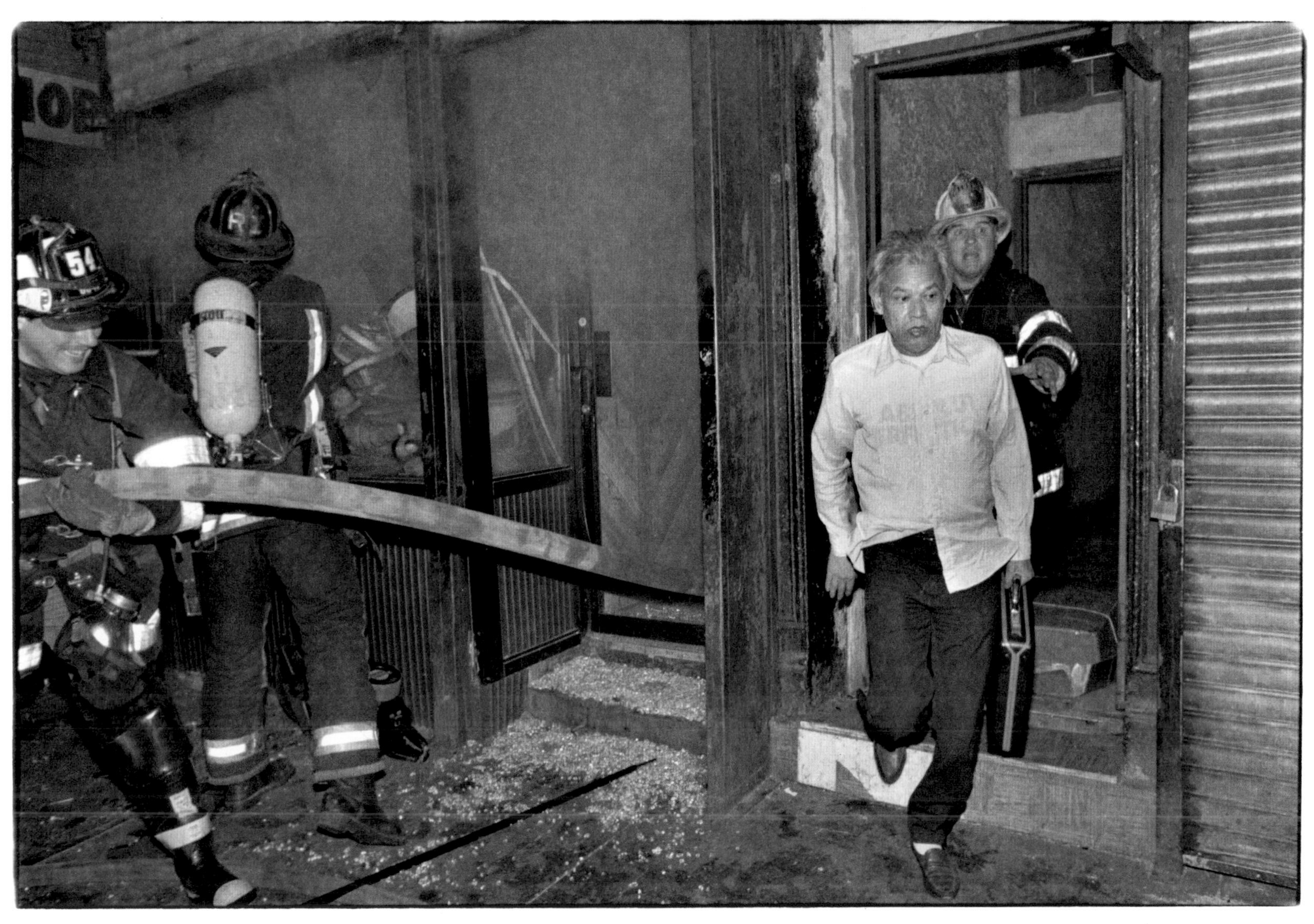

MAN RUNS OUT OF BURNING BUILDING.

1989

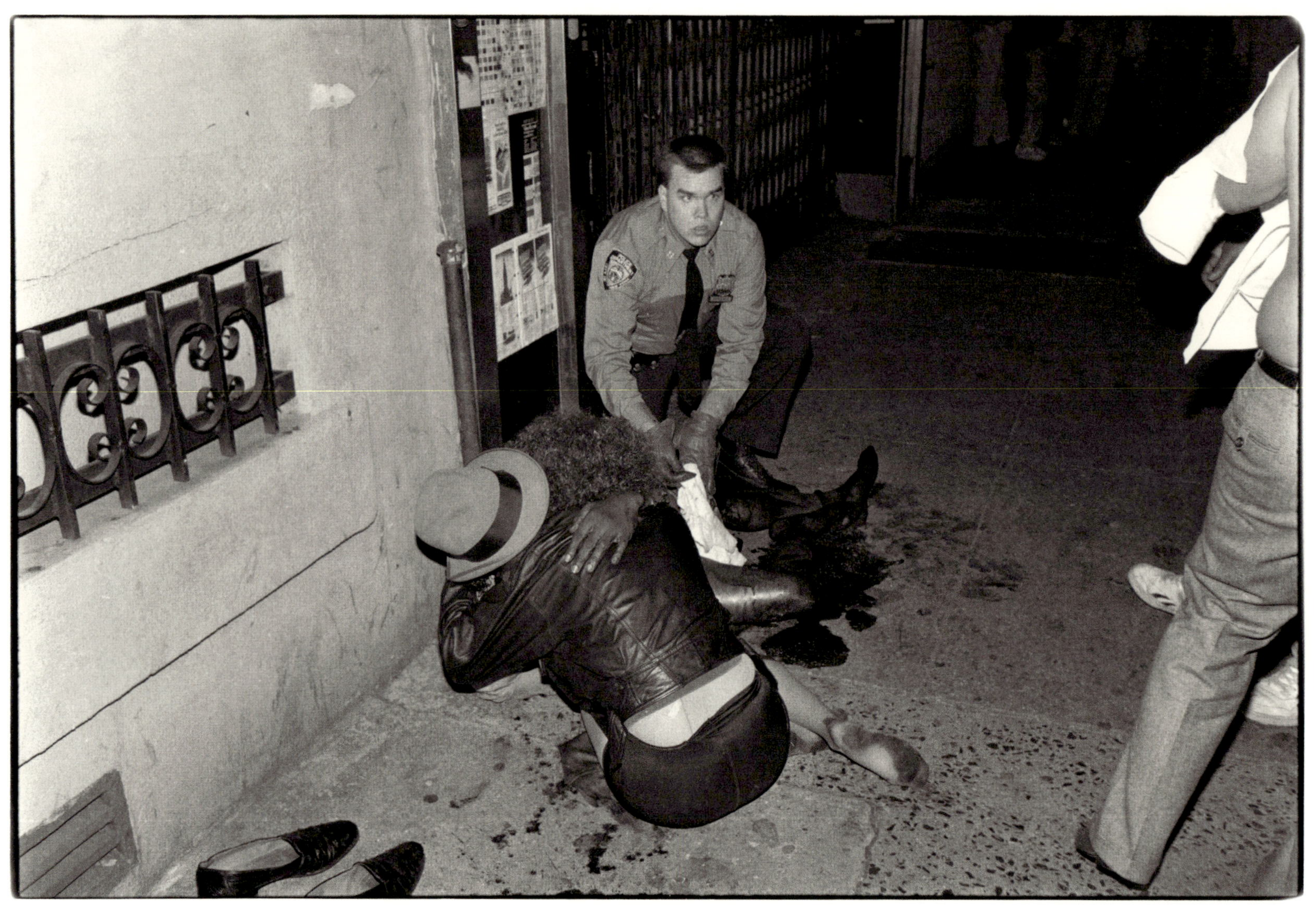

MAN SHOT IN THE LEGS.

1989

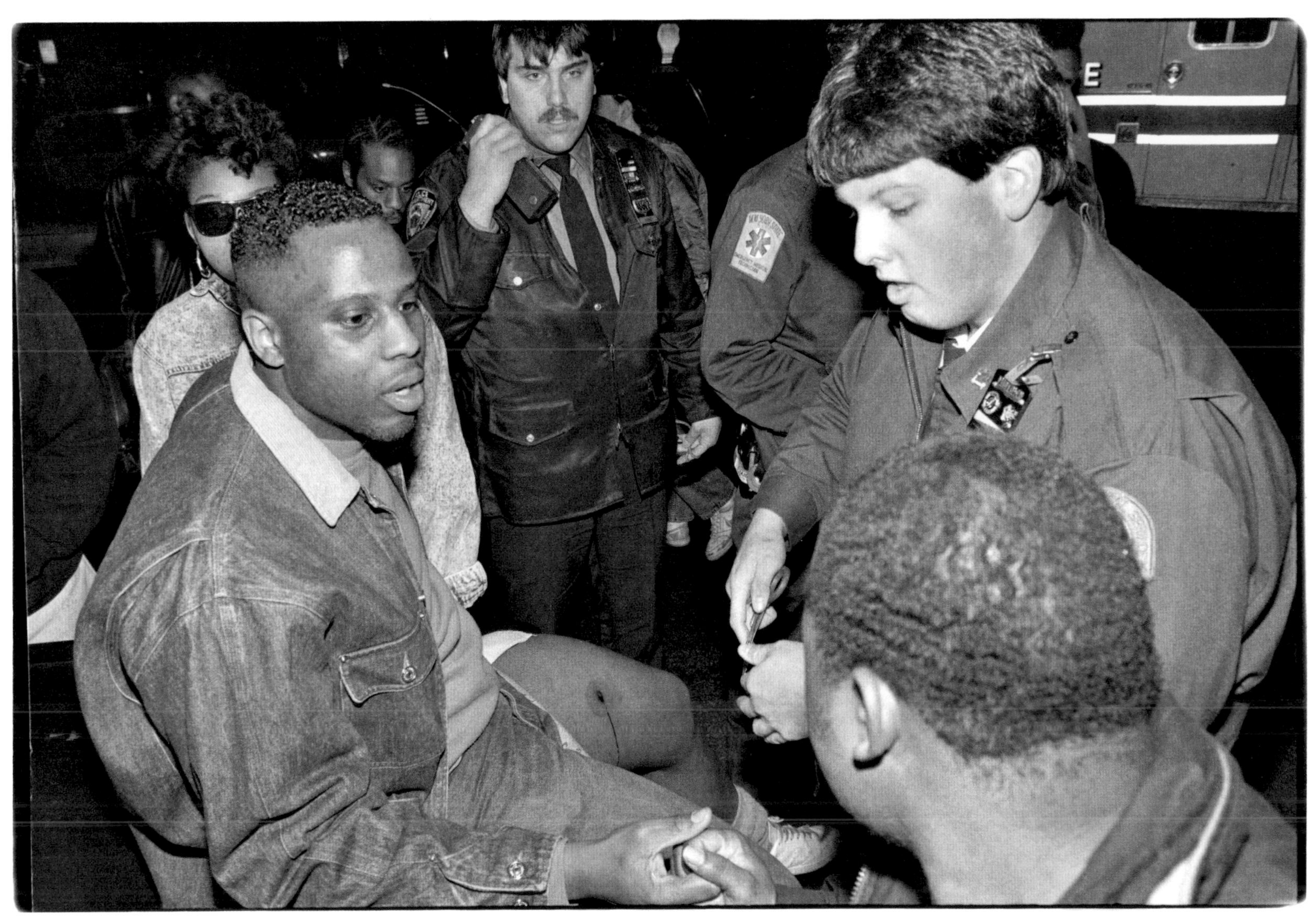

MAN SHOT IN THE LEG.

1989

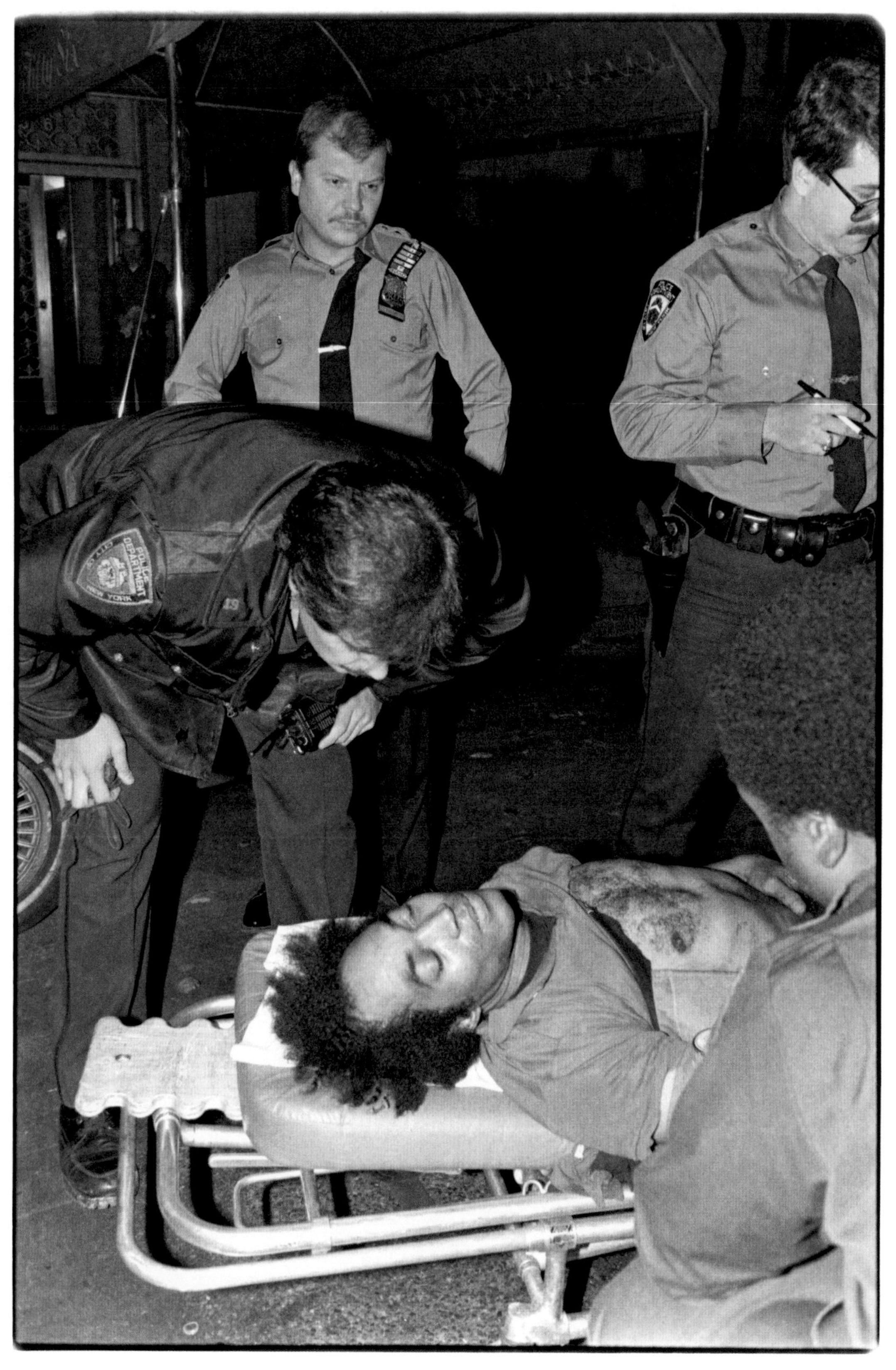

COP ASKS STABBING VICTIM FOR DESCRIPTION OF ATTACKER. 1989

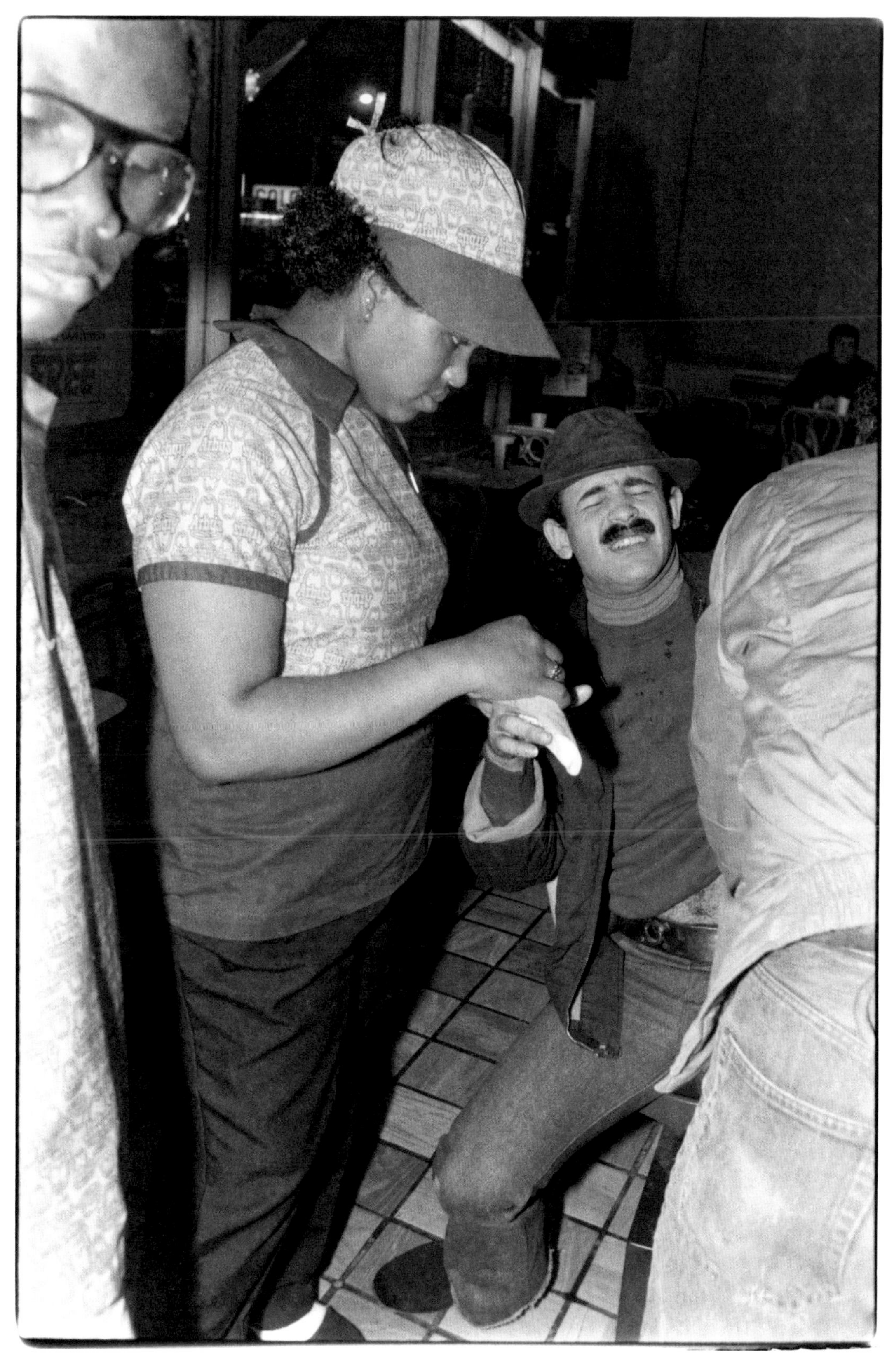

MAN STABBED IN STOMACH AFTER ASKING DISORDERLY MAN TO LEAVE.

1984

SUSPECTS

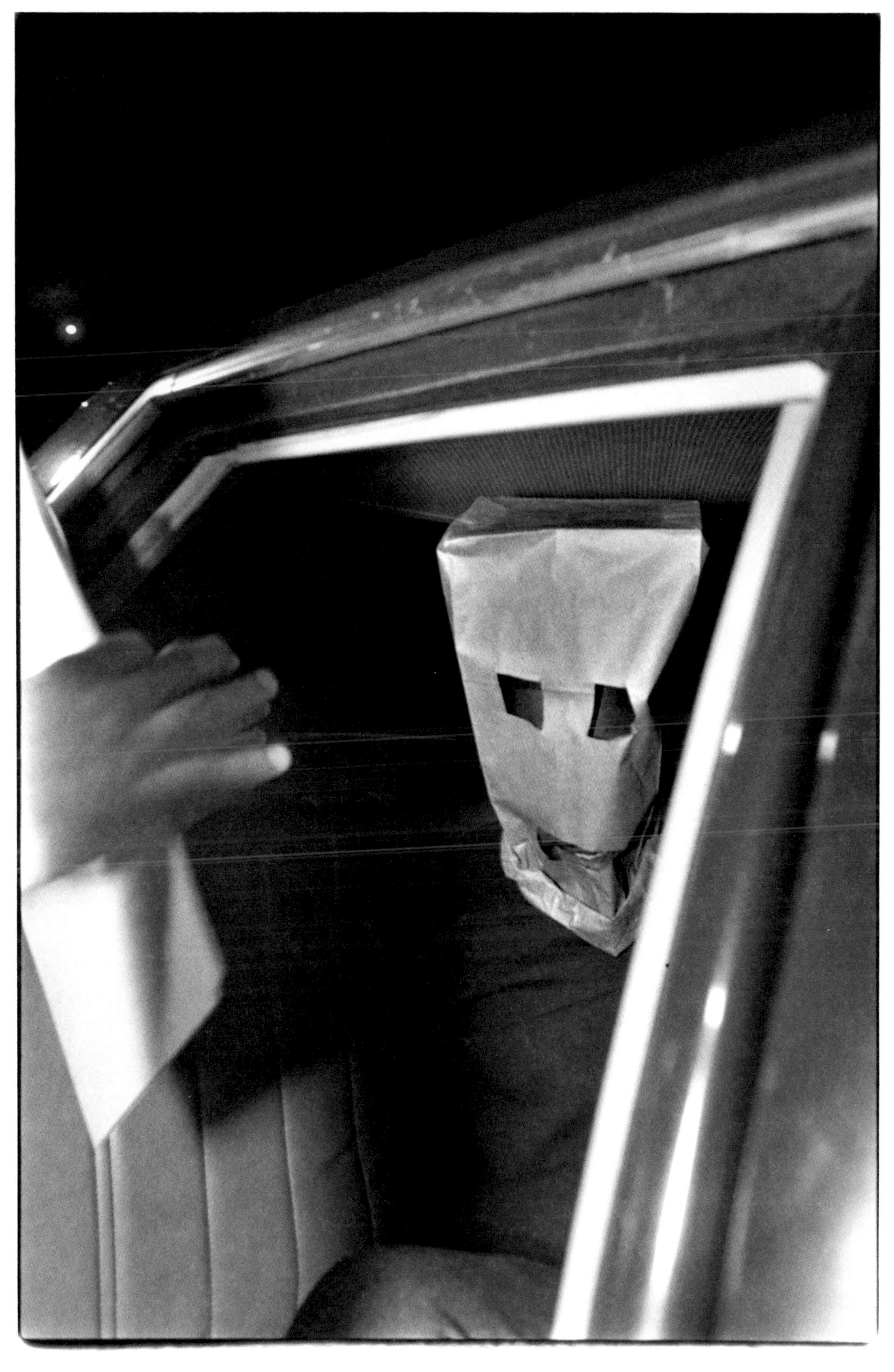

THE EAST SIDE RAPIST. 1985

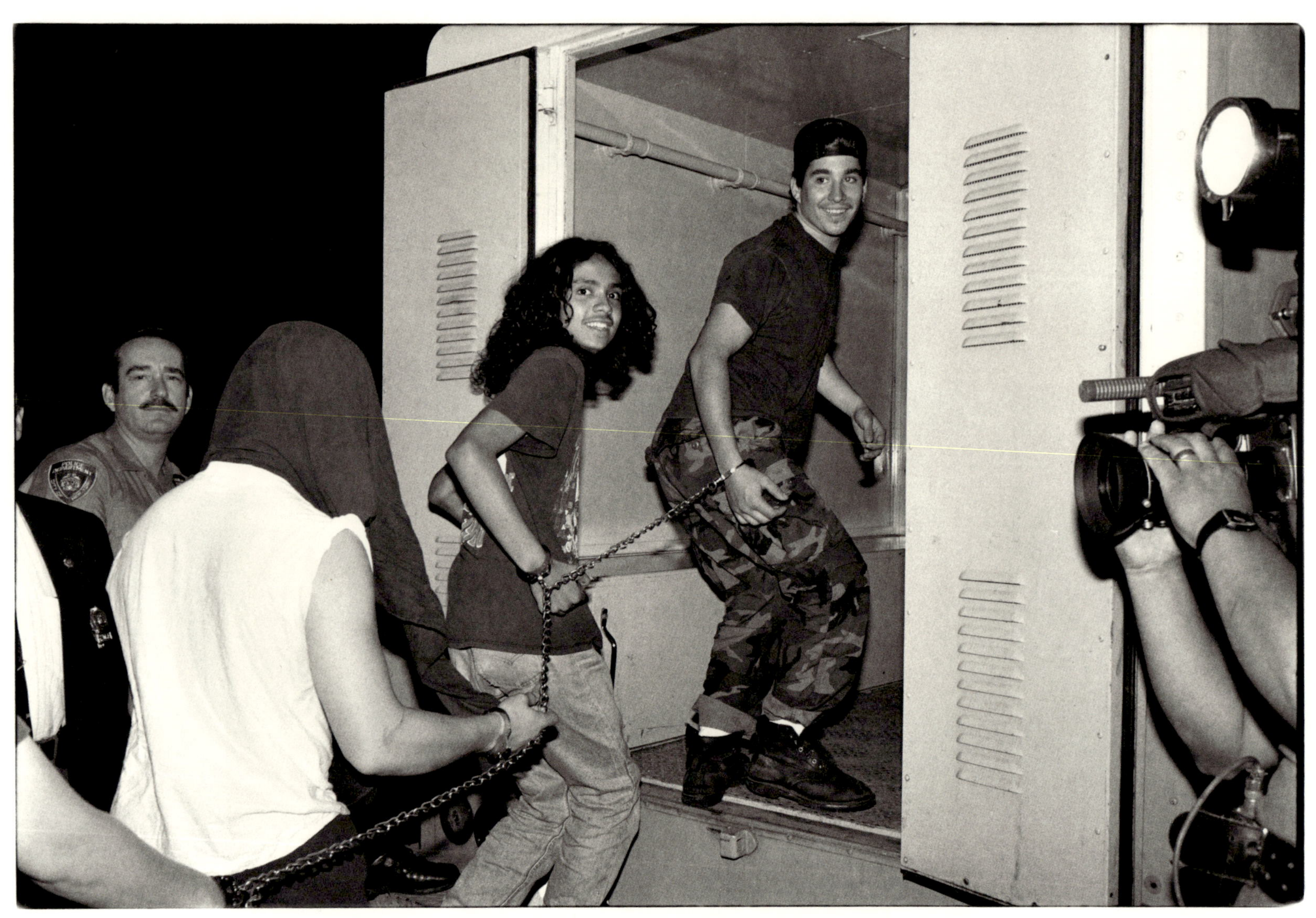

KIDS ARRESTED FOR KNOCKING OVER 838 TOMBSTONES IN QUEENS CEMETERY.

1990

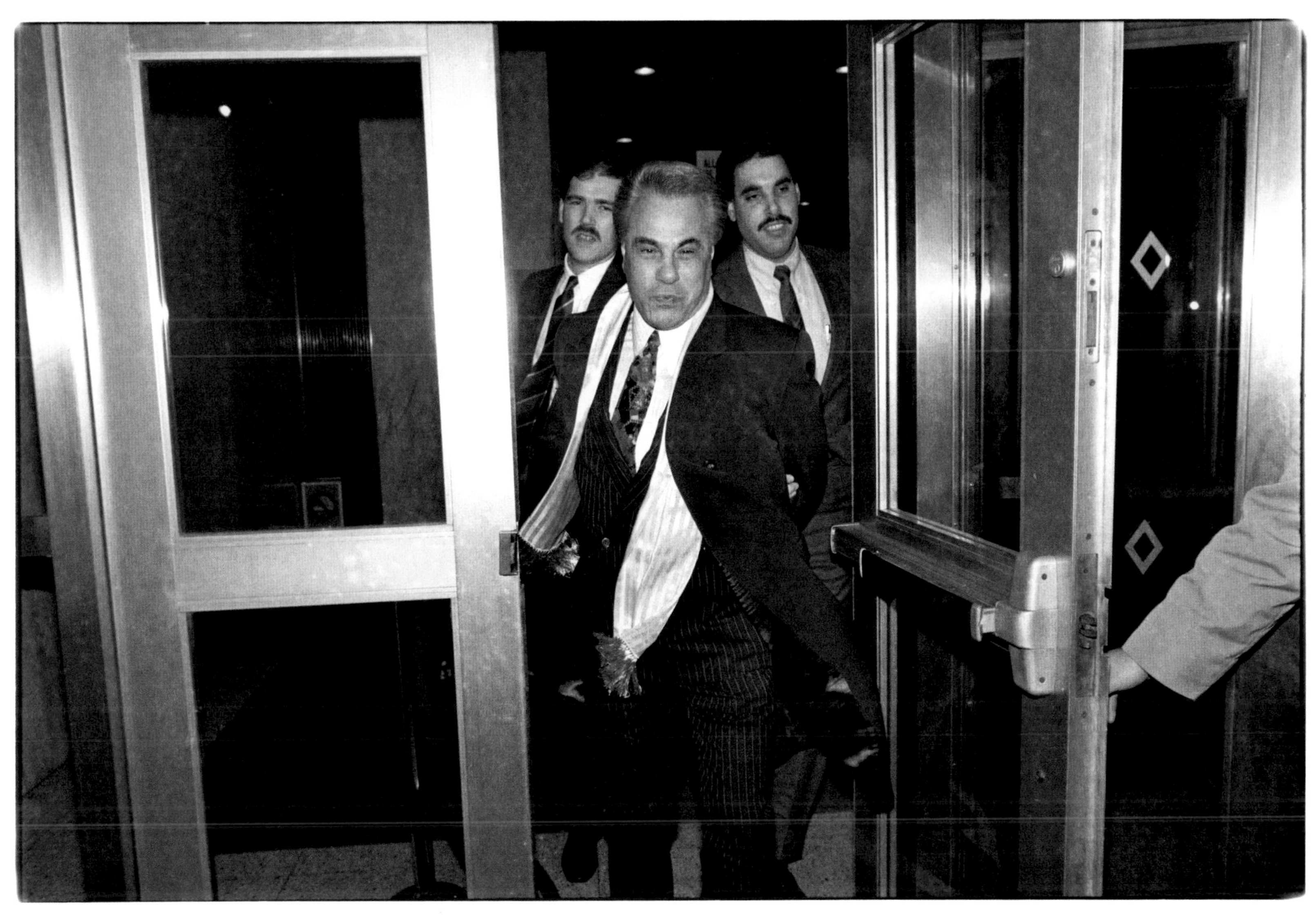

GODFATHER LEAVING F.B.I. BUILDING FOR OVERNIGHT HOLDING CELL.

1990

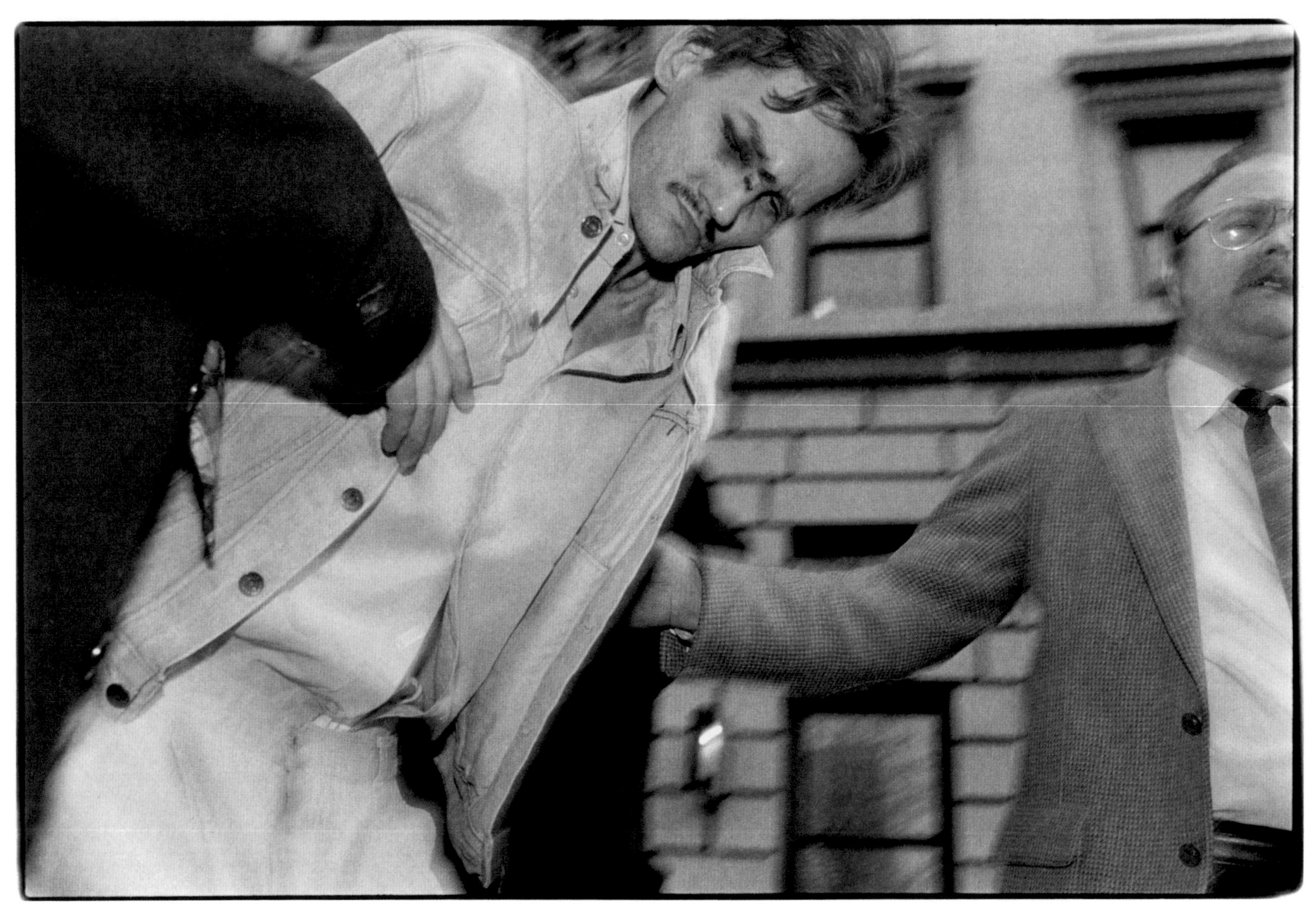

COP SHOOTING SUSPECT LEAVING PRECINCT FOR CENTRAL BOOKING.

1992

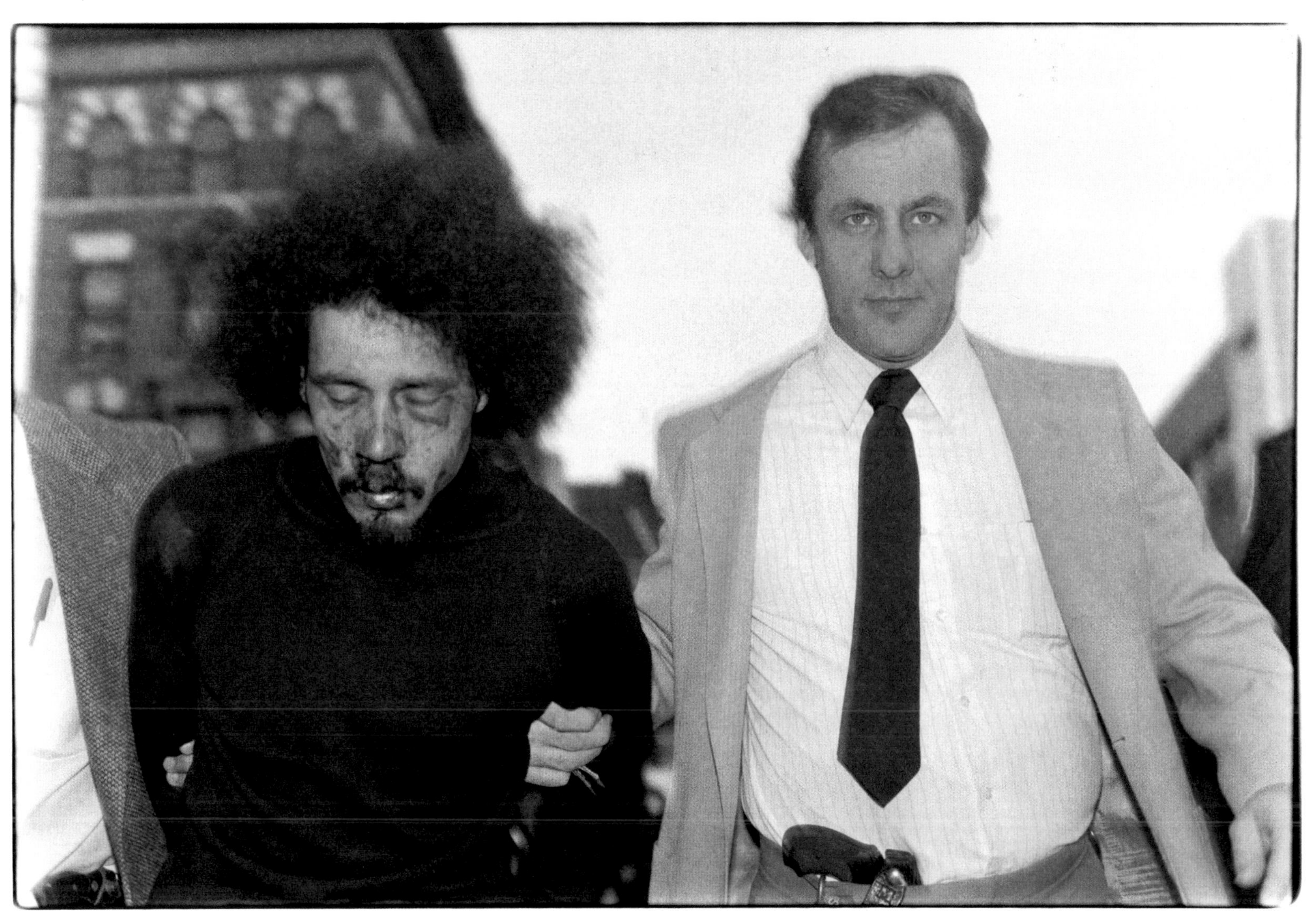

COP SHOOTING — SUSPECT TAKEN IN FOR QUESTIONING.

1982

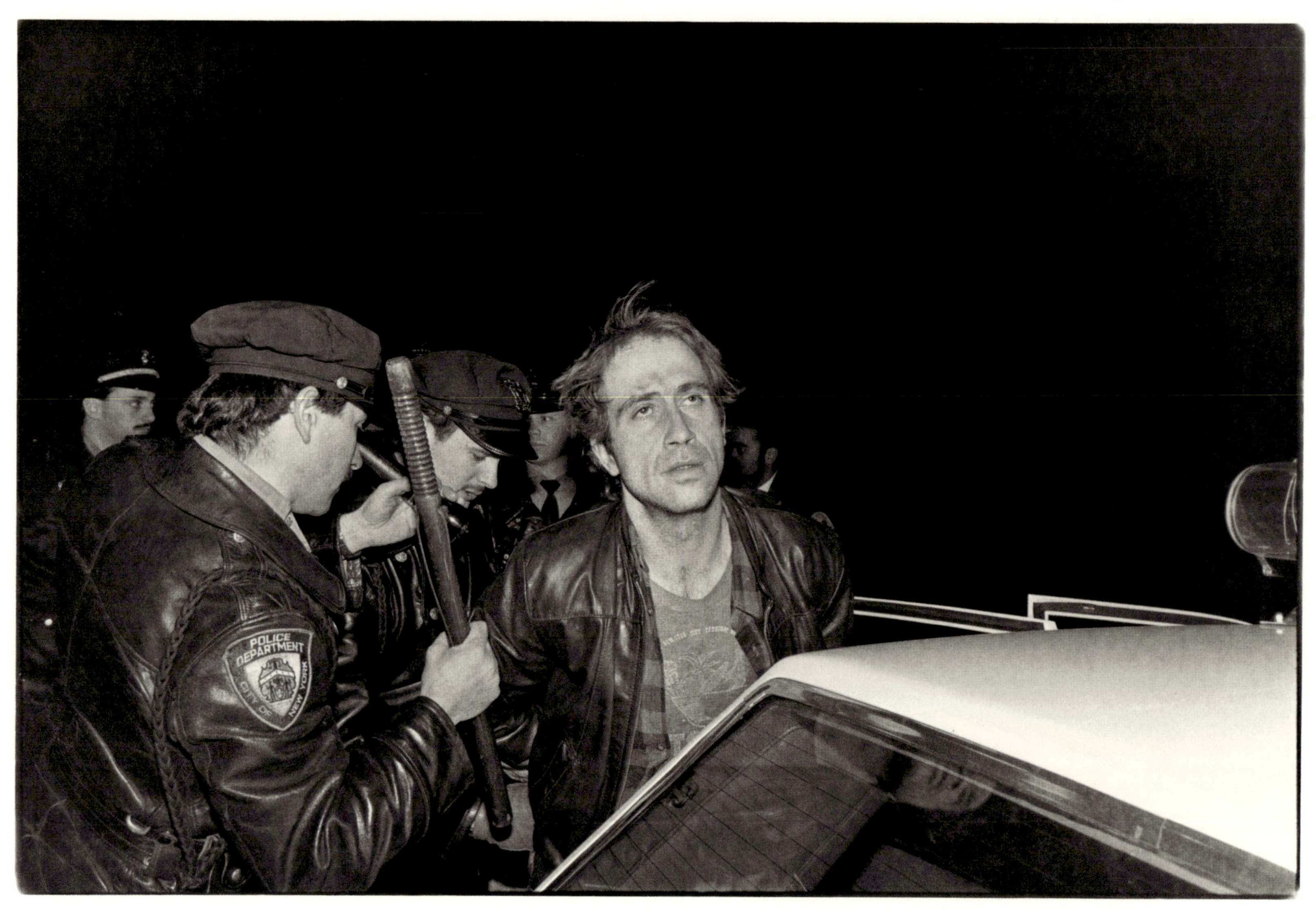

DRUNK DRIVER BEING ARRESTED FOR VEHICULAR HOMICIDE.

1989

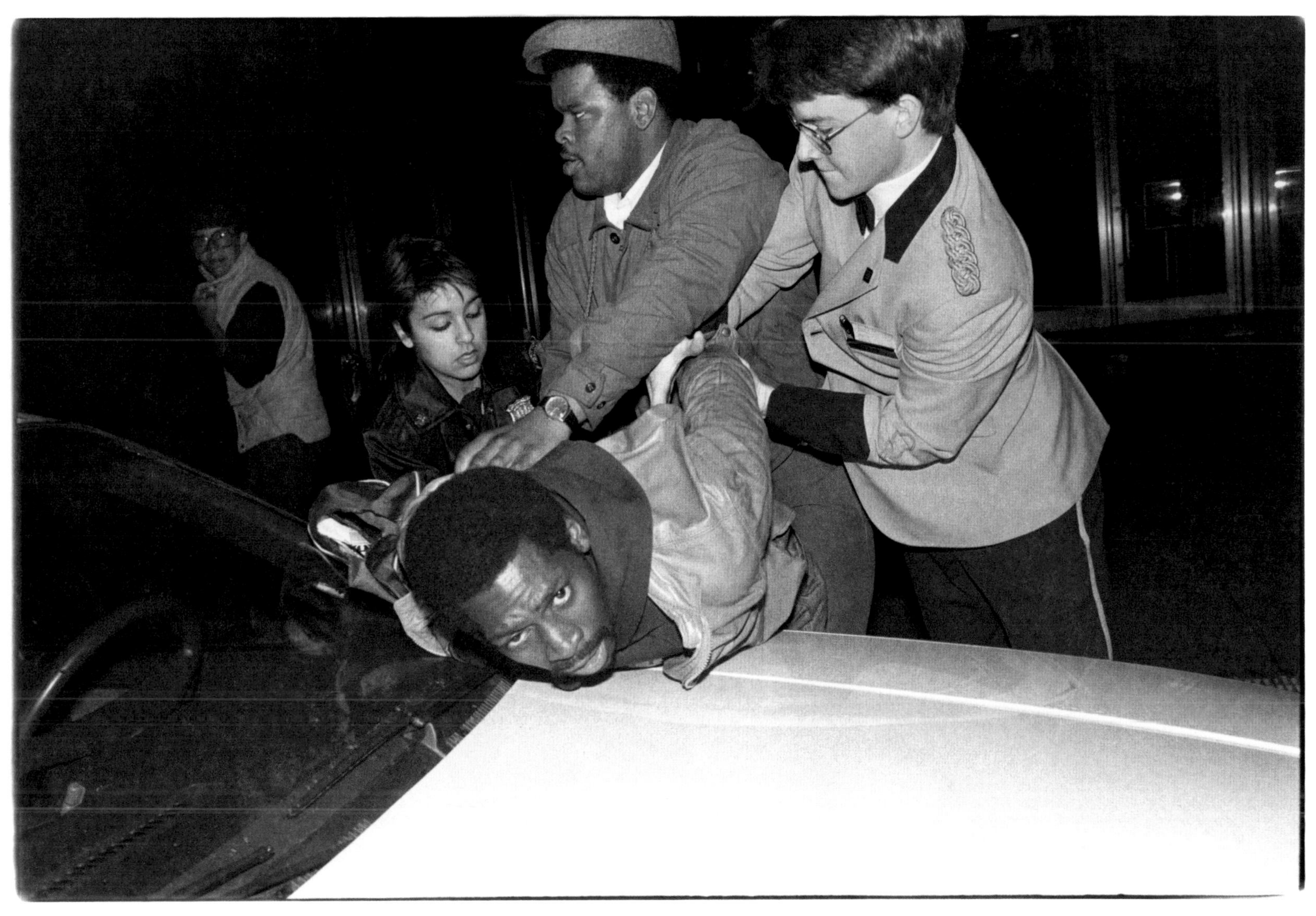

HOTEL DOORMAN AND TAXI DRIVER HELP TRANSIT COP ARREST ALLEGED TOKEN SUCKER.

1989

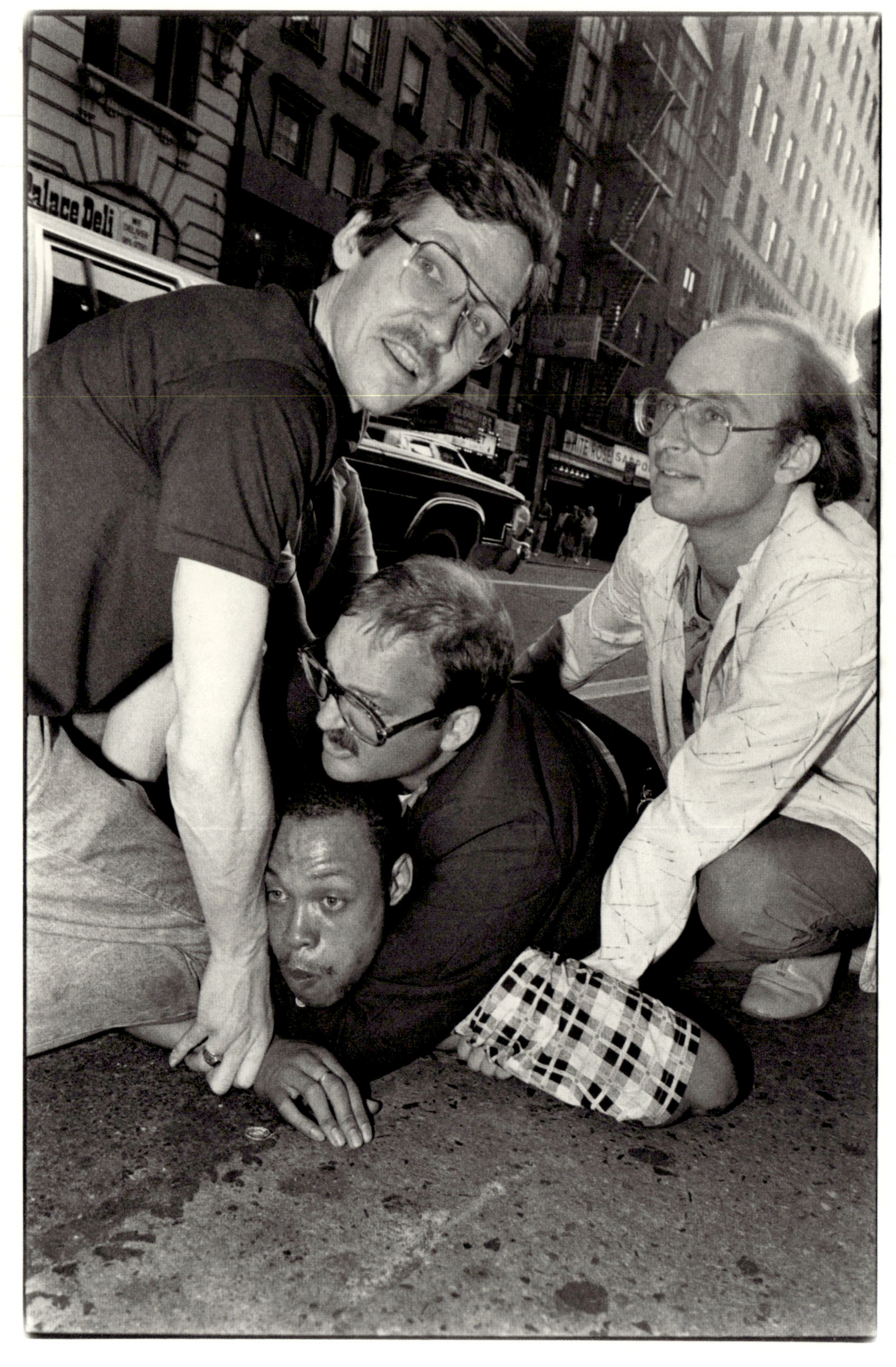

CITIZENS' ARREST OF ALLEGED PICKPOCKET. 1984

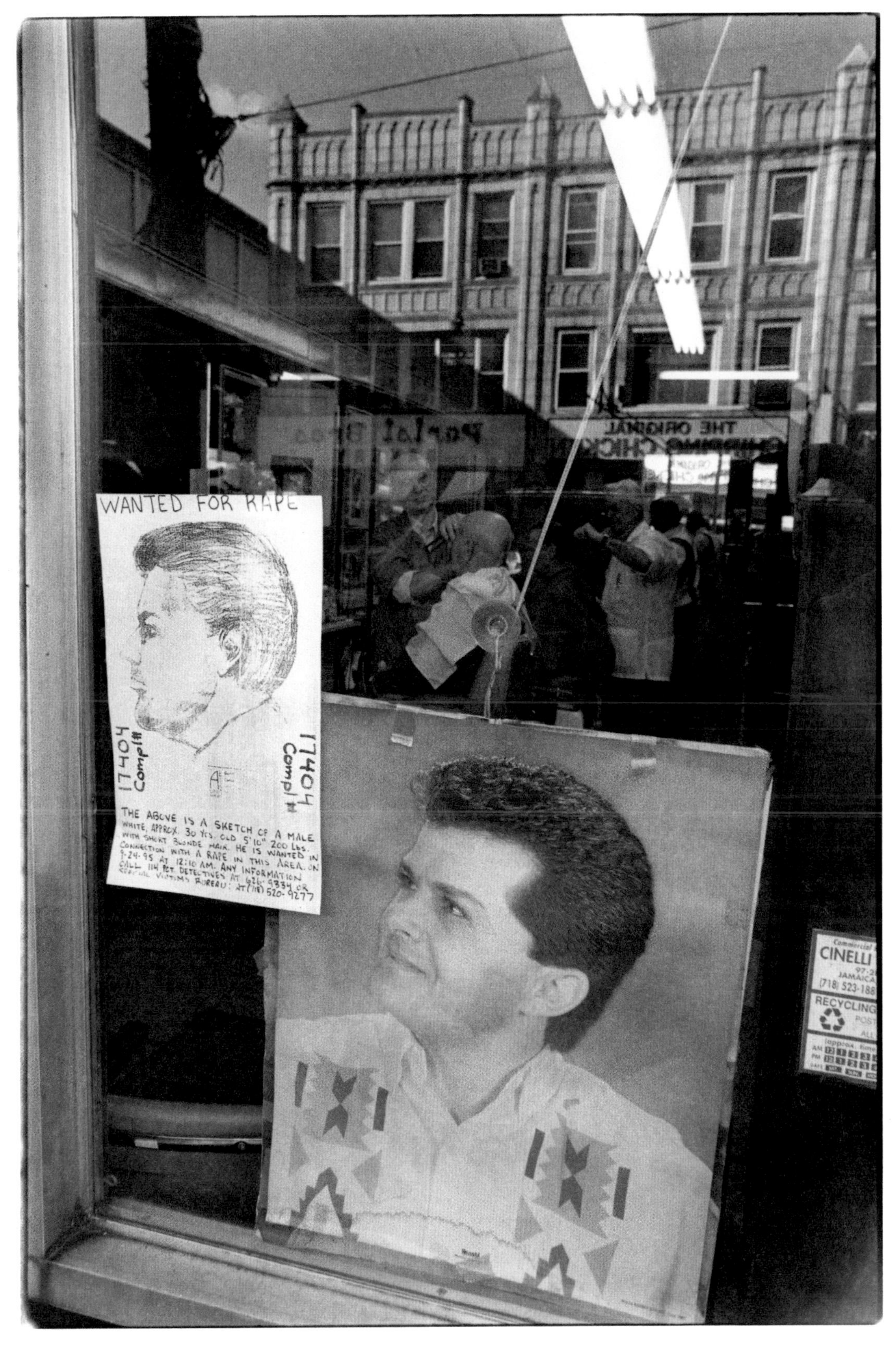

POLICE SKETCH OF RAPE SUSPECT DISPLAYED IN BARBER SHOP WINDOW. 1995

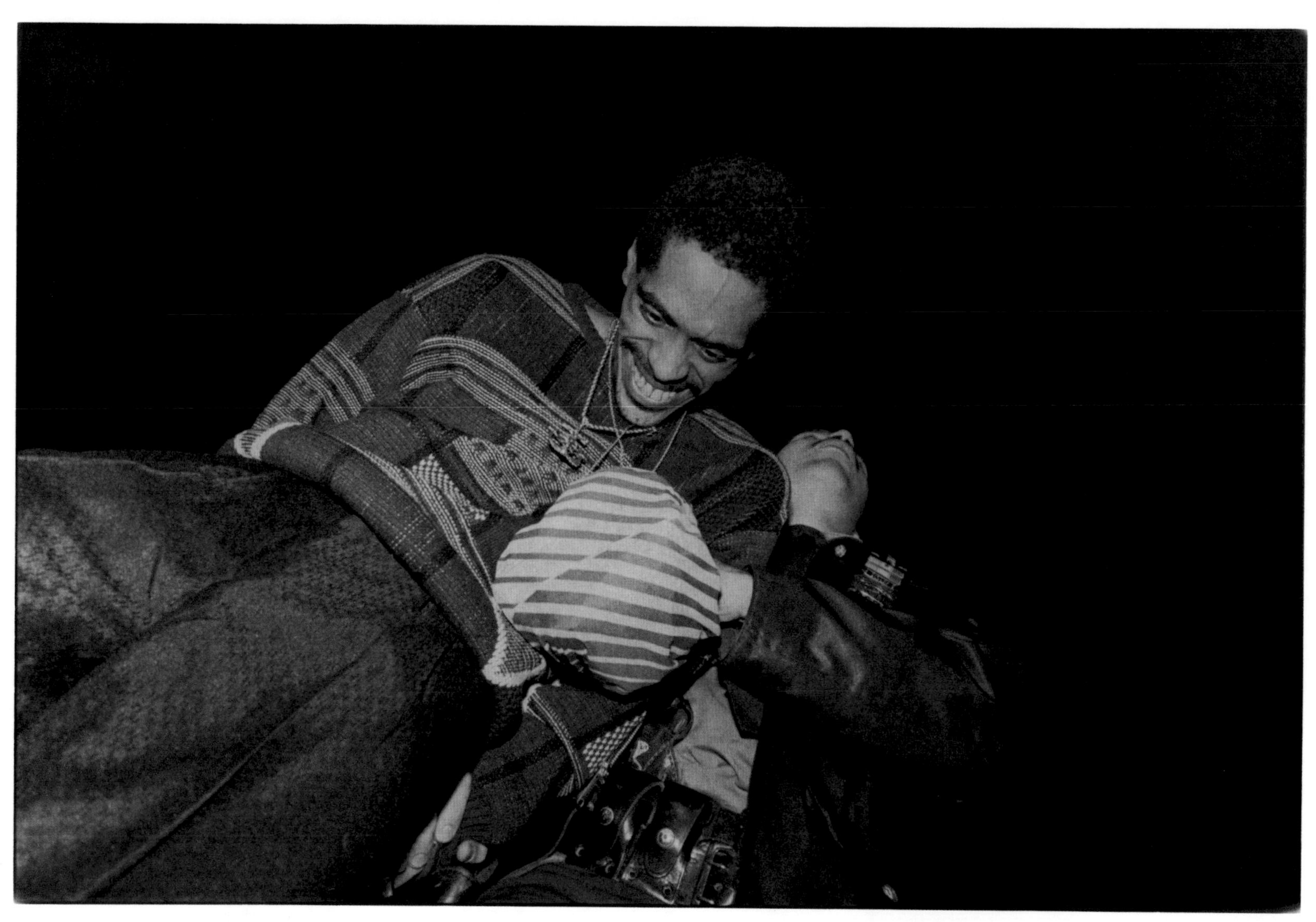

MAN ARRESTED FOR SEllING DRUGS.

1989

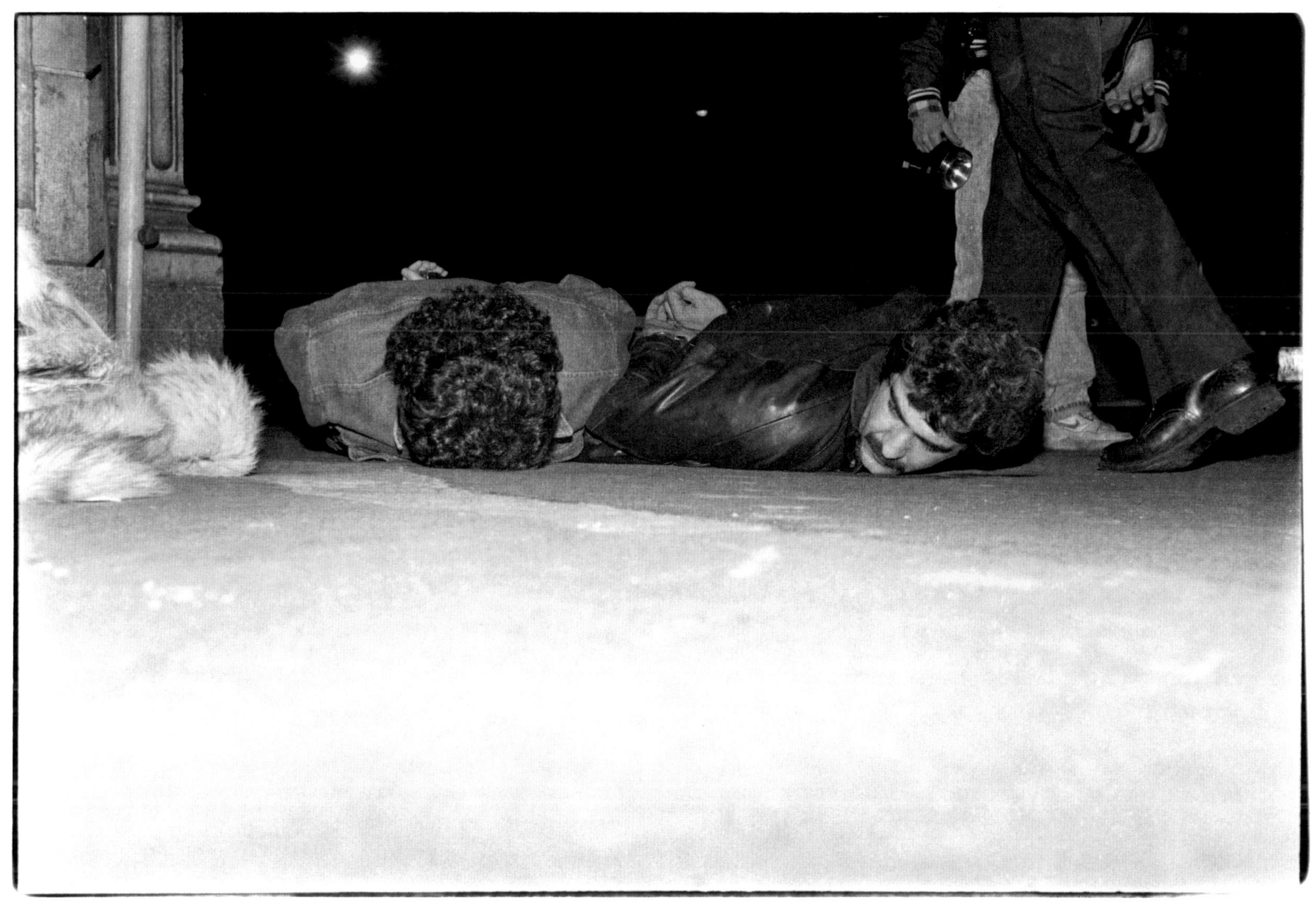

ARRESTED FUR THIEVES

1989

OUTSIDERS

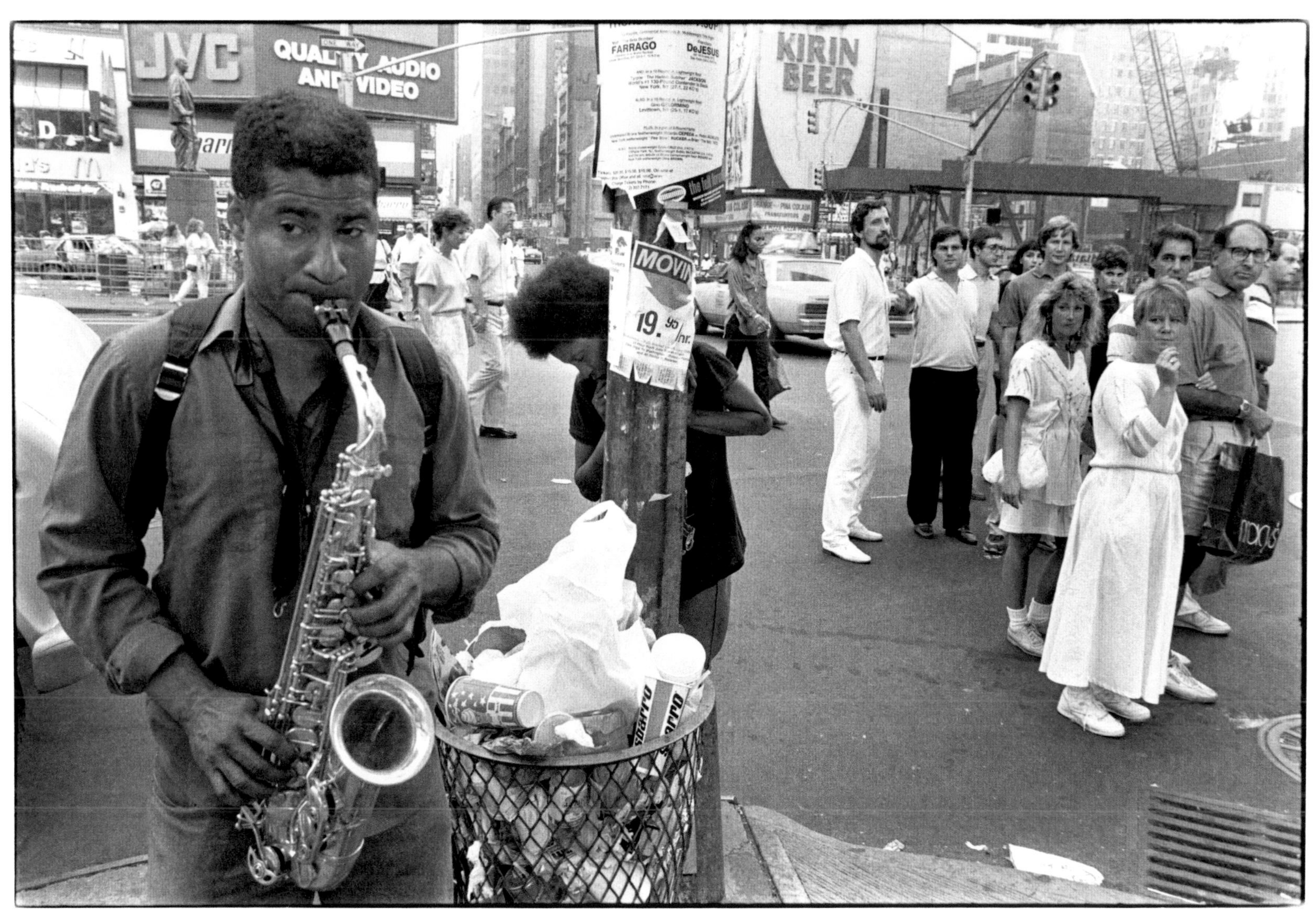

TOURISTS PASSING MAN PLAYING SAX AND WOMAN ON DRUGS.

1988

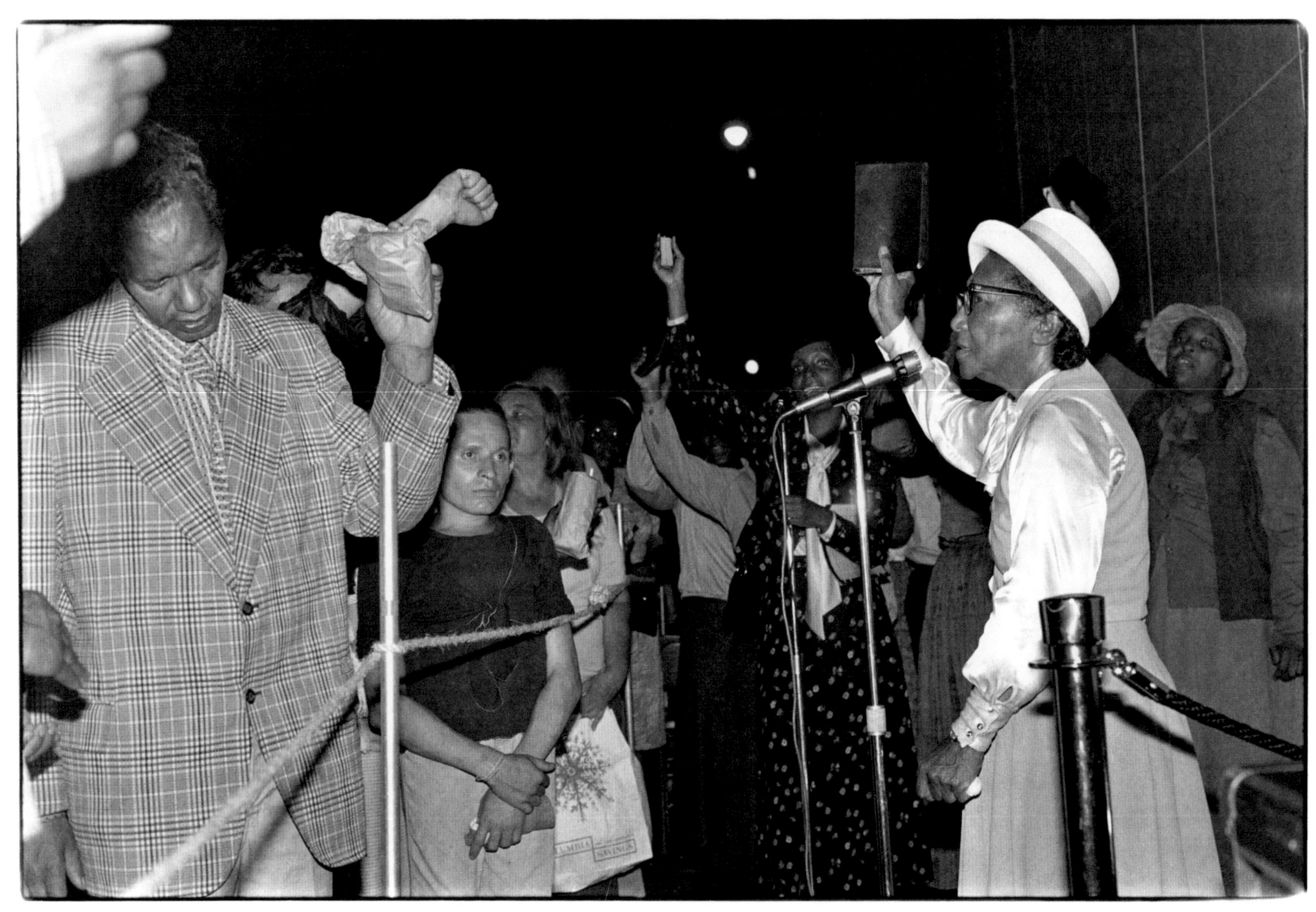

SATURDAY NIGHT GOSPEL WITH SISTER WILLIAMS — TIMES SQUARE.

1982

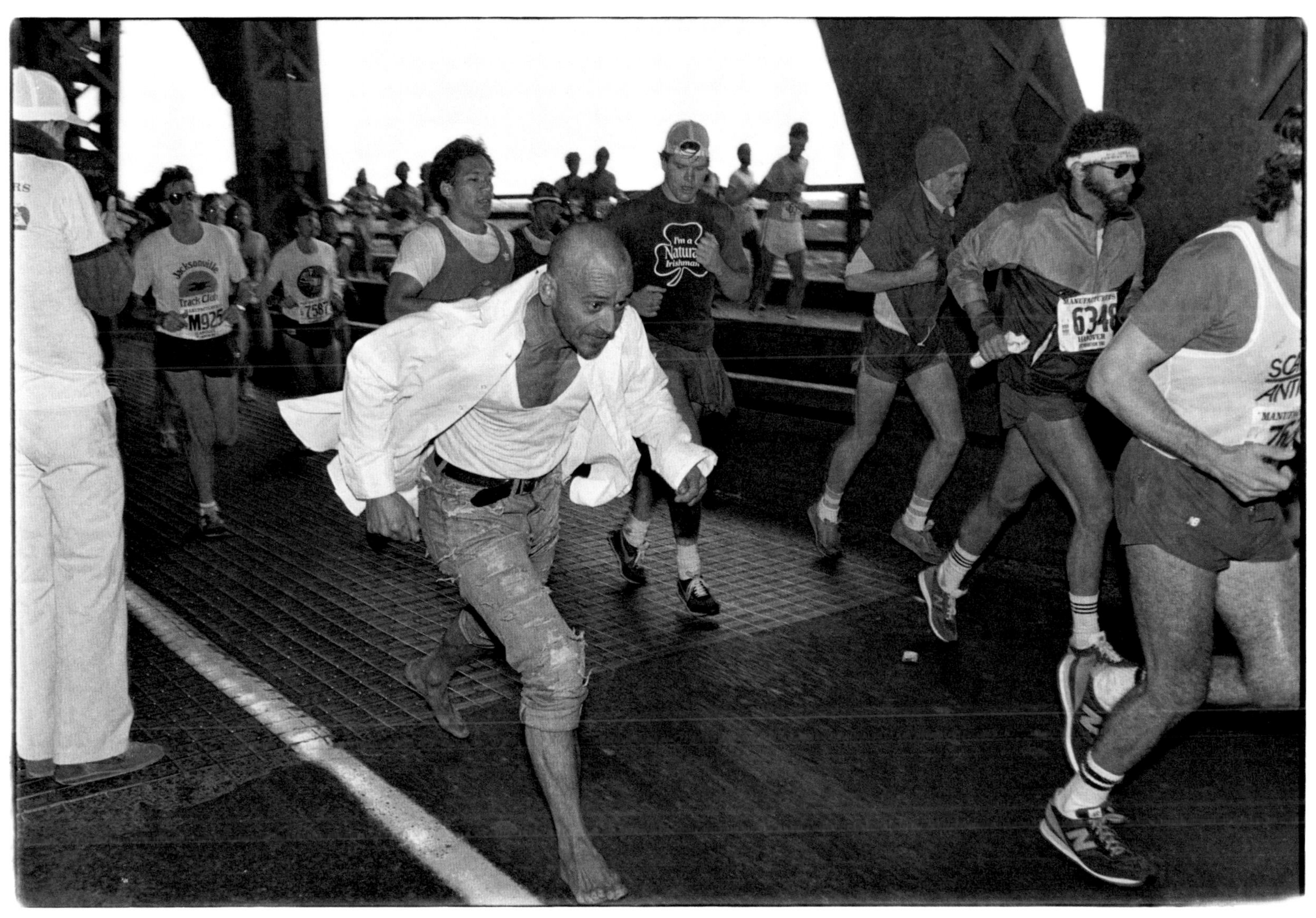

MARATHON RUNNERS CROSSING THE 59th STREET BRIDGE.

1982

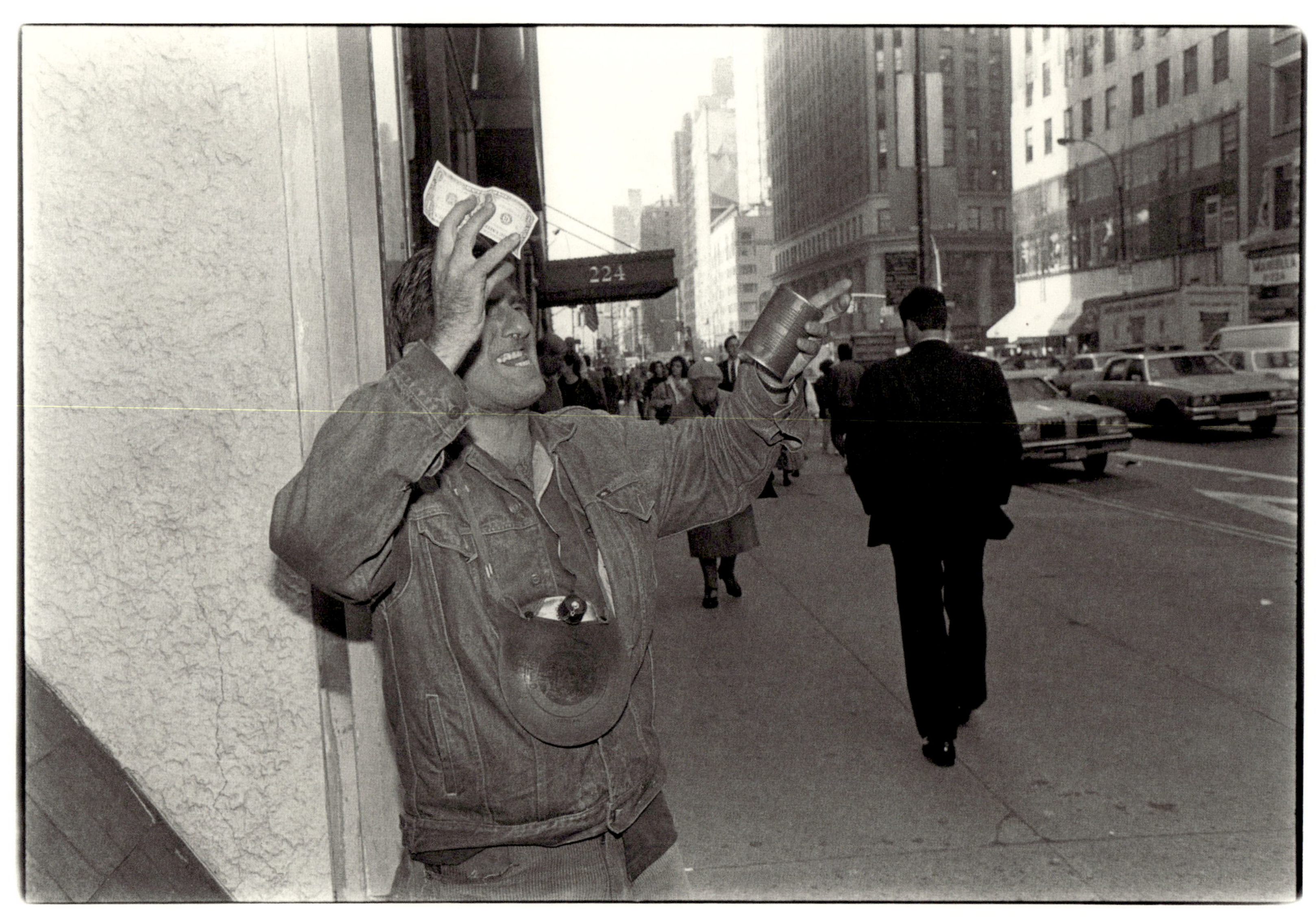

MAN SINGING OPERA— W57 ST.

1989

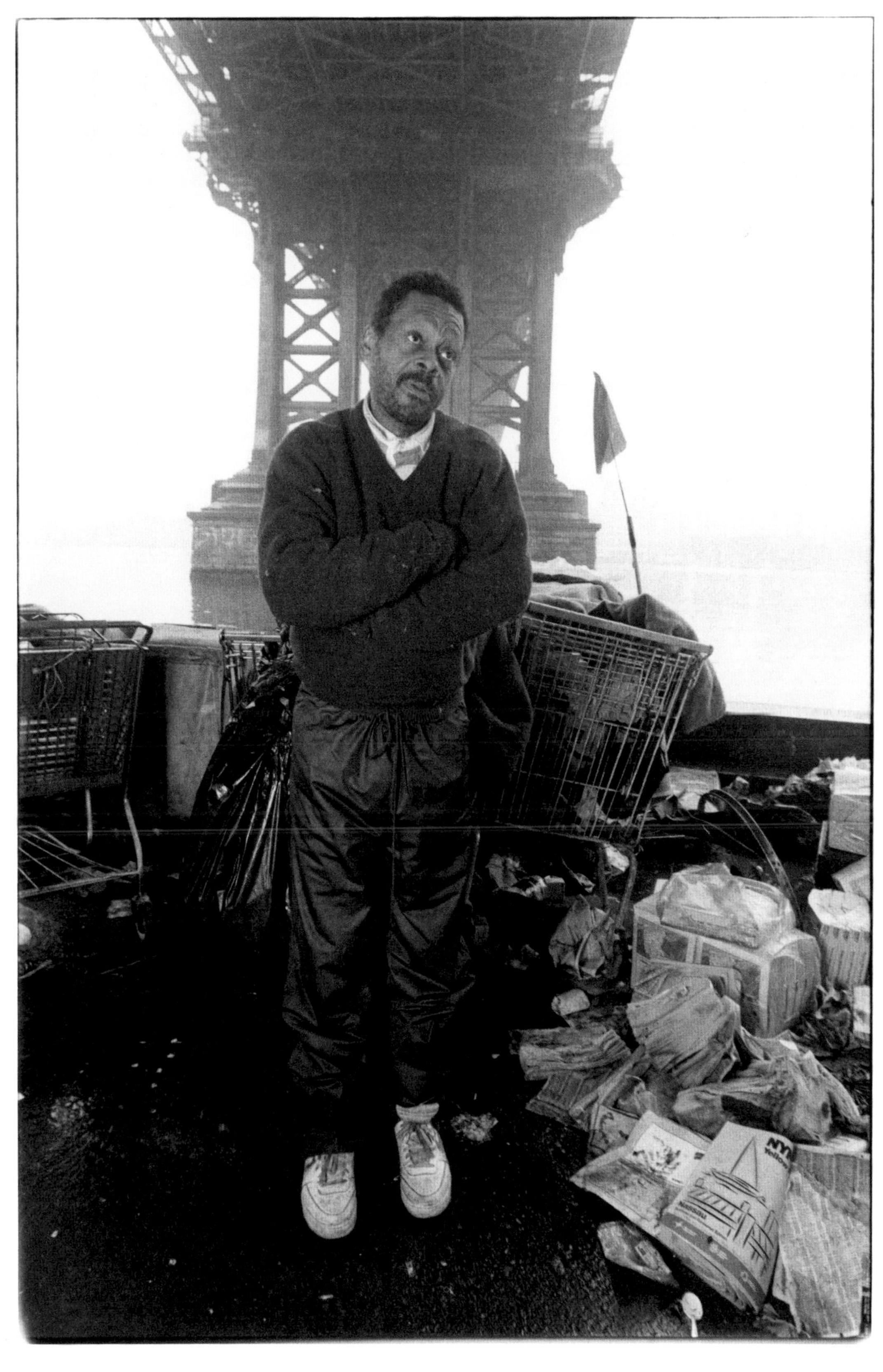

MAN DESCRIBES LIFE IN EAST RIVER SHANTY TOWN. 1995

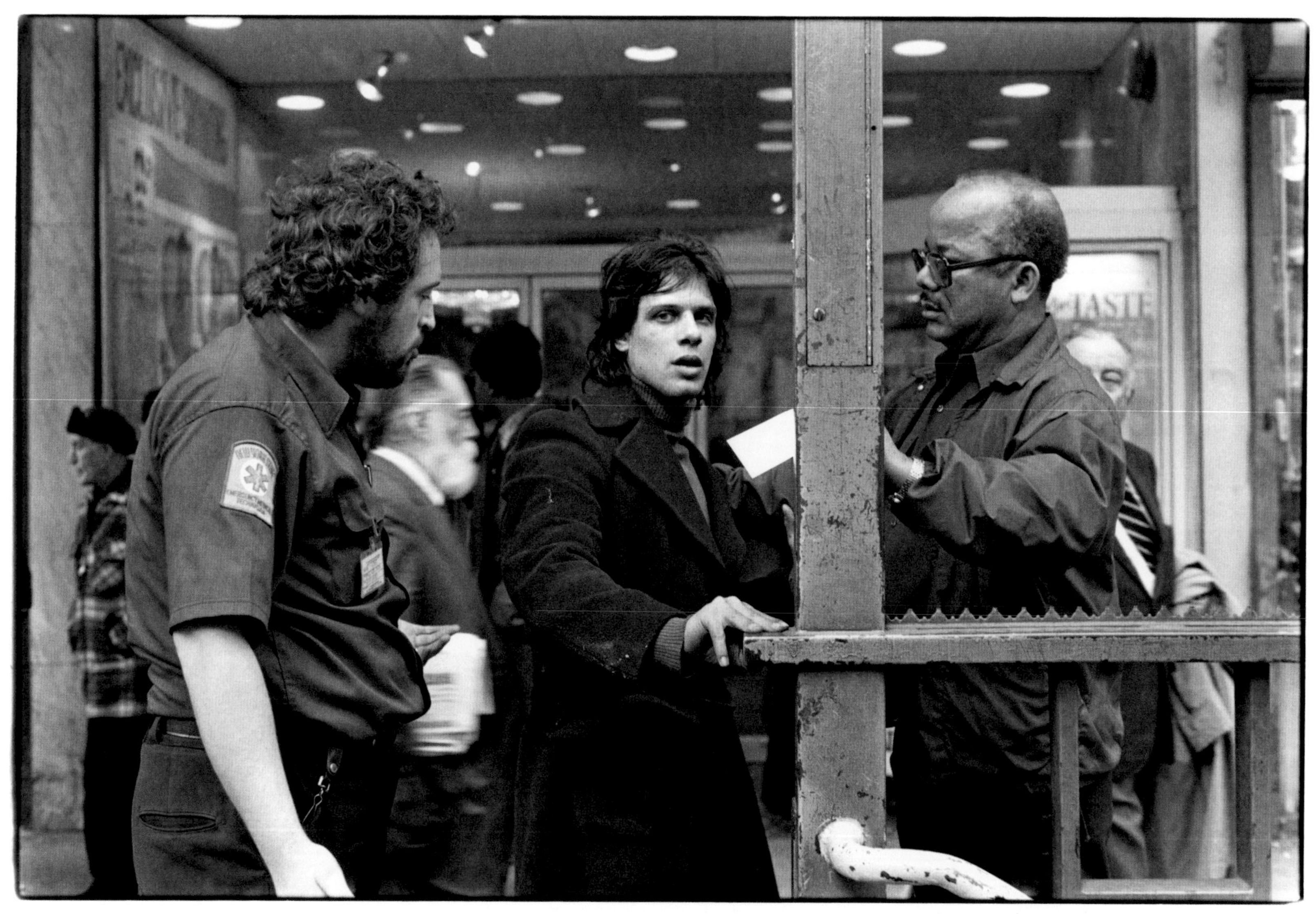

DRUG OVERDOSE BEING ASKED IF HE WOULD LIKE TO GO TO A HOSPITAL.

1981

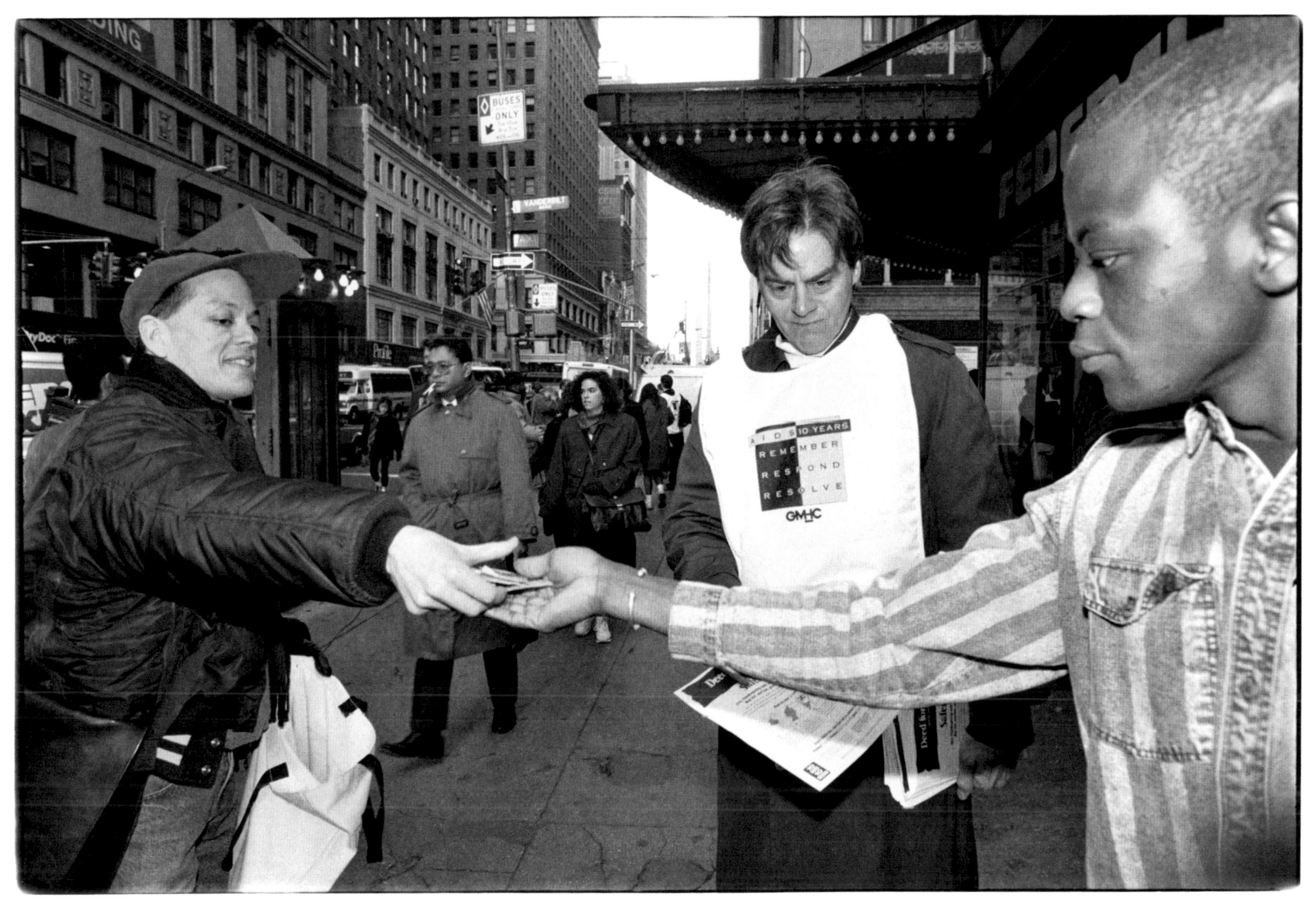

MEN HANDING OUT CONDOMS AND SAFE SEX FLYERS.

1991

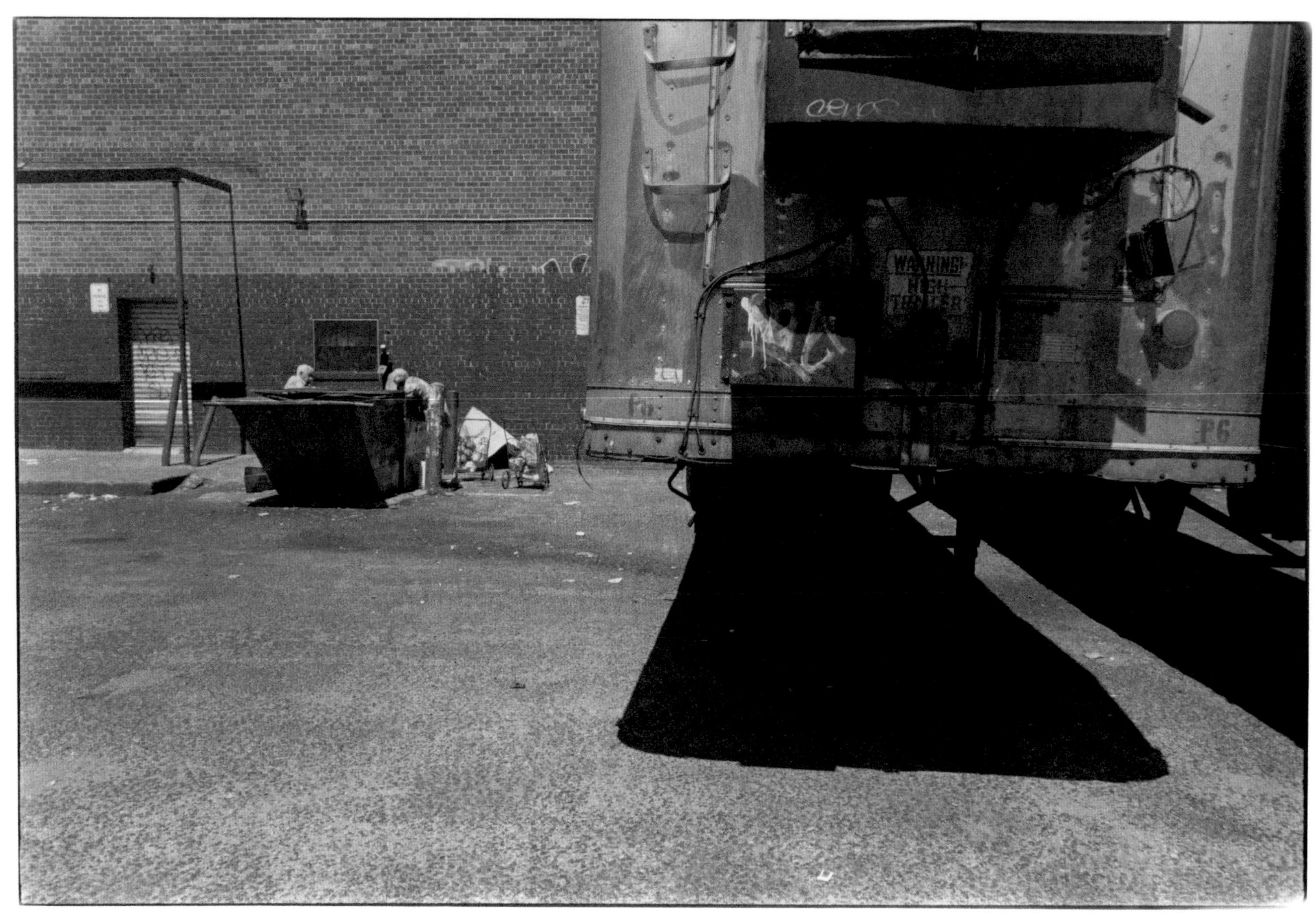

ELDERLY COUPLE SEARCHING SUPERMARKET DUMPSTER FOR FOOD.

1995

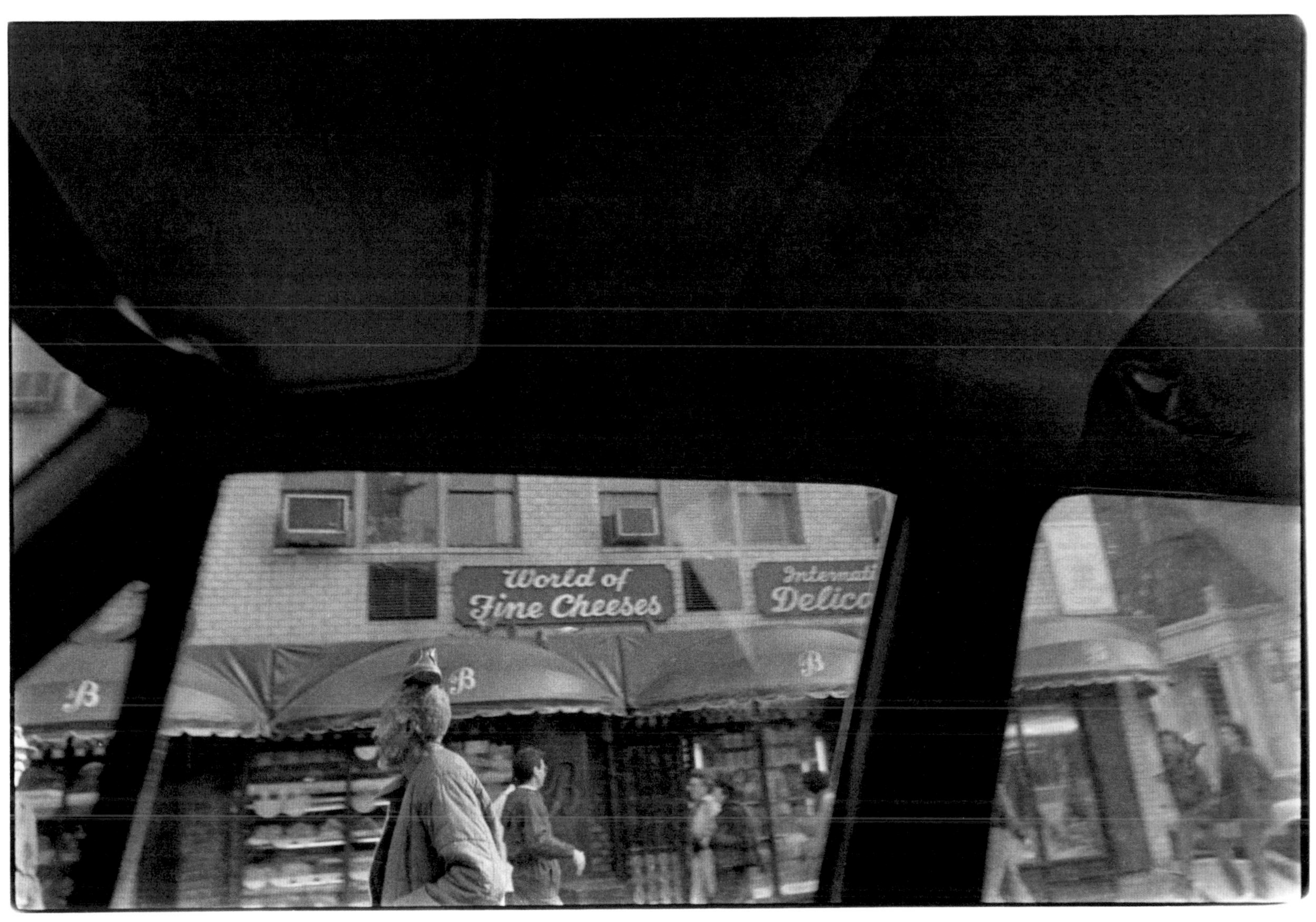

MAN WALKING AROUND WITH A SHOE ON HIS HEAD.

1990

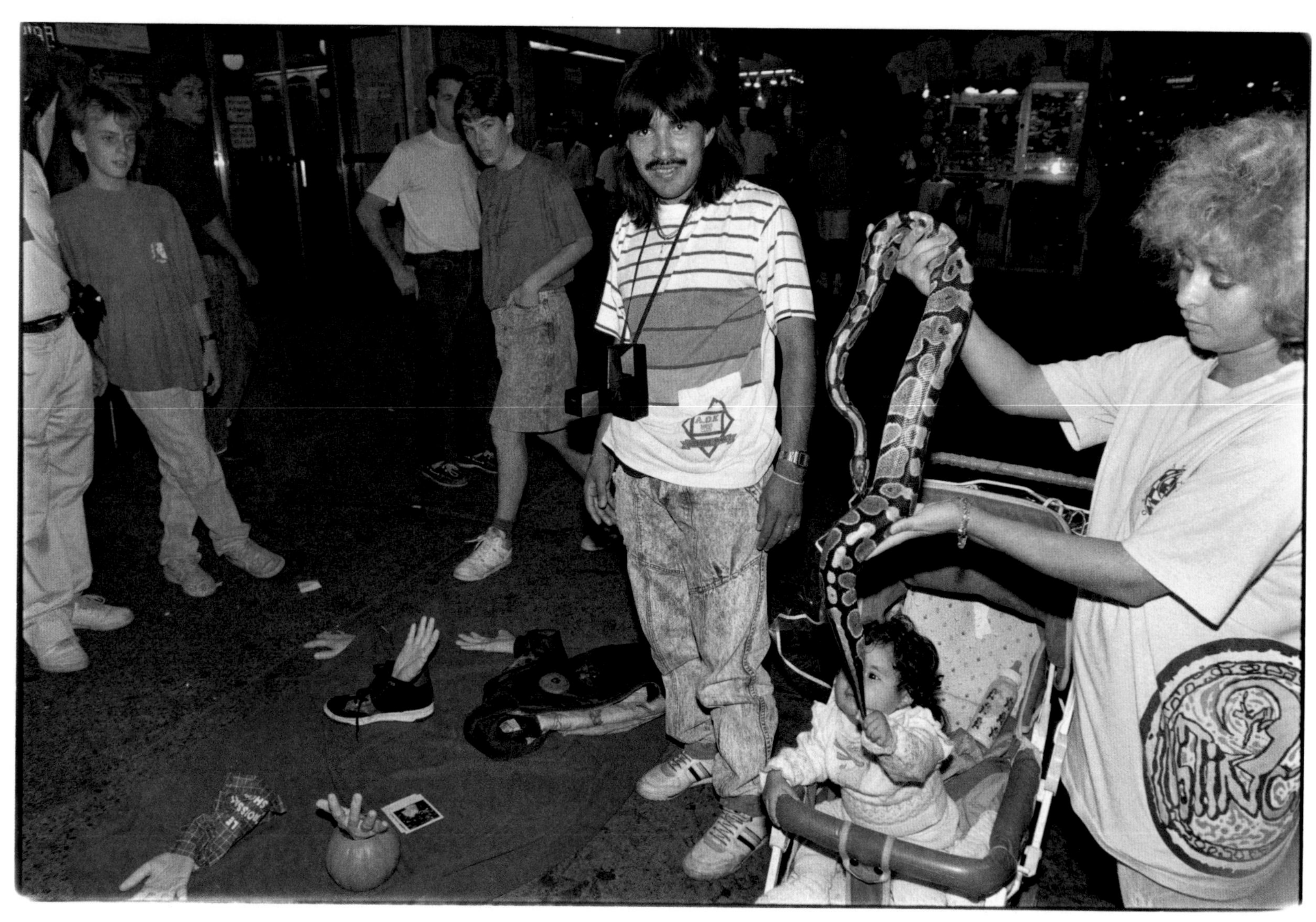

YOUNG FAMILY SELLING POLAROID PORTRAITS WITH PYTHON.

1991

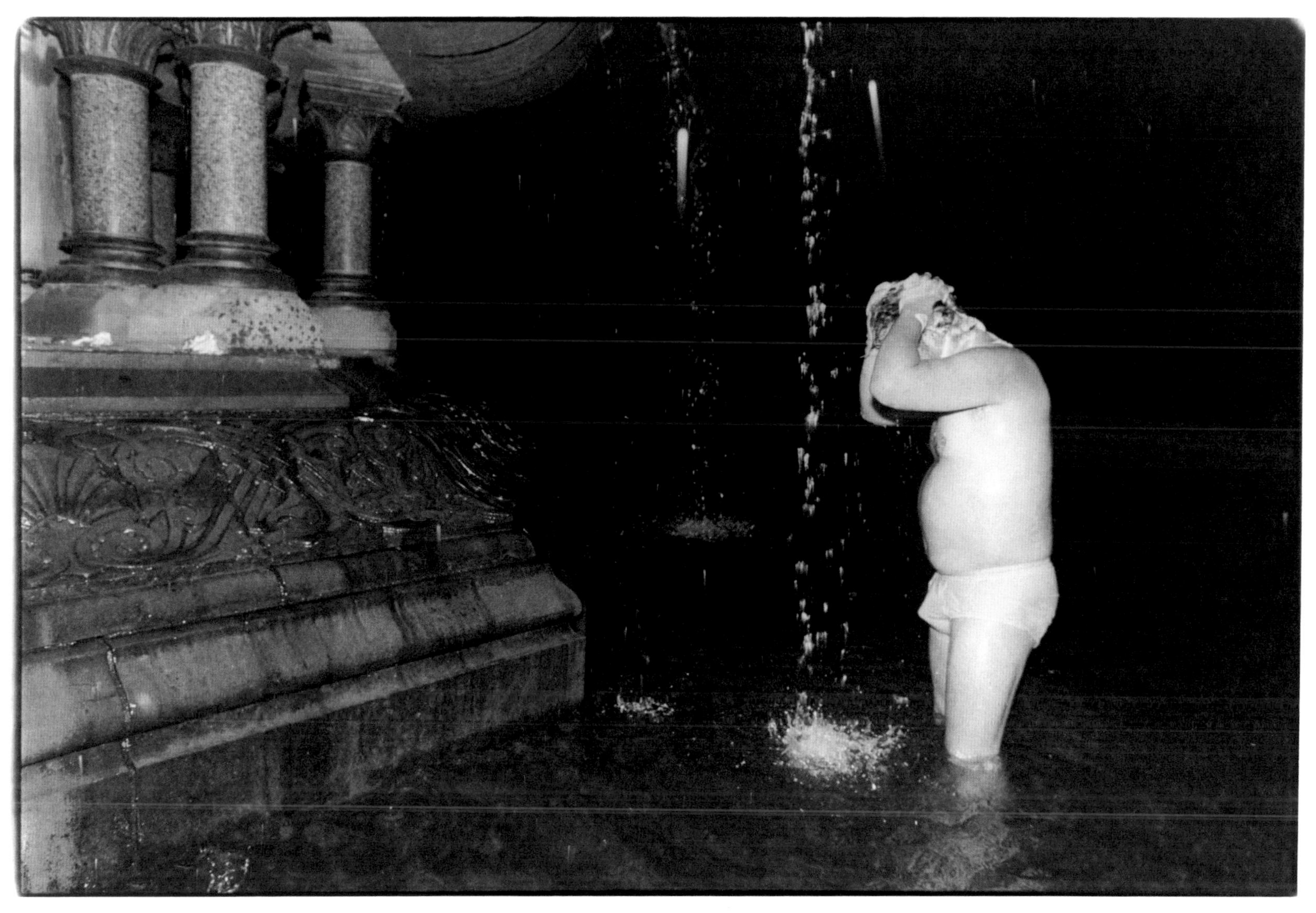

MAN BATHING AT DAWN IN CENTRAL PARK FOUNTAIN.

1994

DESPERATE PEOPLE

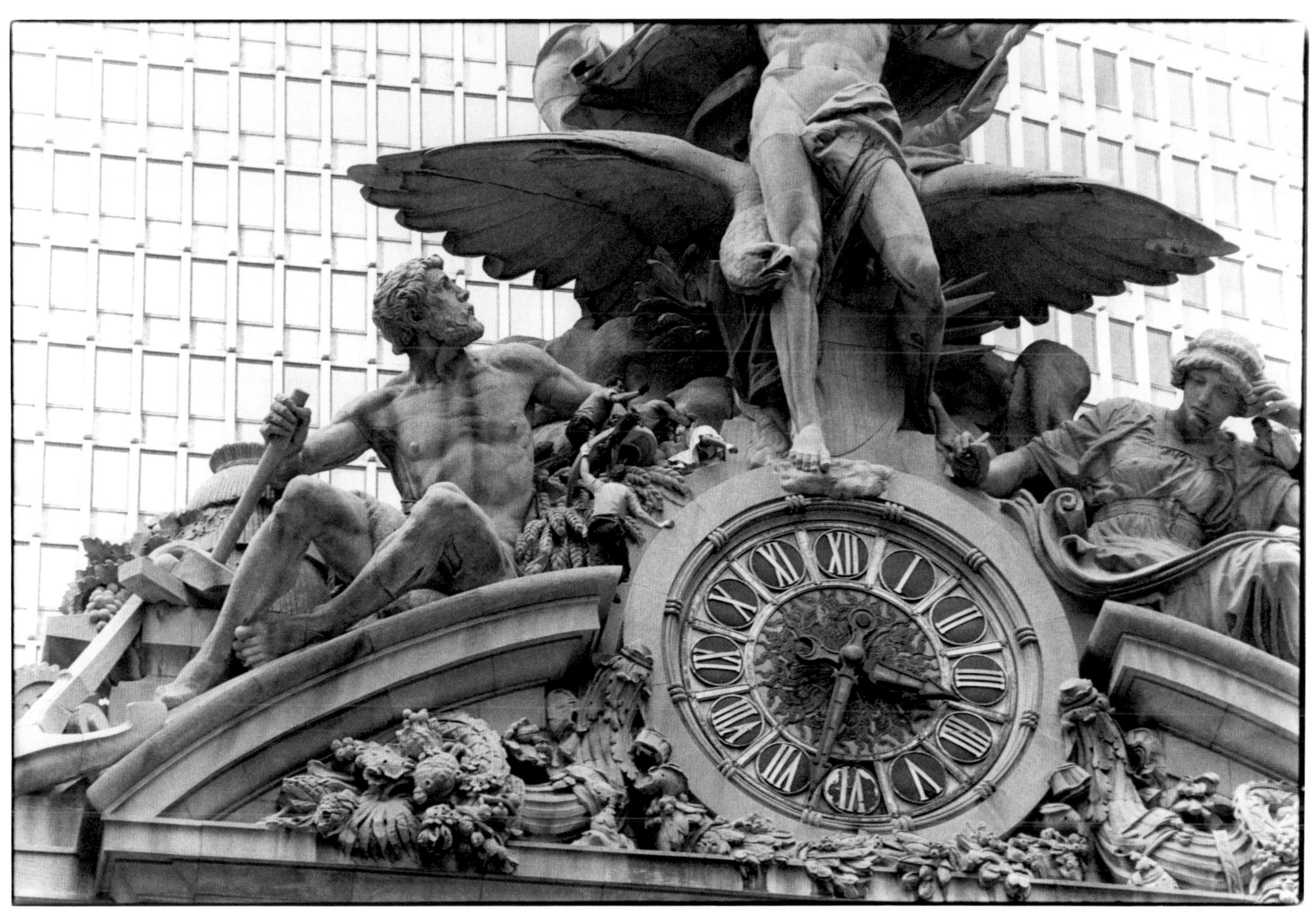

POLICE PREVENT WOMAN FROM JUMPING OFF GRAND CENTRAL STATION.

1990

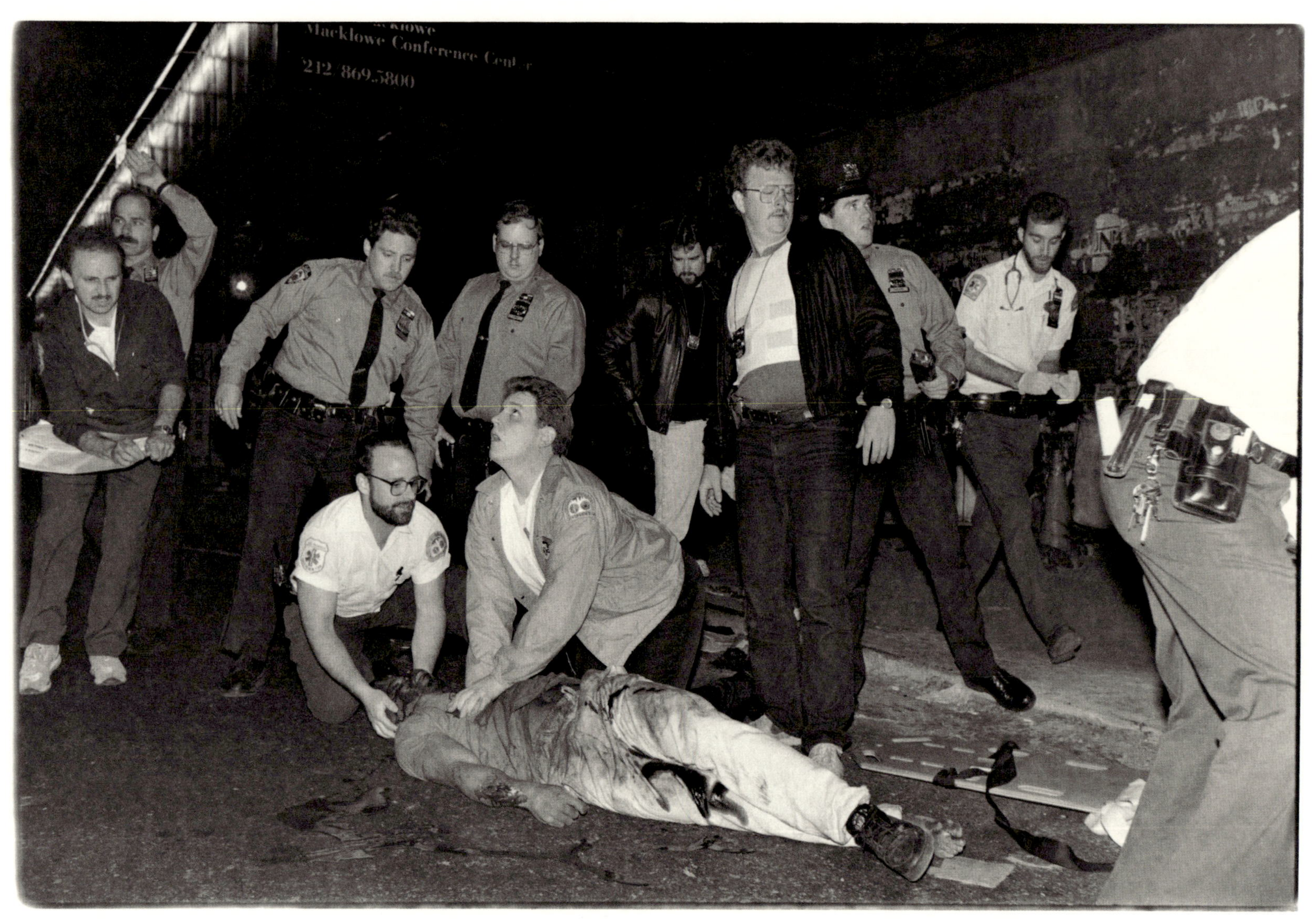

MAN JUMPS OFF HIGH RISE BUILDING.

1989

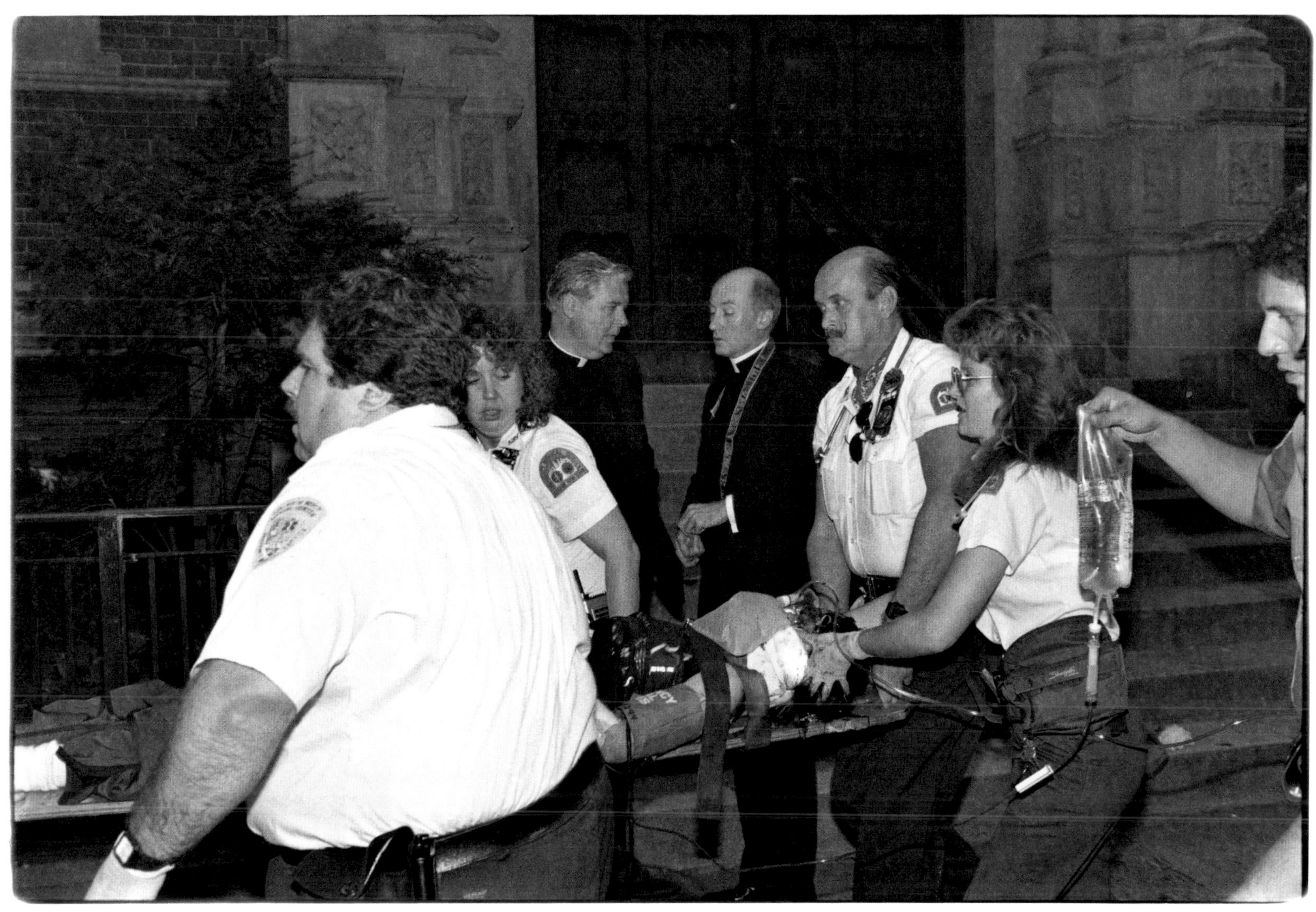

19 YR. OLD HOMELESS WOMAN SHOOTS HERSELF ON CHURCH STEPS WITH GUN SHE TRIED TO SELL EARLIER.

1987

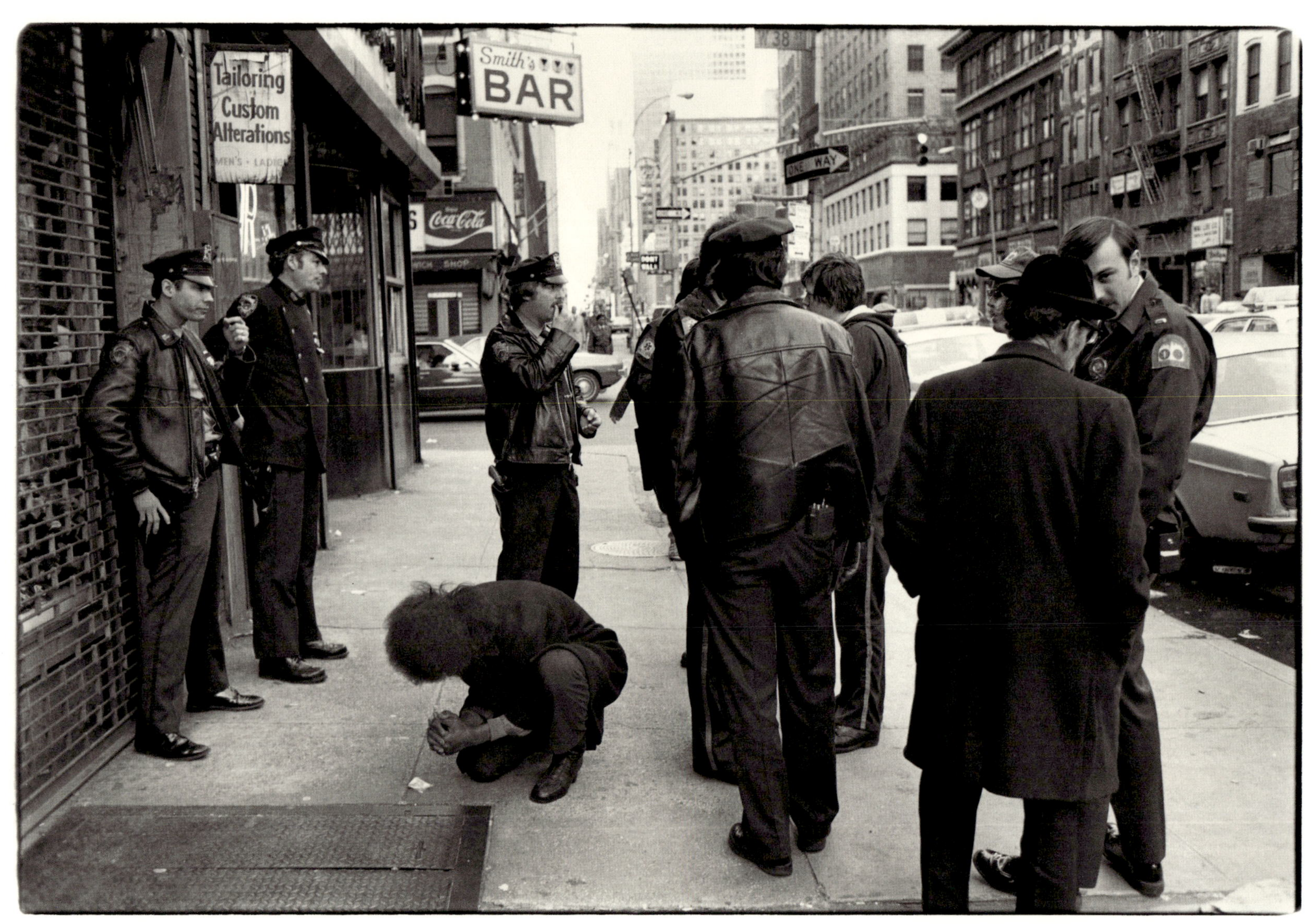

MAN PRAYS FOR A long TIME.

1980

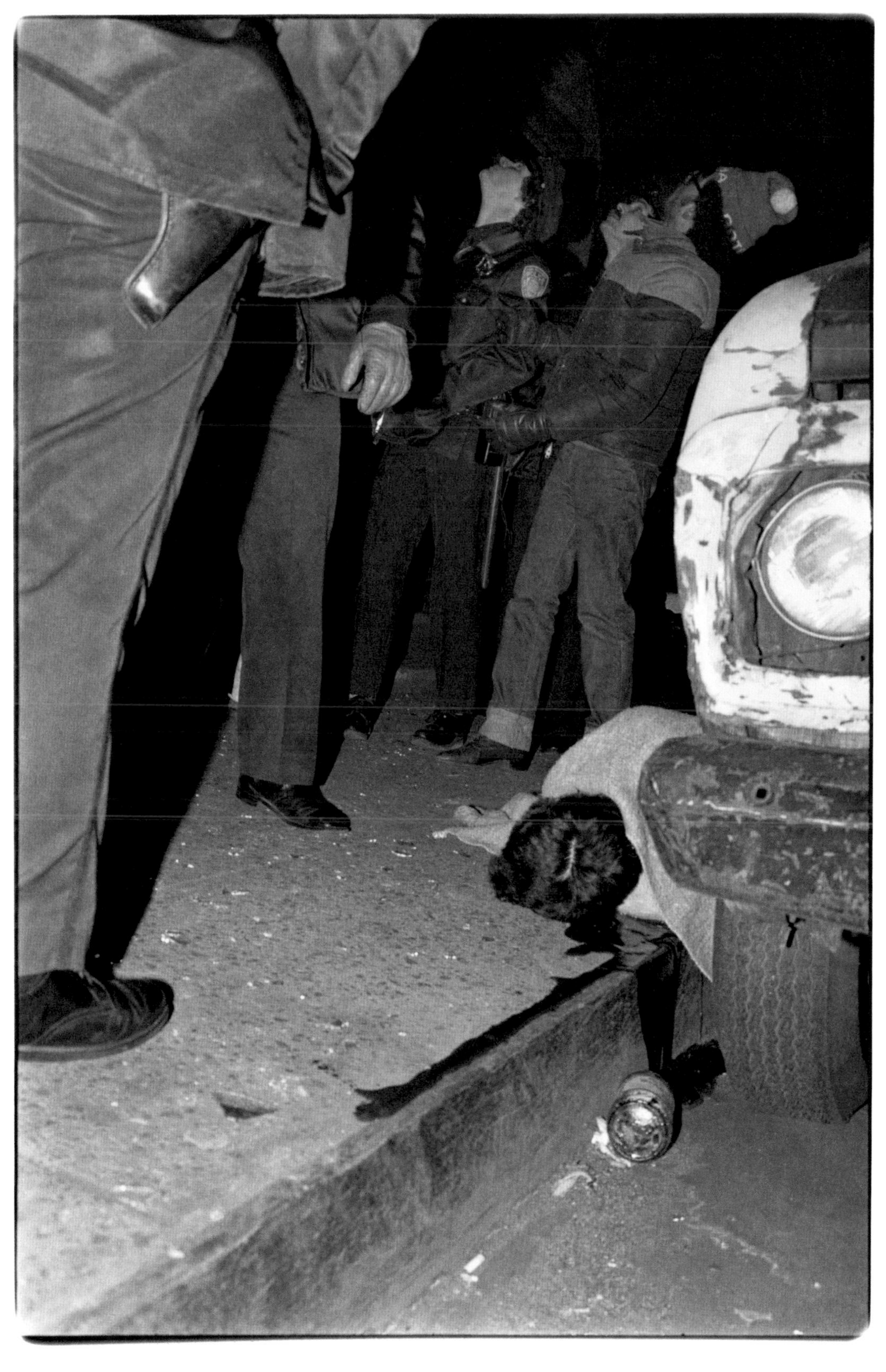

MAN FAllS FROM TENEMENT. 1989

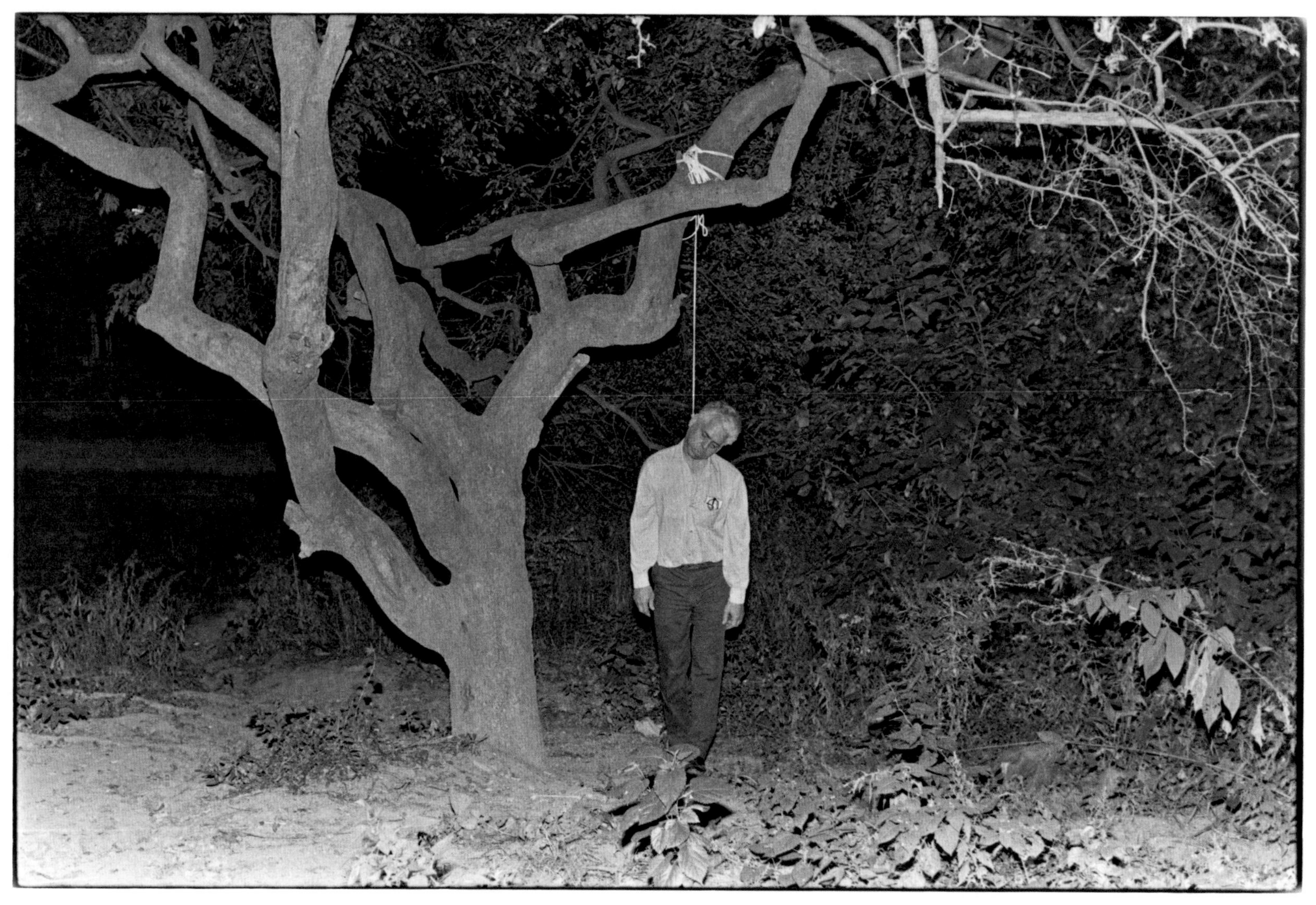

MAN HANGING FROM CRAB TREE.

1987

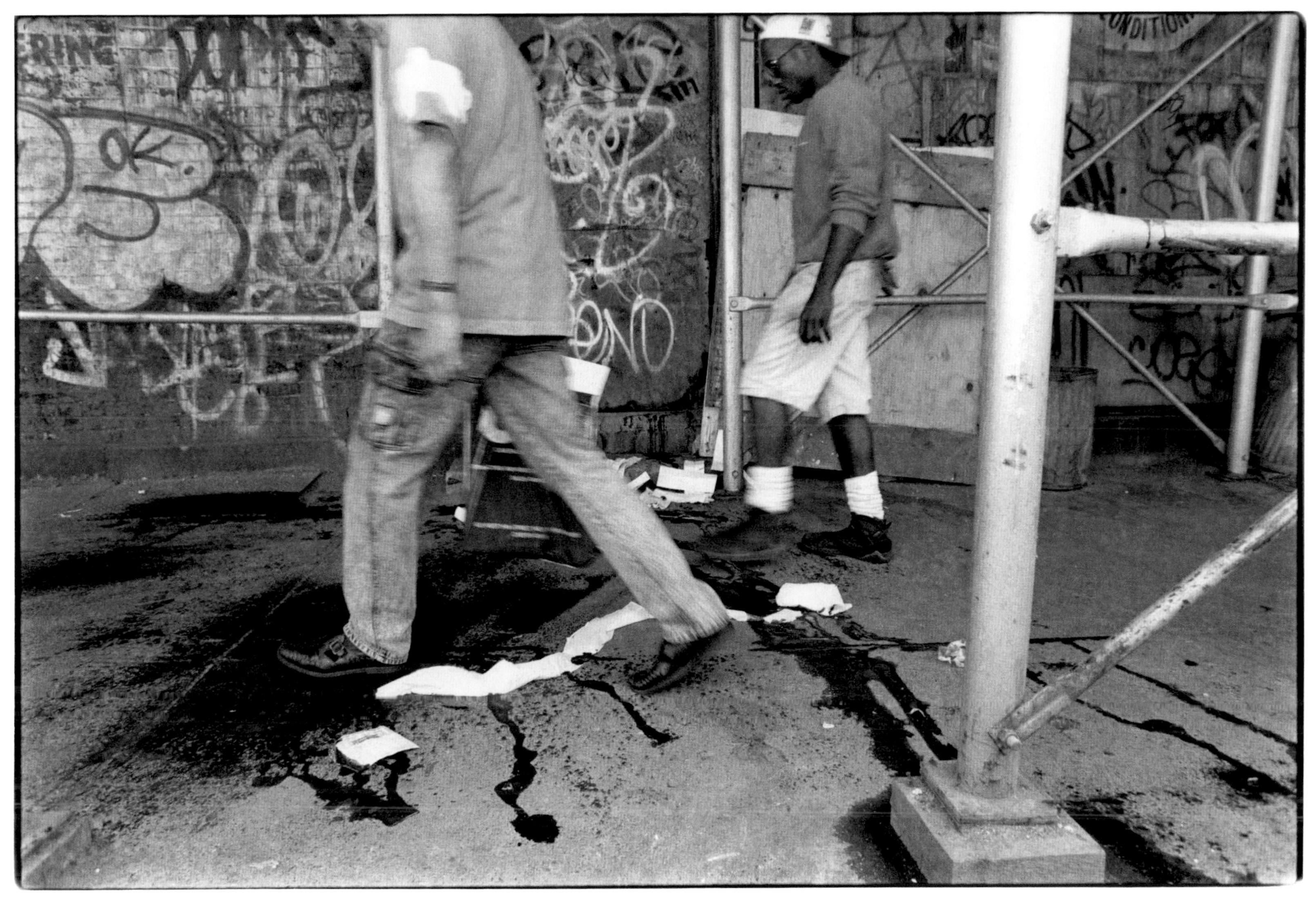

DISTRAUGHT MAN SLASHES HIS WRISTS AFTER HIS WIFE LEFT HIM.

1992

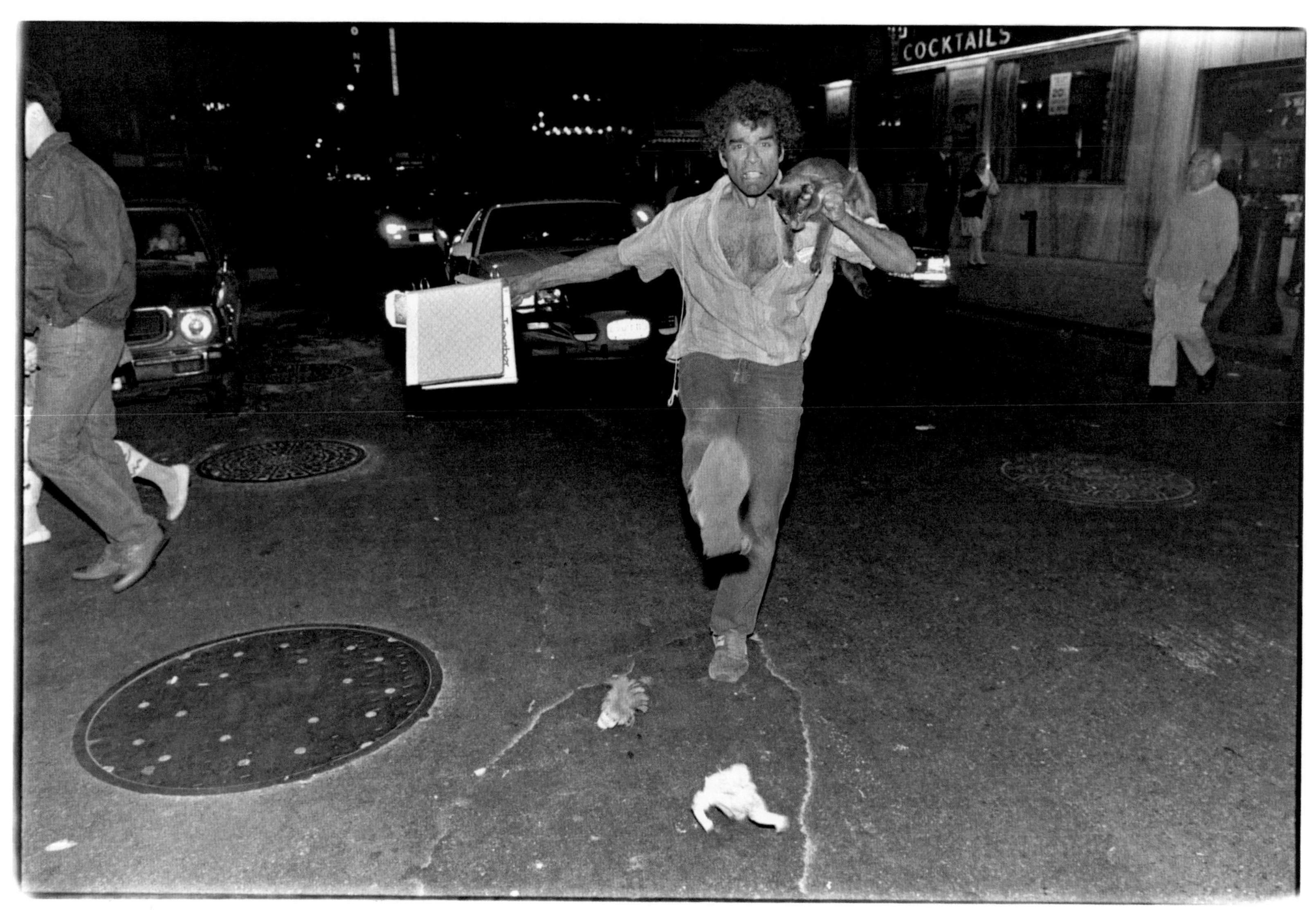

MAN KICKING THE HEAD OFF HIS DOLL.

1985

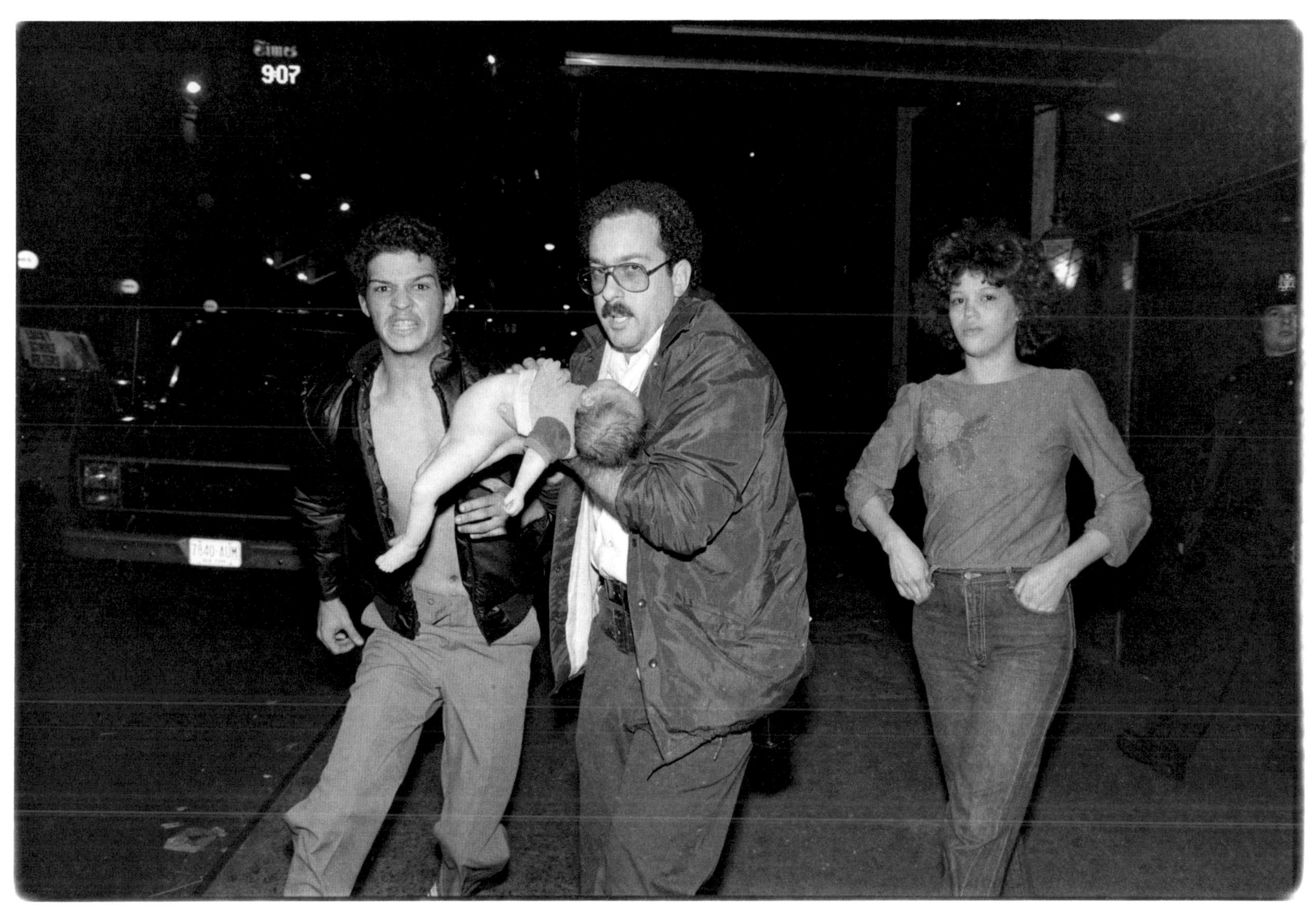

FATHER CHARGED WITH KILLING CRYING BABY.

1985

DEATH

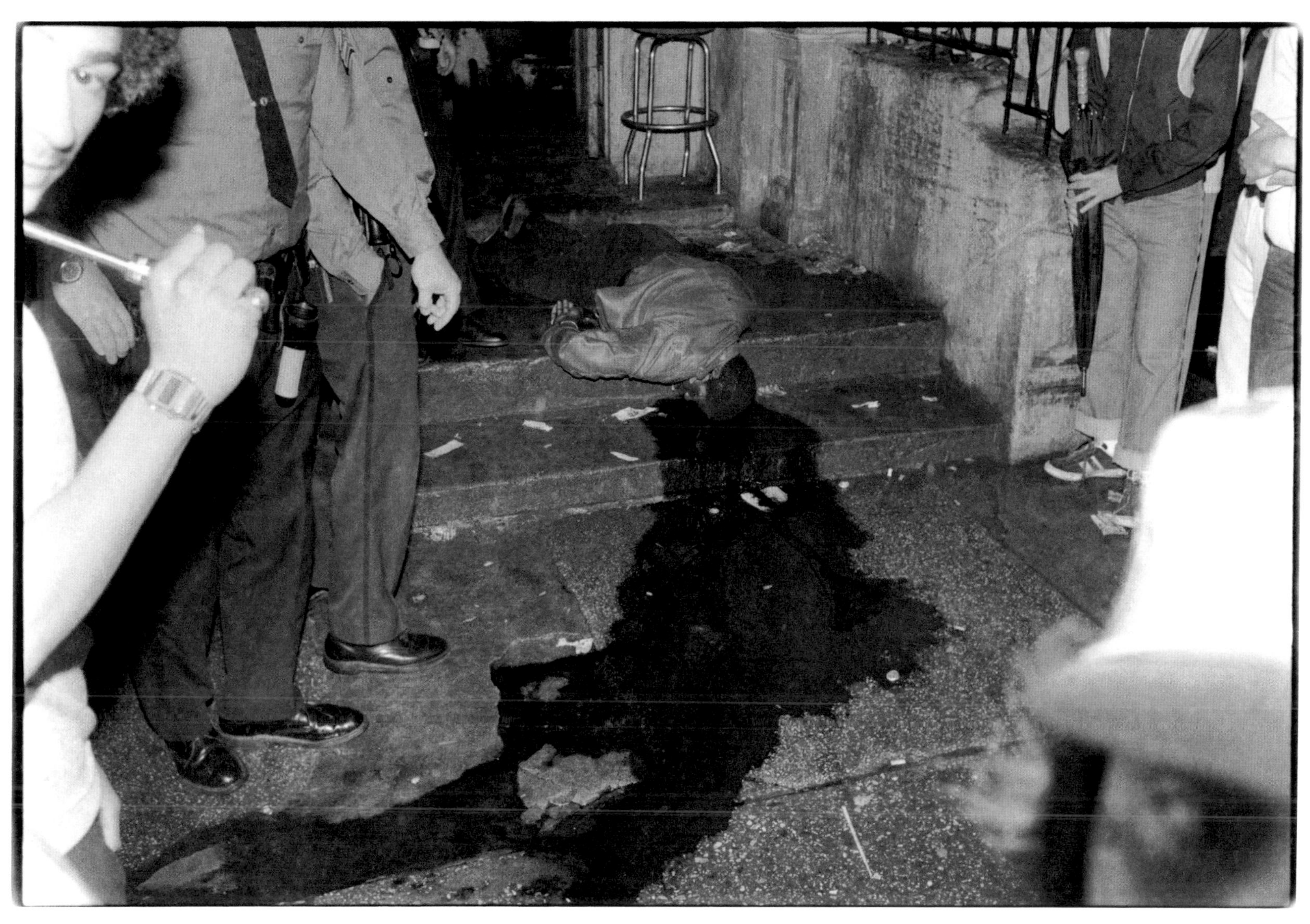

MAN SHOT IN THE HEAD.

1982

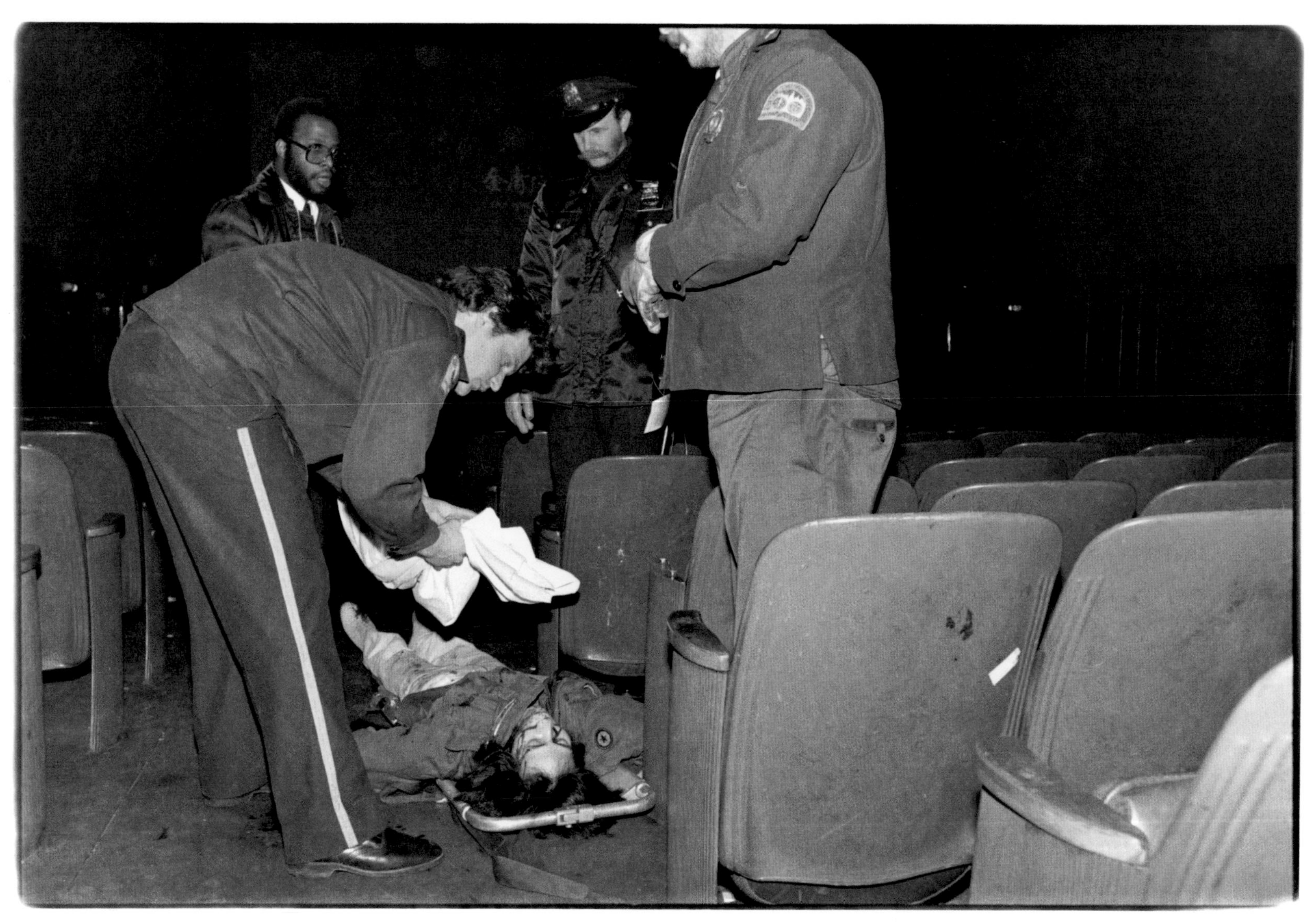

GHOST SHADOW SHOT IN THE HEAD WHILE WATCHING MOVIE.

1981

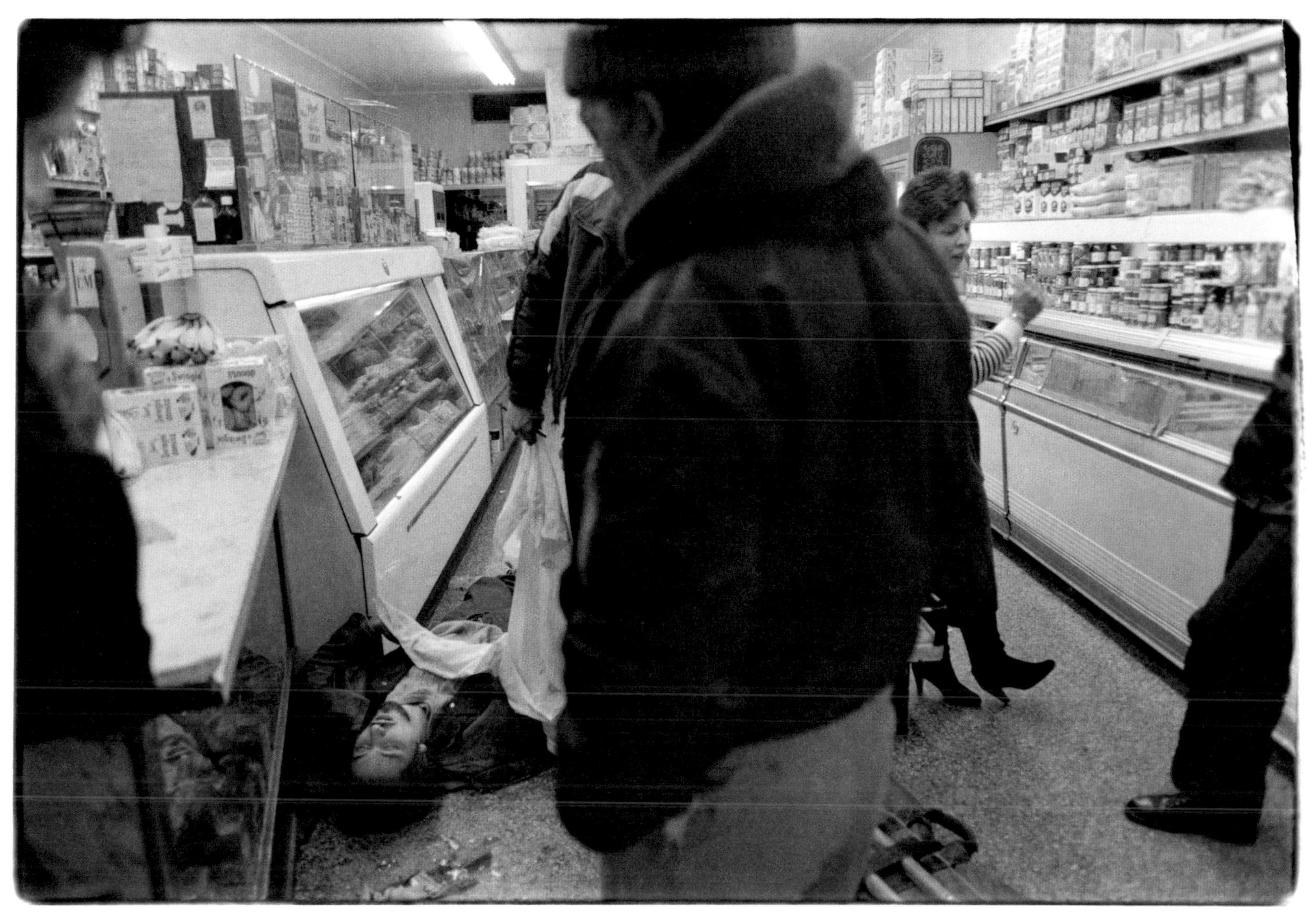

BODEGA OWNER SHOOTS AND KILLS TWO ROBBERY SUSPECTS.

1982

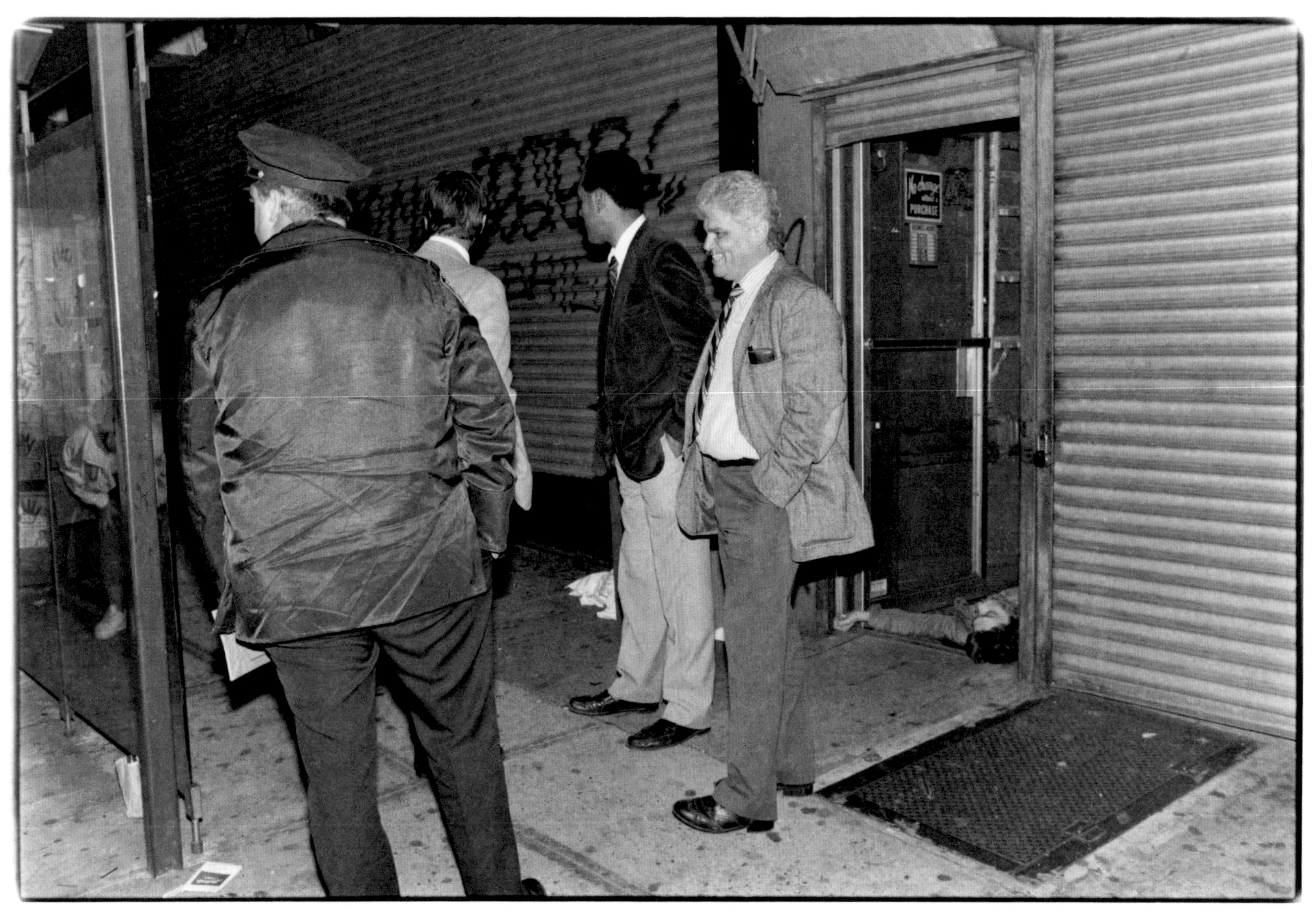

MAN IS SHOT WITH HIS OWN GUN WHILE ROBBING TROPICAL FISH STORE.

1982

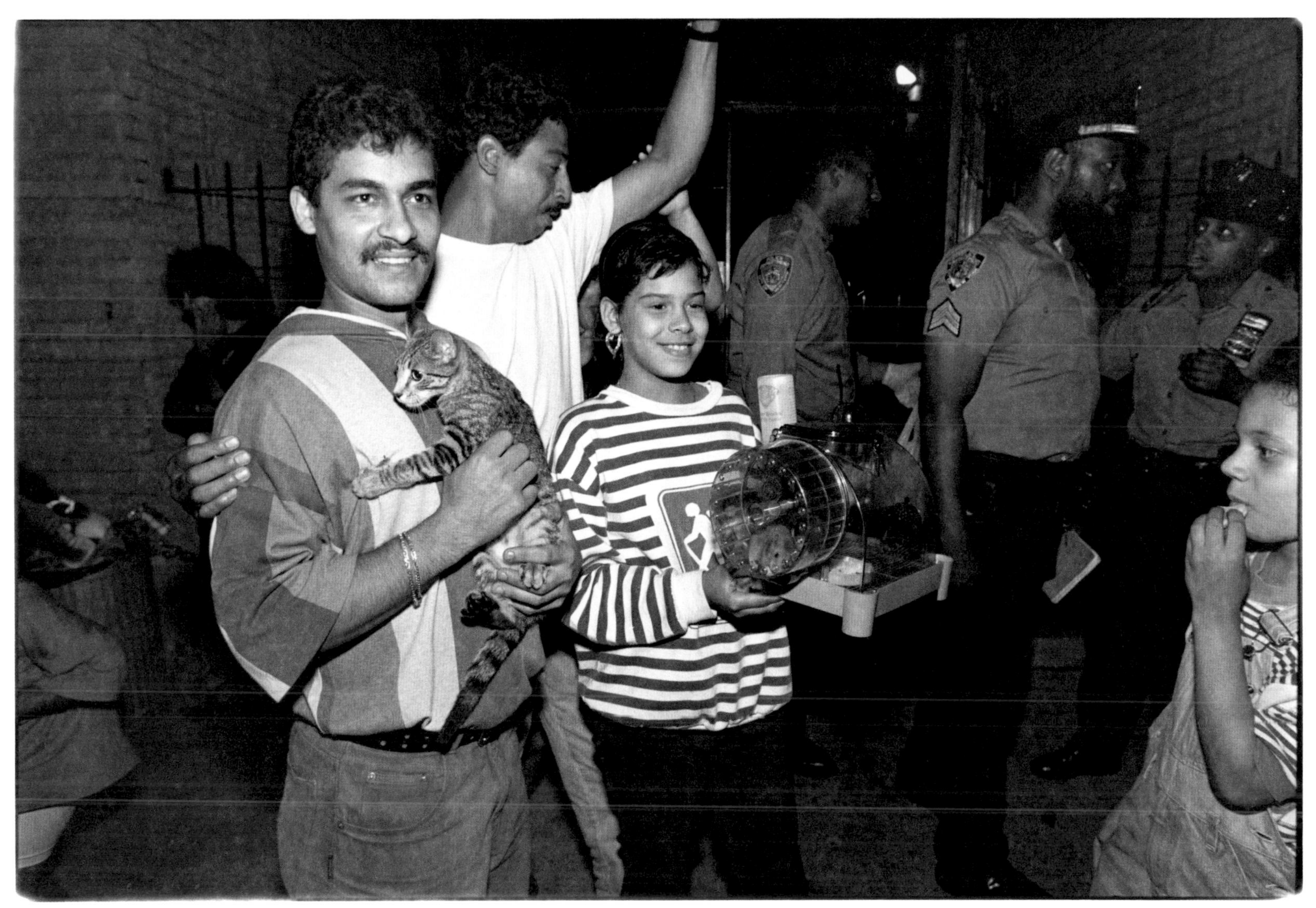

POLICE GIVE NEIGHBORS CAT AND HAMSTER FOUND INSIDE APT. CONTAINING HOMICIDES.

1993

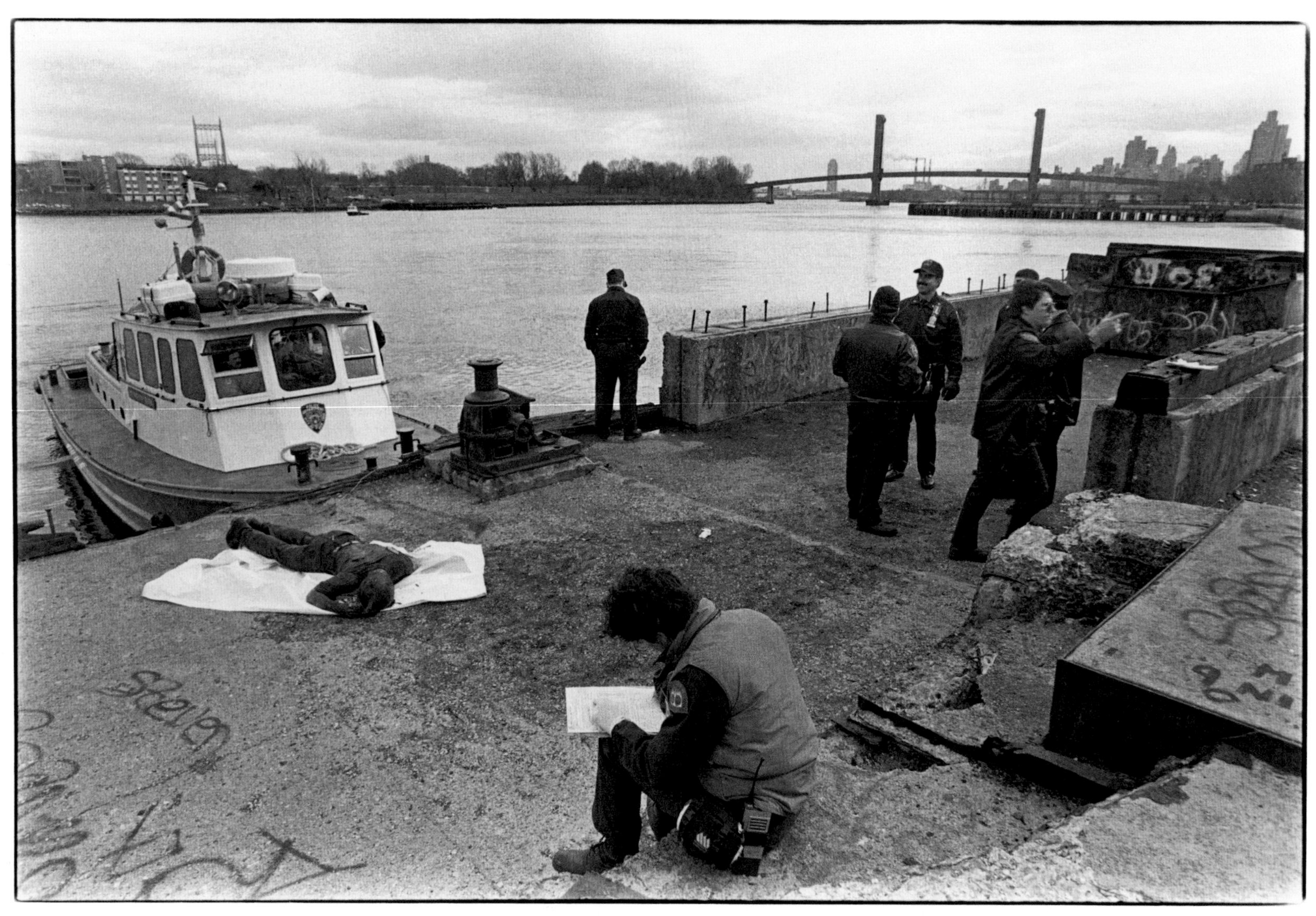

BODY RECOVERED FROM THE EAST RIVER.

1990

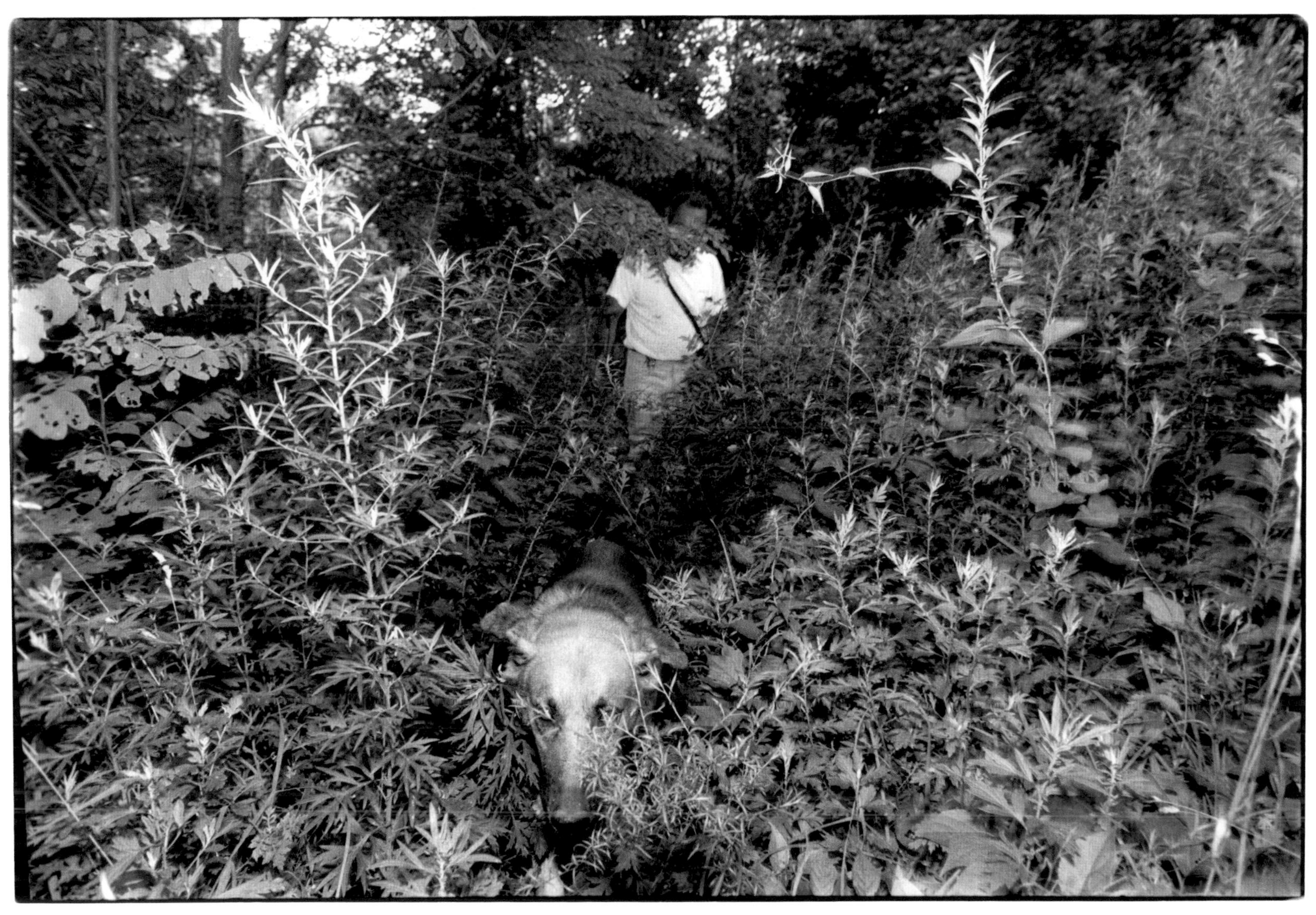

CADAVER DETECTION DOG SEARCHING FOR THE FIFTH VICTIM OF THE ZODIAC II.

1993

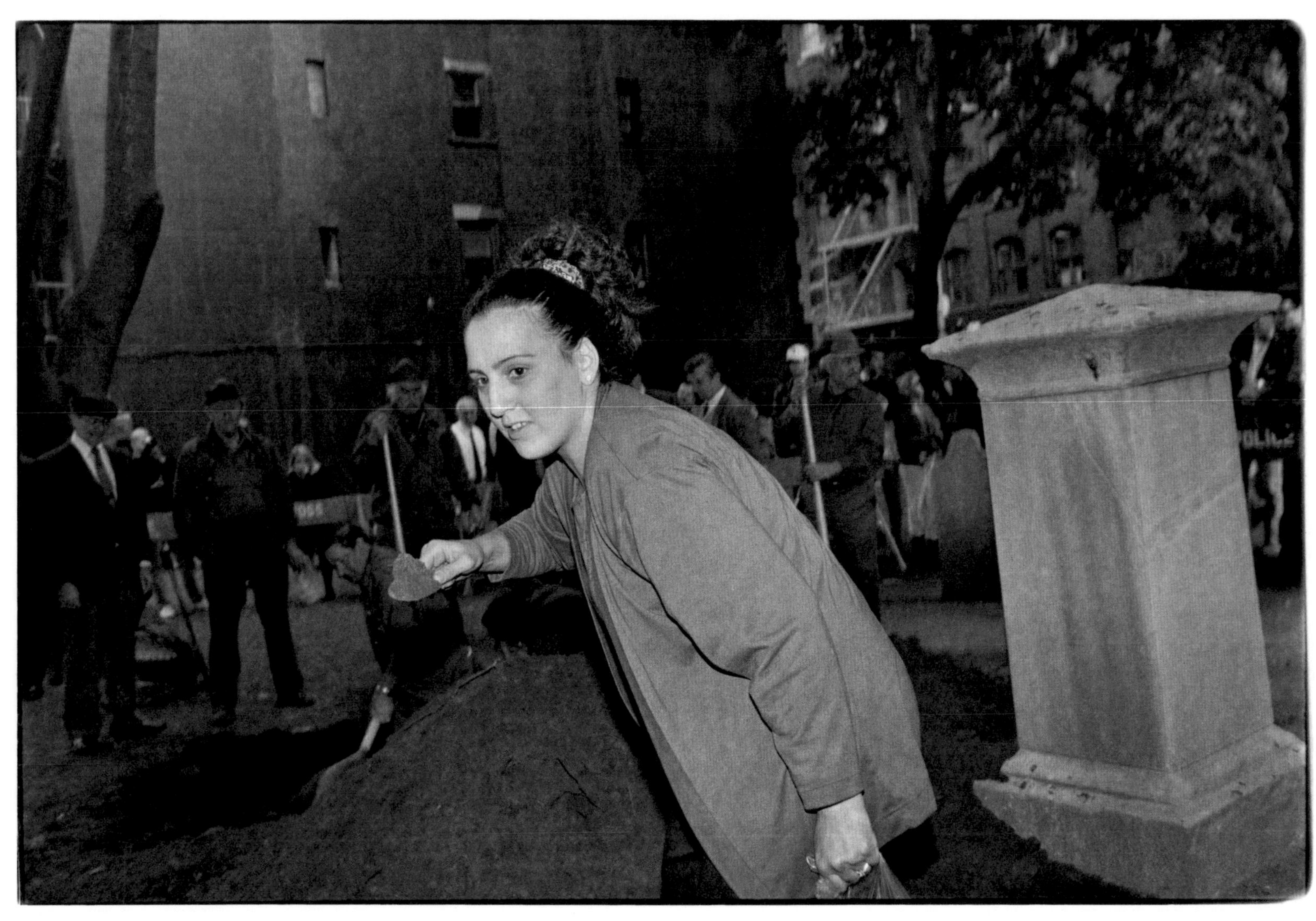

WOMAN TAKING DIRT FROM EXHUMED GRAVE.

1990

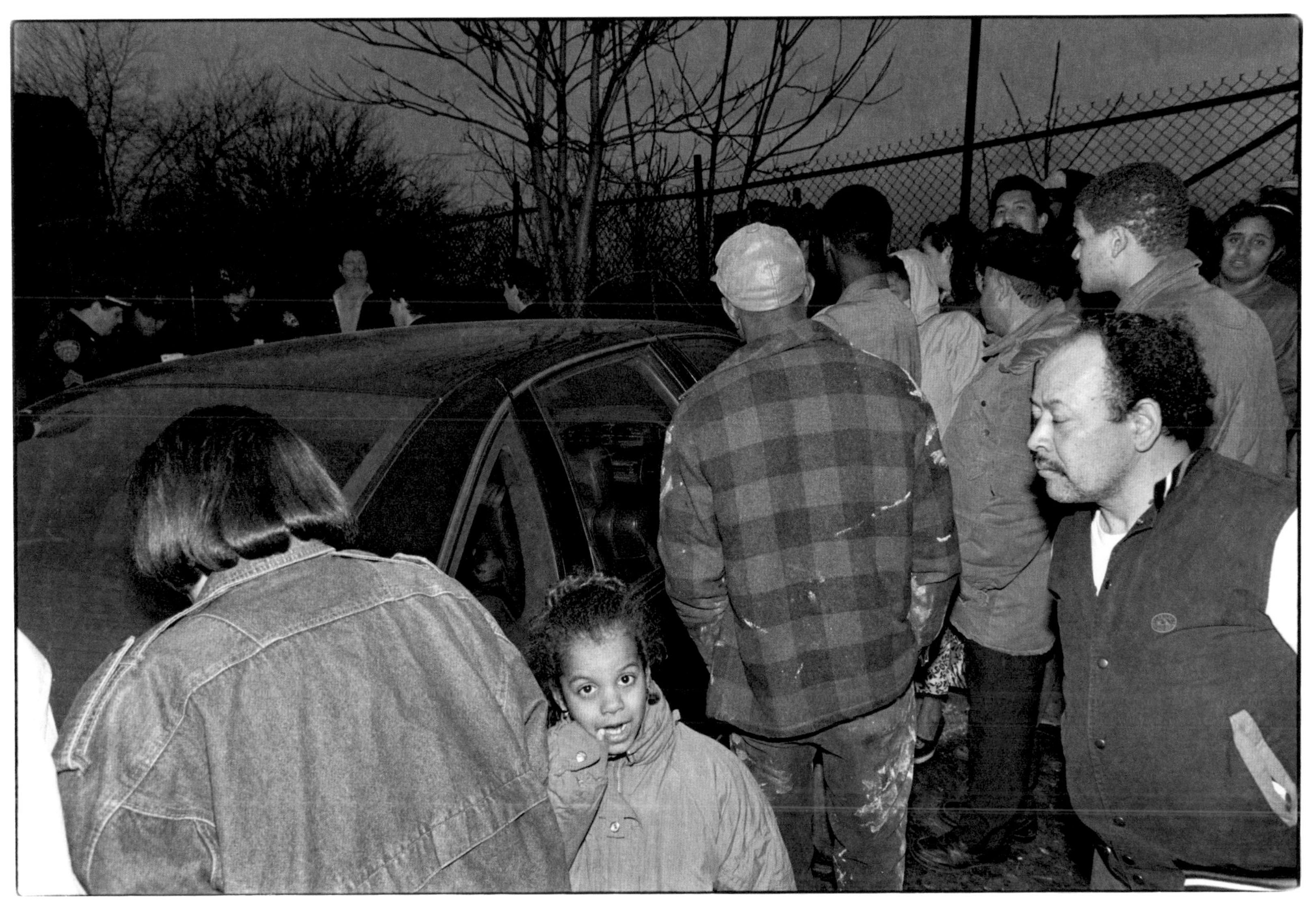

MISSING WOMAN IS FOUND INSIDE PLASTIC BAG IN VACANT LOT.

1993

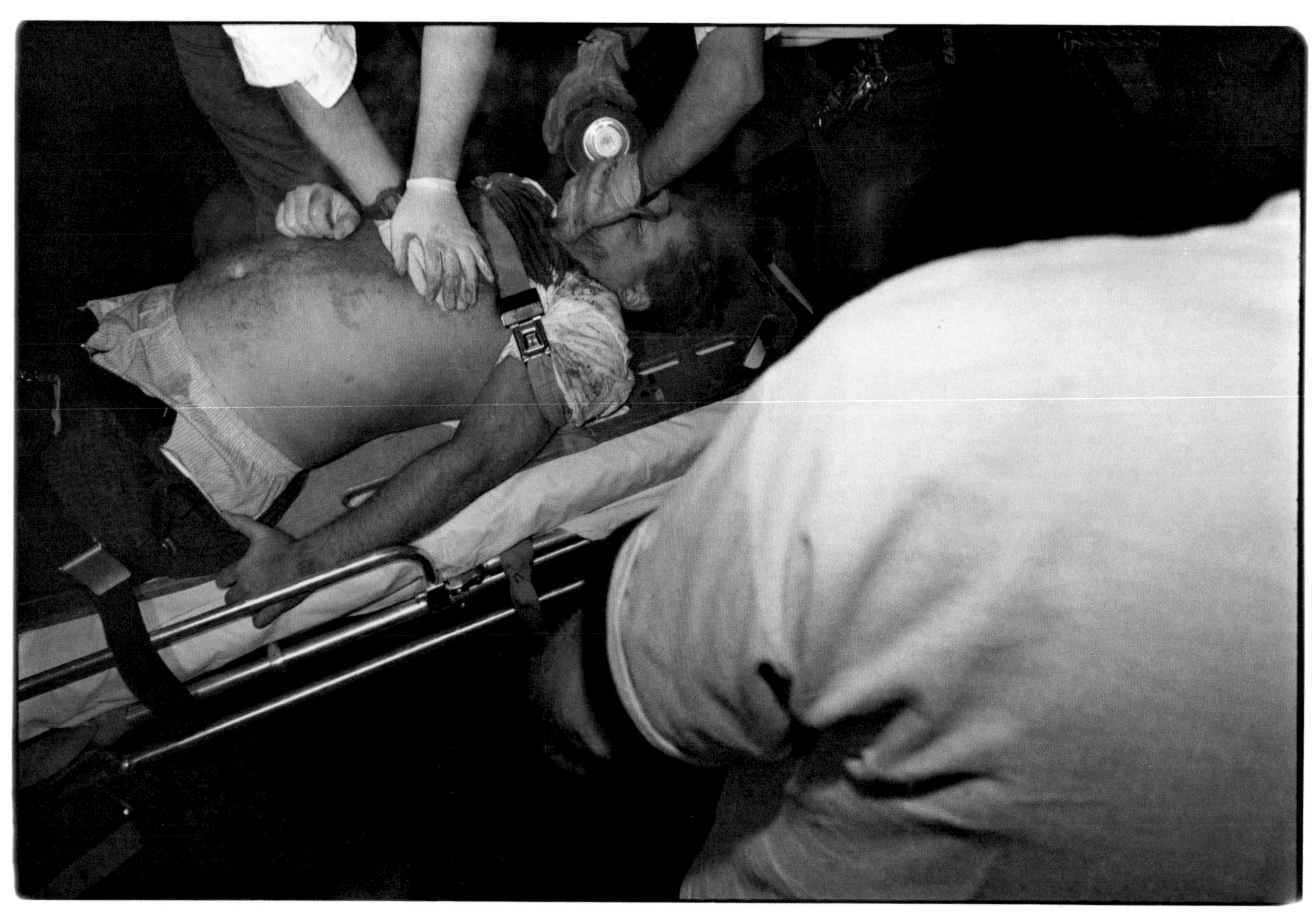

BARTENDER SHOT DEAD DURING ATTEMPTED ROBBERY.

1989

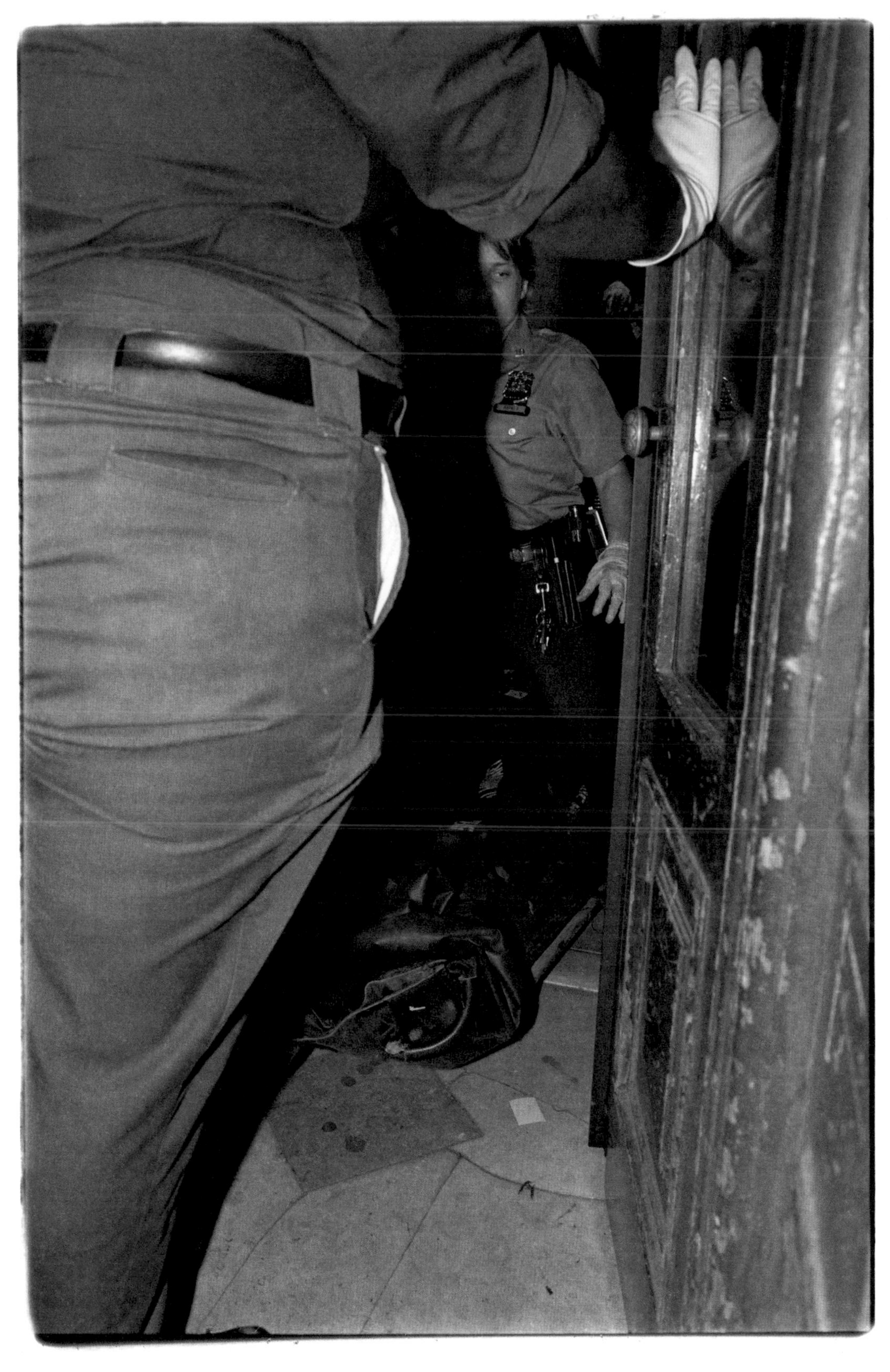

DOUBLE HOMICIDE FOUND INSIDE CHELSEA APT. 1988

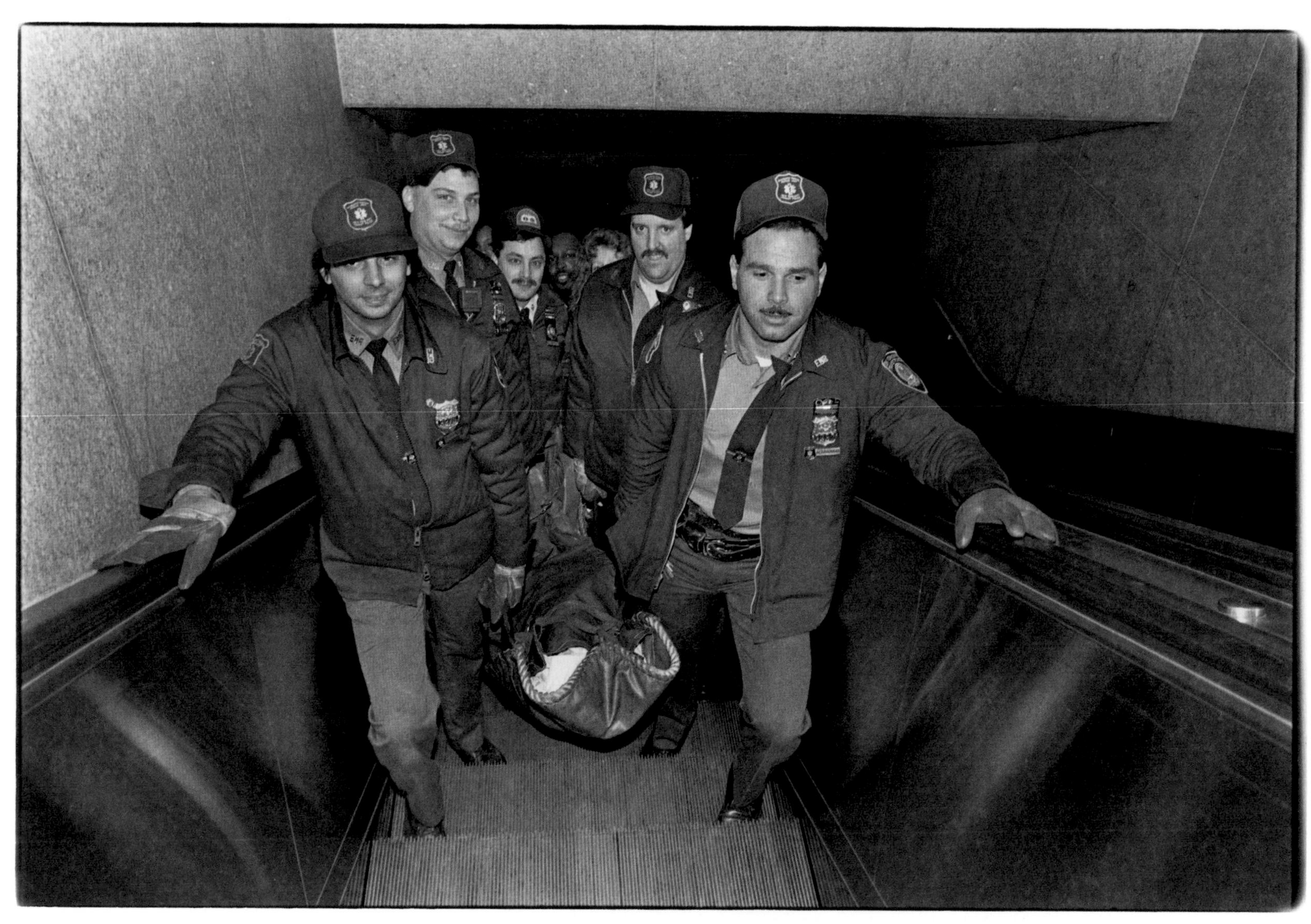

BODY BEing REMOVED FROM SUBWAY TRACKS.

1986

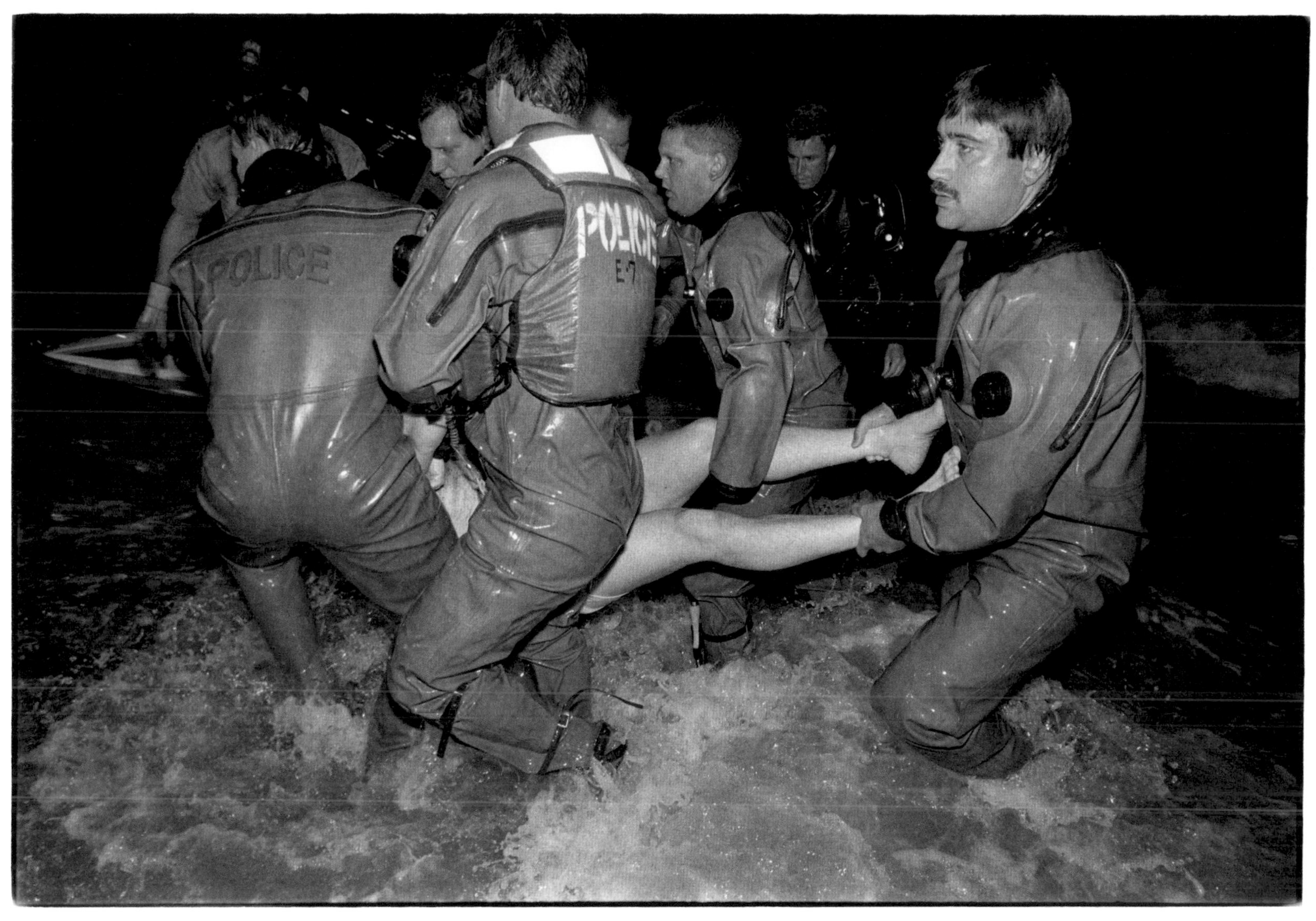

MAN DROWNS TRYING TO SAVE GIRL WHO WAS RESCUED.

1993

SEX

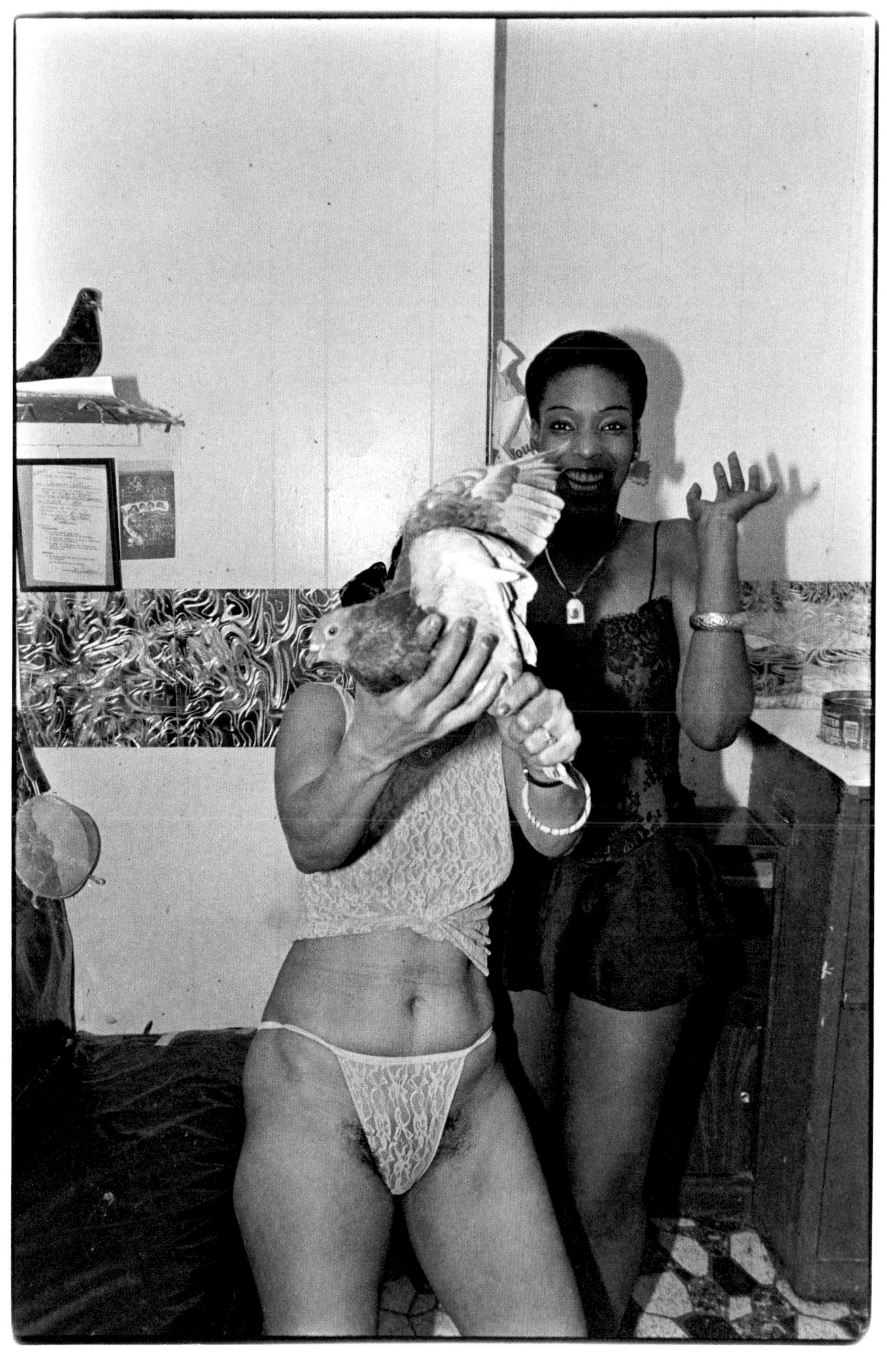

PEEP SHOW WOMEN WITH PIGEON. 1985

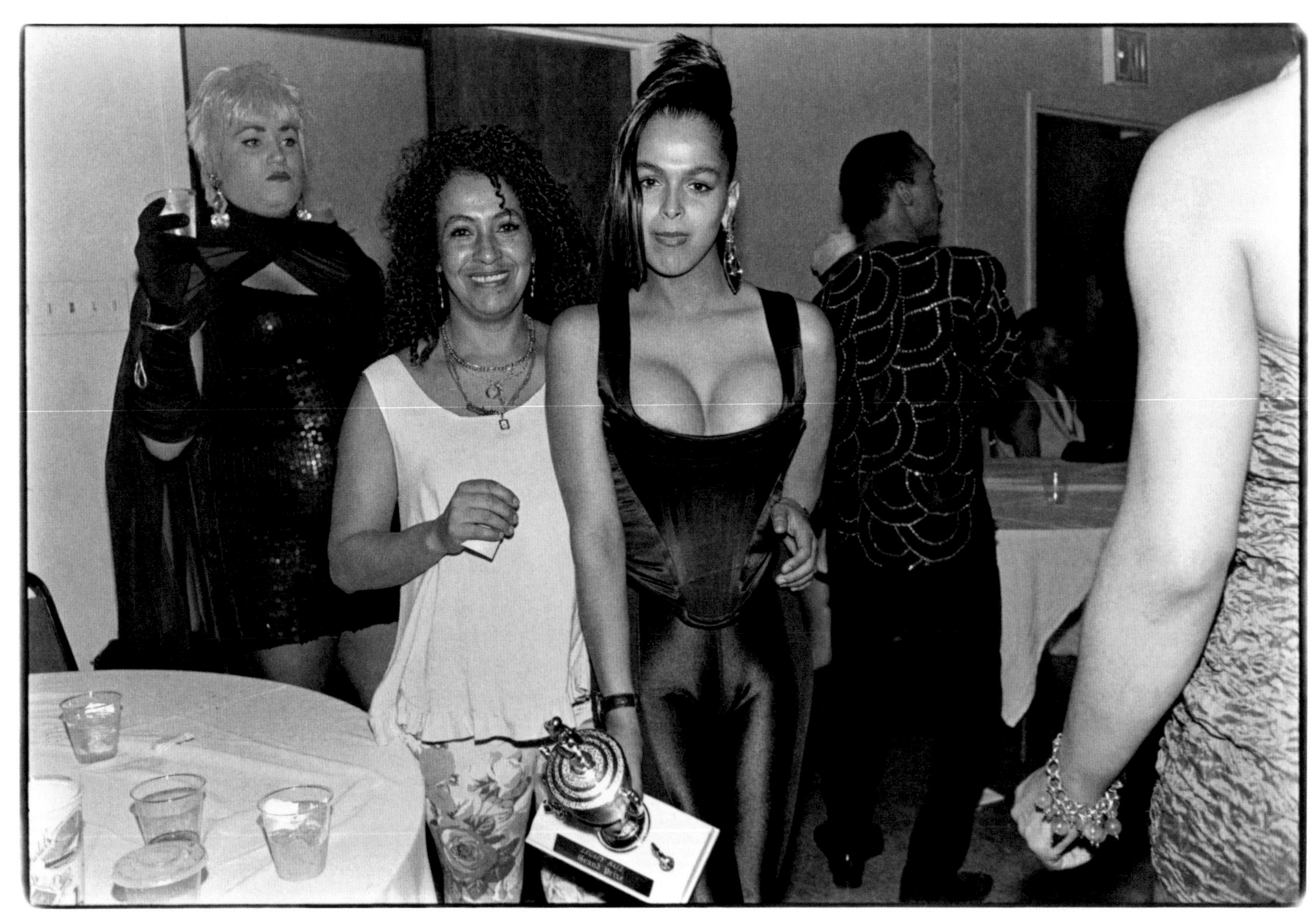

MOTHER AND SON AT VOGUING BALL.

1992

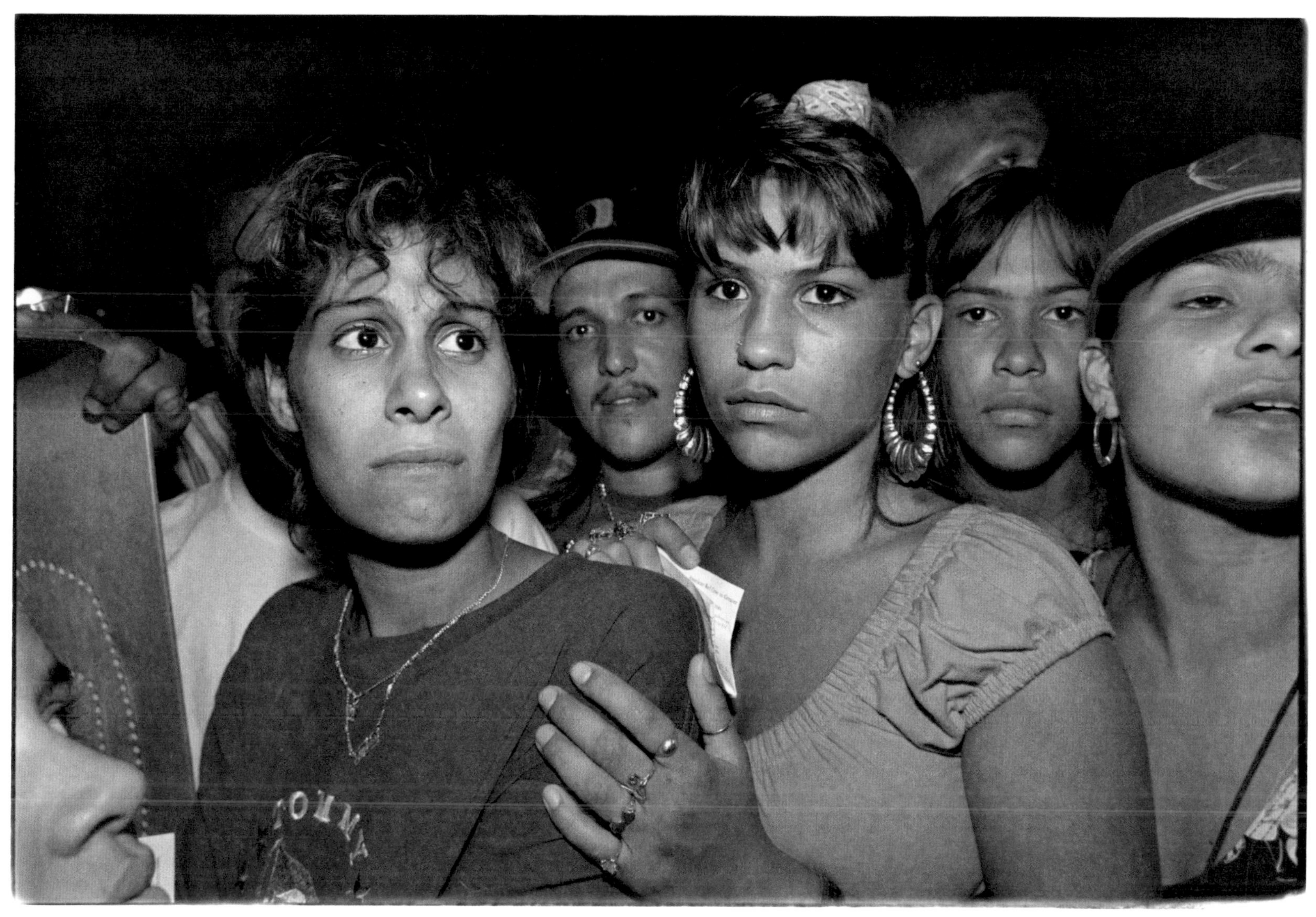

JEALOUS BOYFRIEND STARTS FIRE THAT LEAVES OVER ONE HUNDRED PEOPLE HOMELESS.

1993

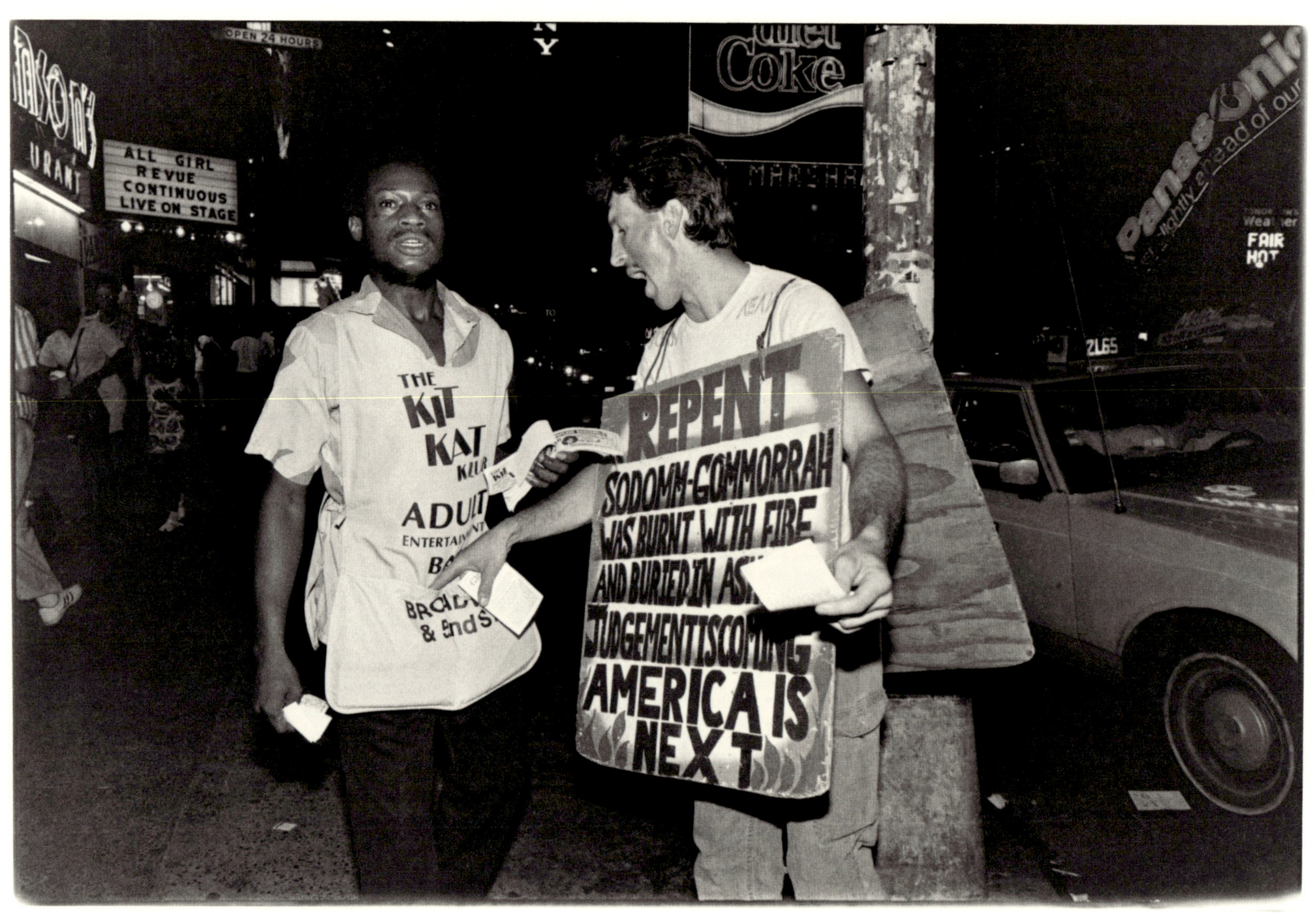

MEN DEBATING MORALITY — TIMES SQUARE.

1990

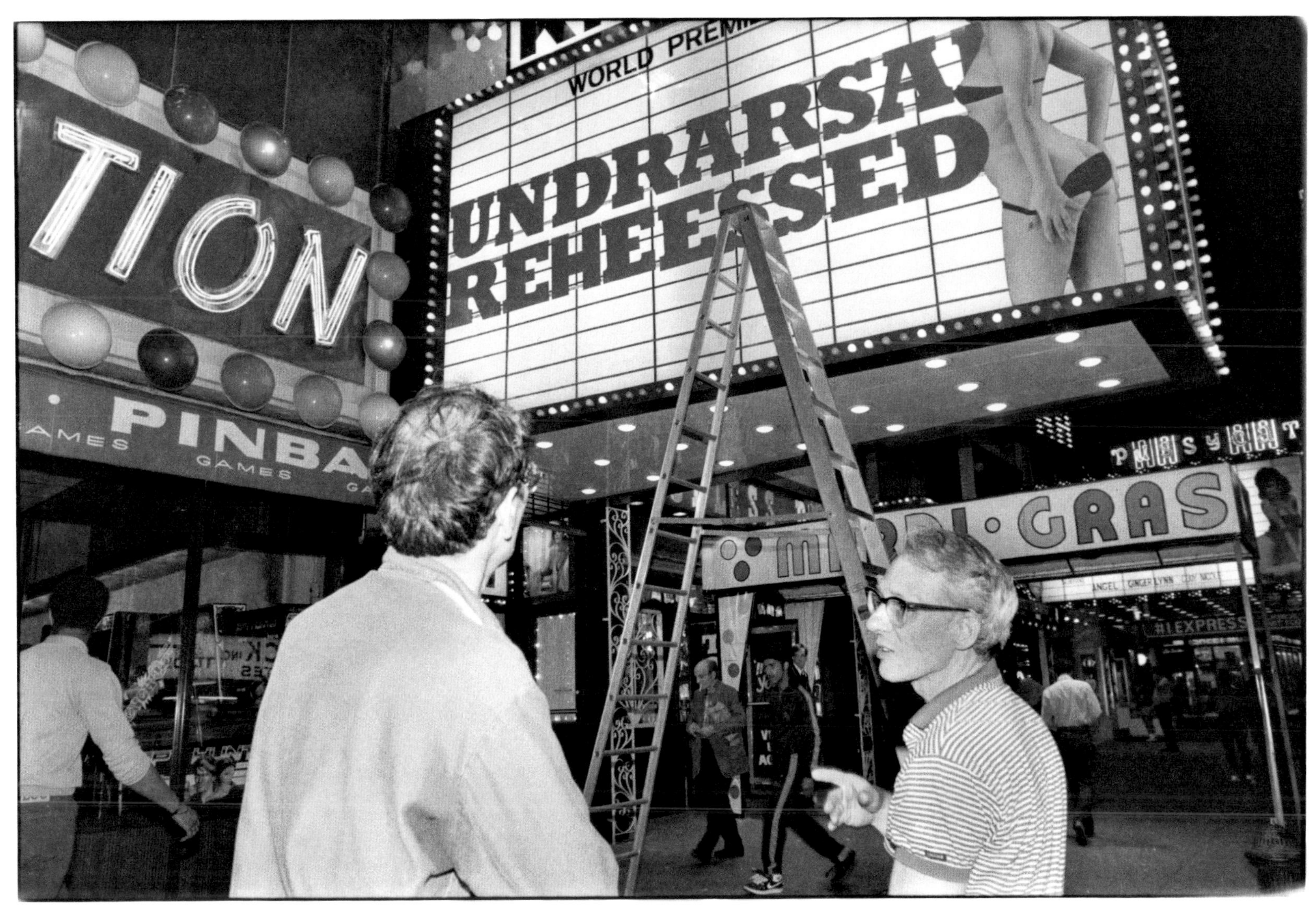

MEN CONFUSED ABOUT THE SPElling OF NEW MOViE.

1985

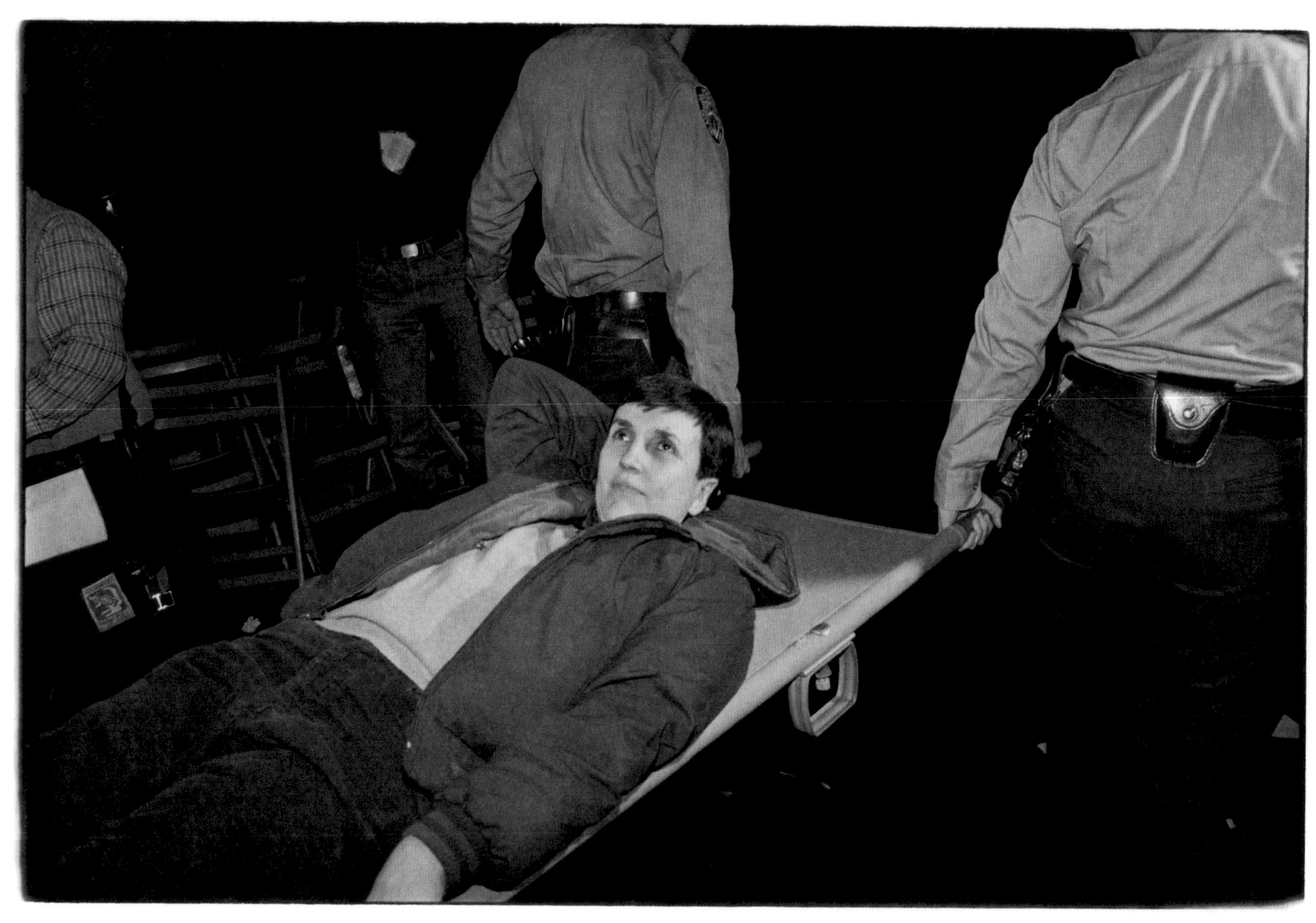

gAY Rights sit-in DEMONSTRATOR being ARRESTED.

1982

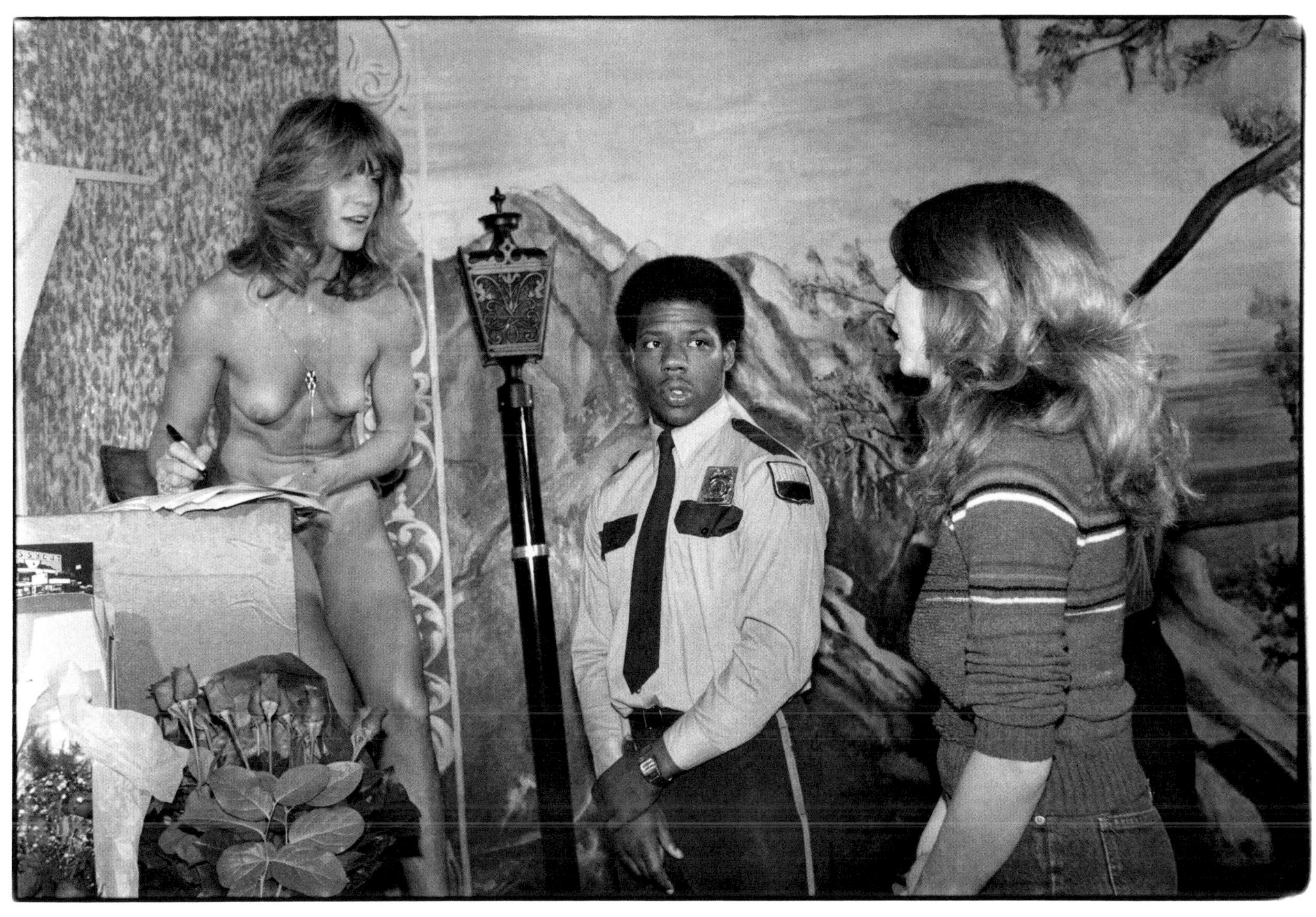

WOMAN ASKING PORN STAR FOR HER AUTOGRAPH.

1982

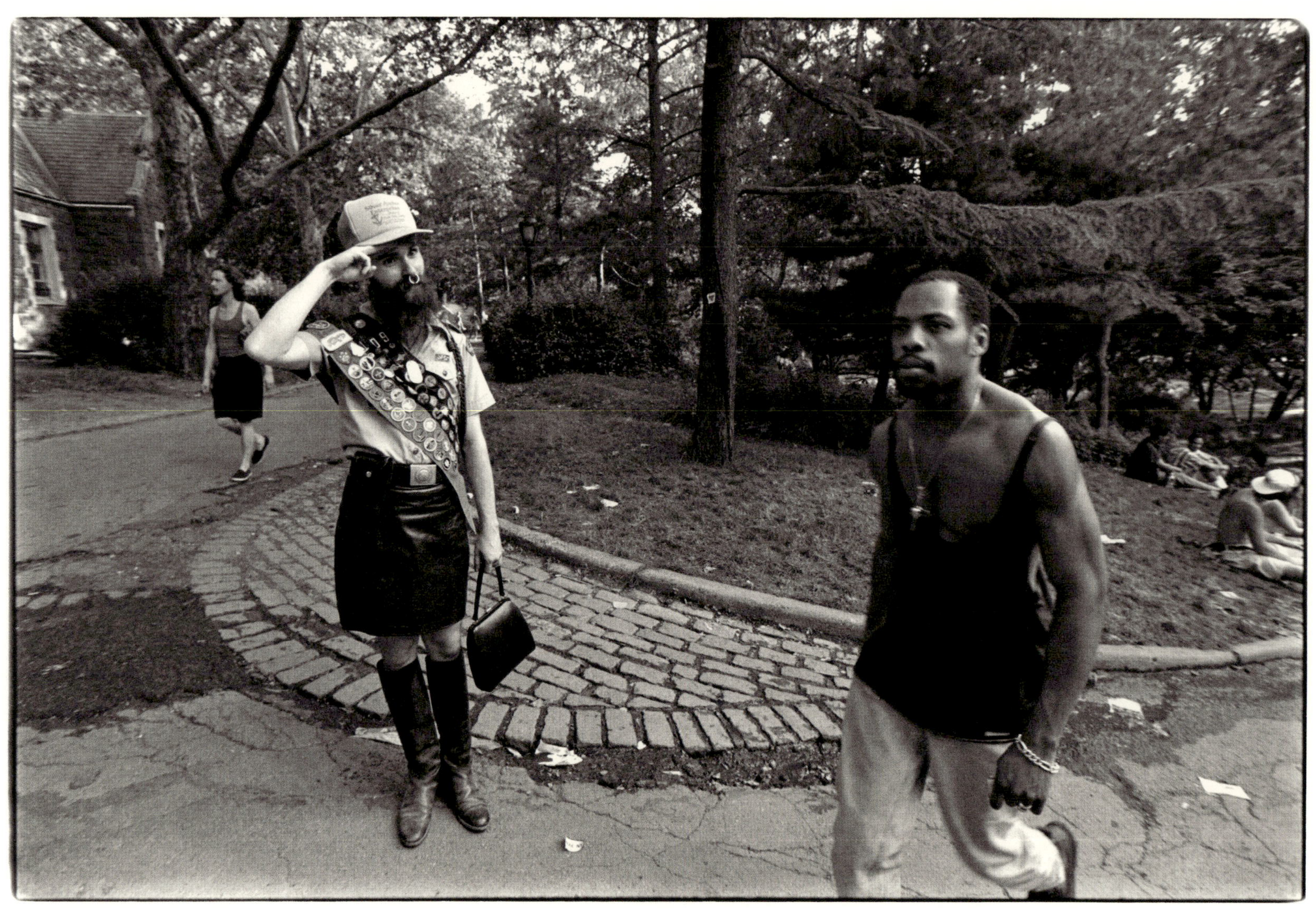

MAN WALKING PAST MAN DRESSED AS BOTH BOY SCOUT AND GIRL SCOUT.

1994

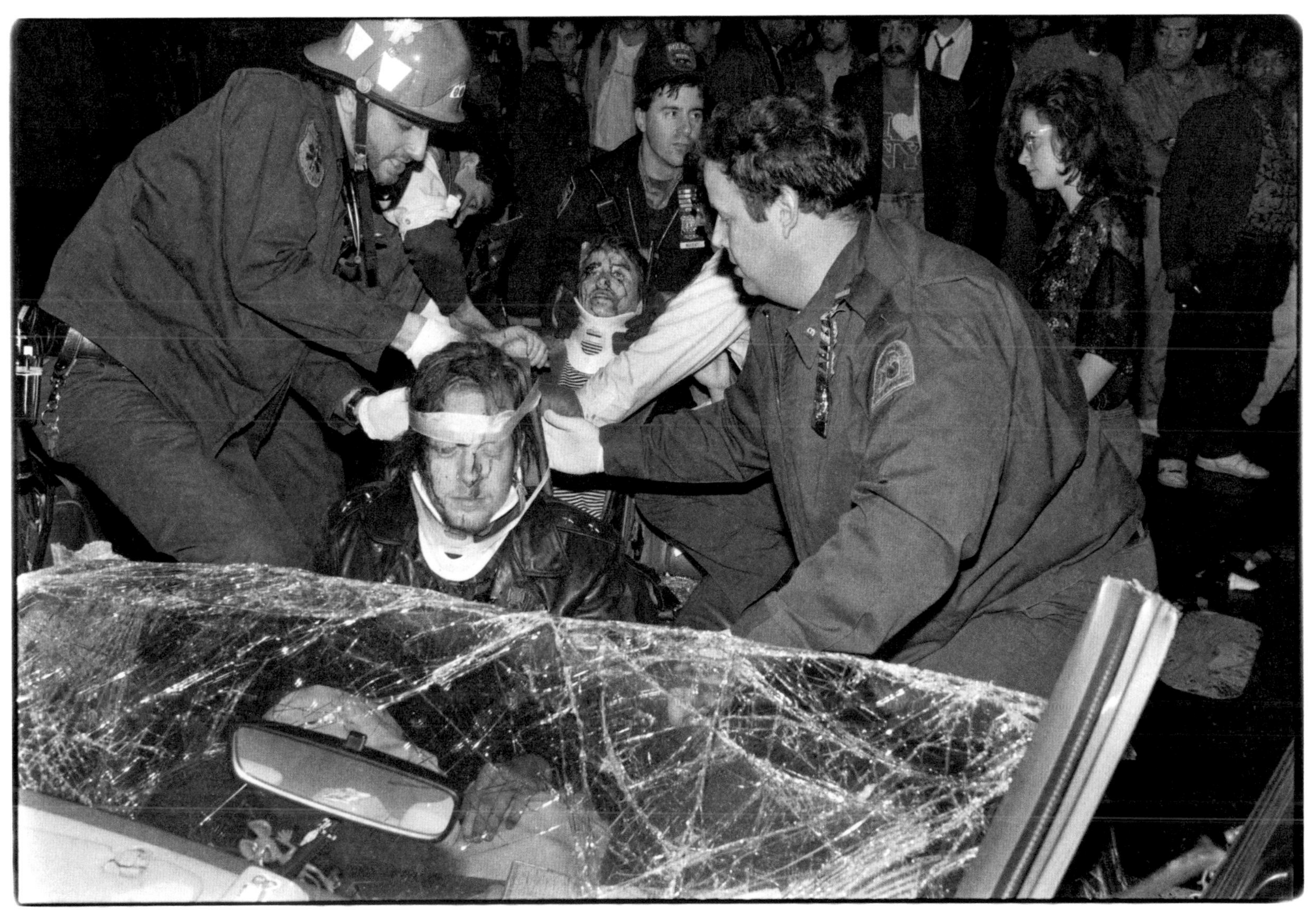

WHILE THE CAR WRECK VICTIMS ARE BEING TREATED — COP & BYSTANDER HAVE EYE CONTACT.

1990

STREET

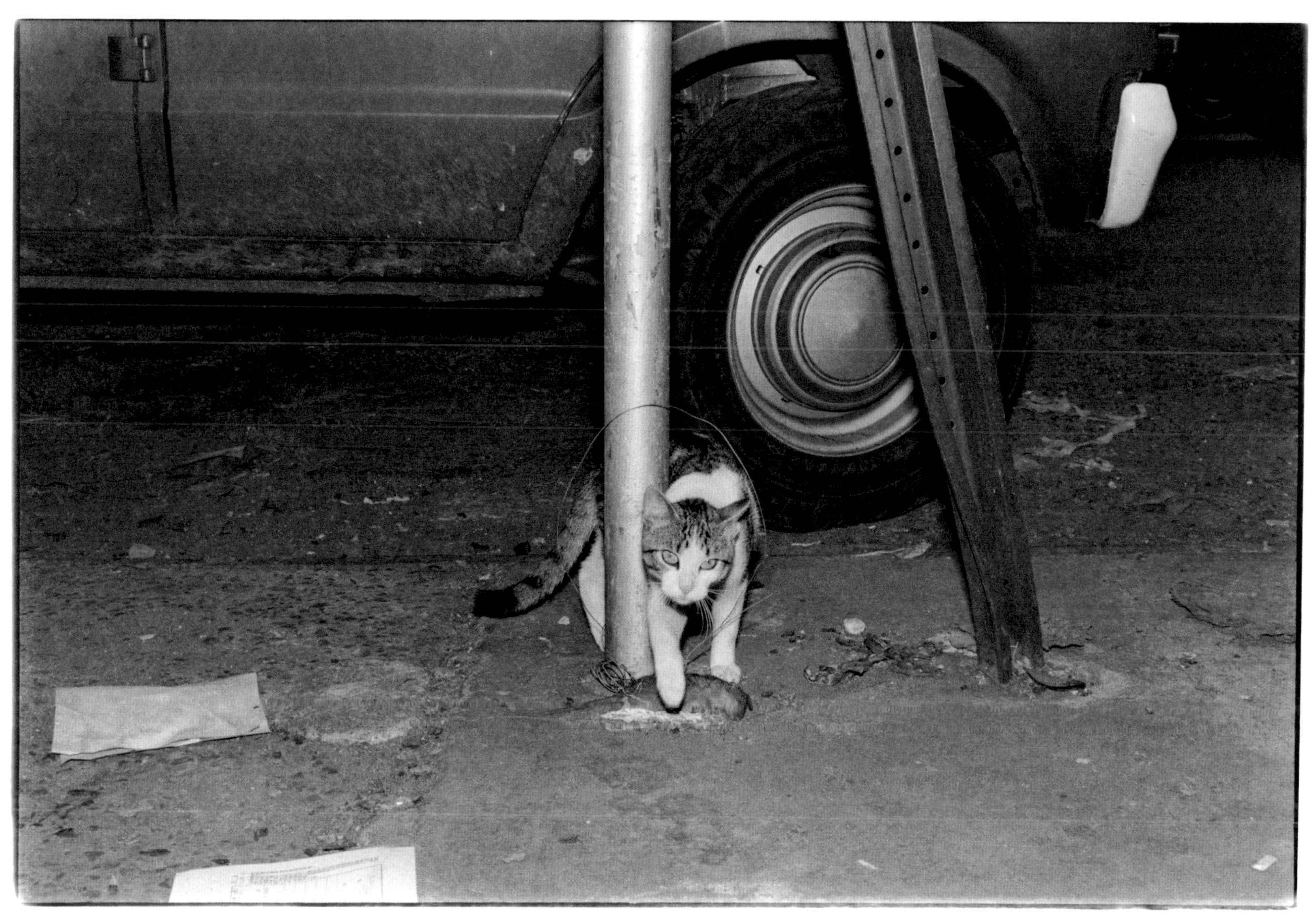

CAT PLAYING WITH DEAD RAT.

1980

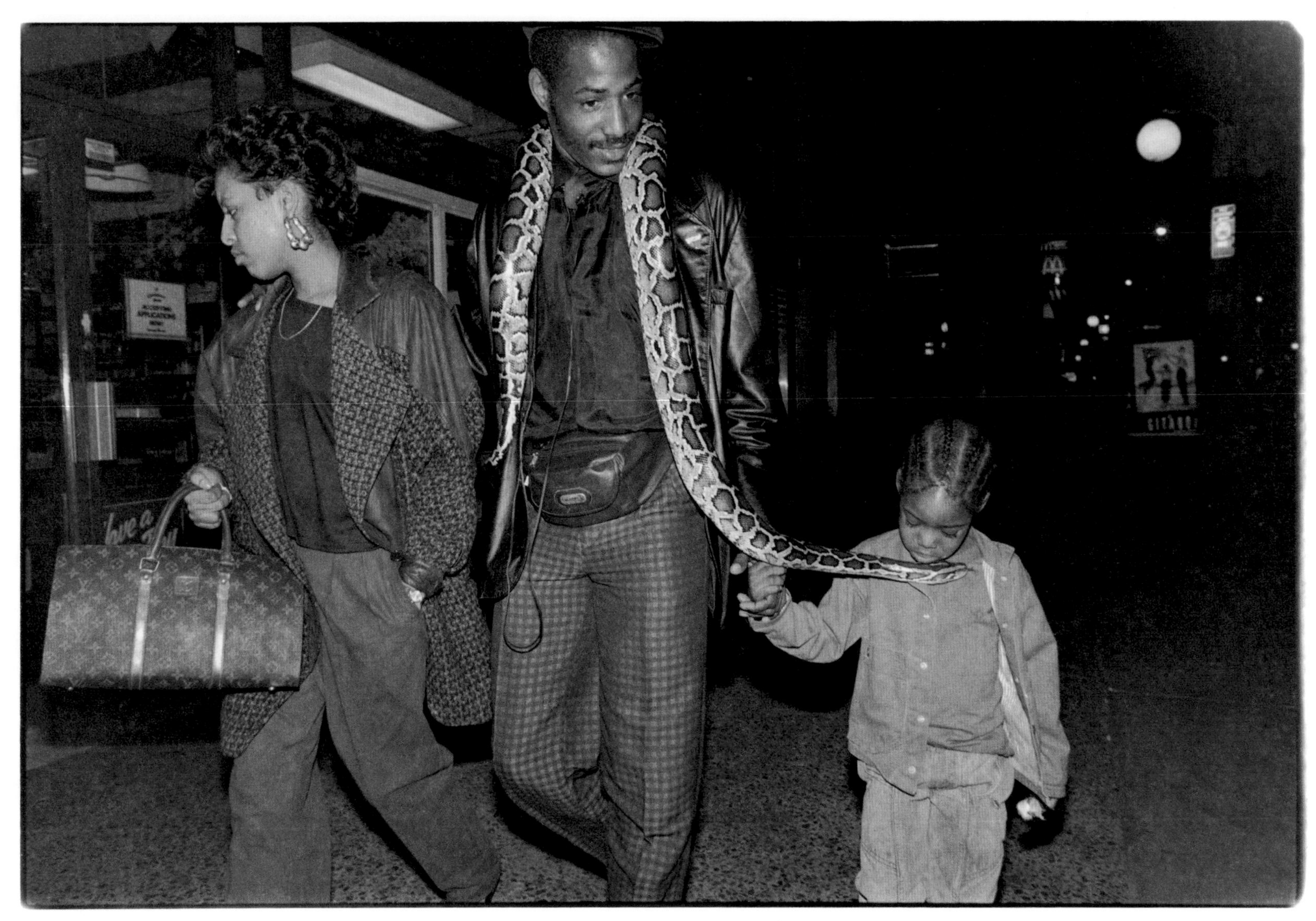

YOUNG FAMILY WALKING WITH PYTHON.

1988

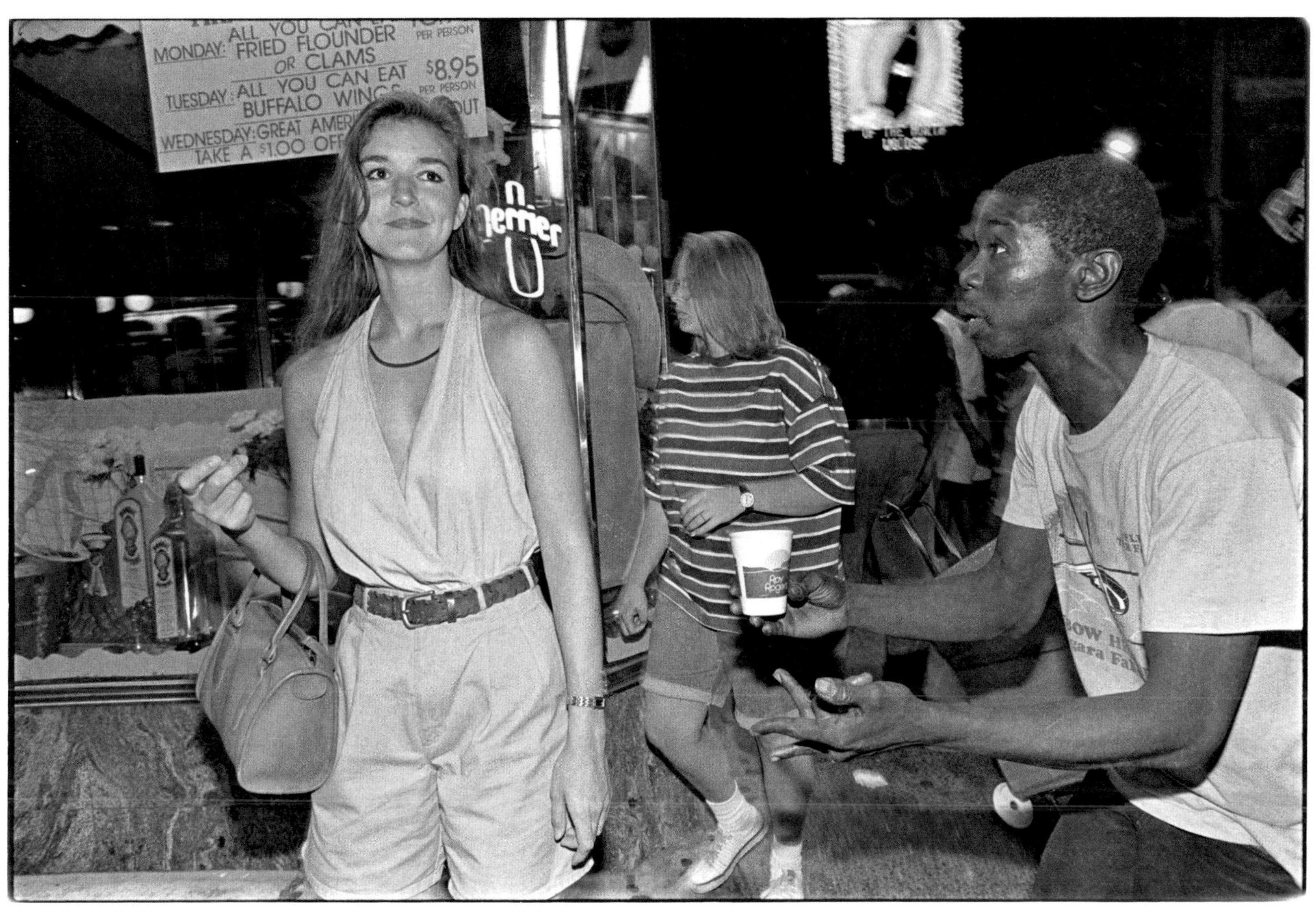

MAN SINGING STEVIE WONDER SONGS FOR SPARE CHANGE.

1992

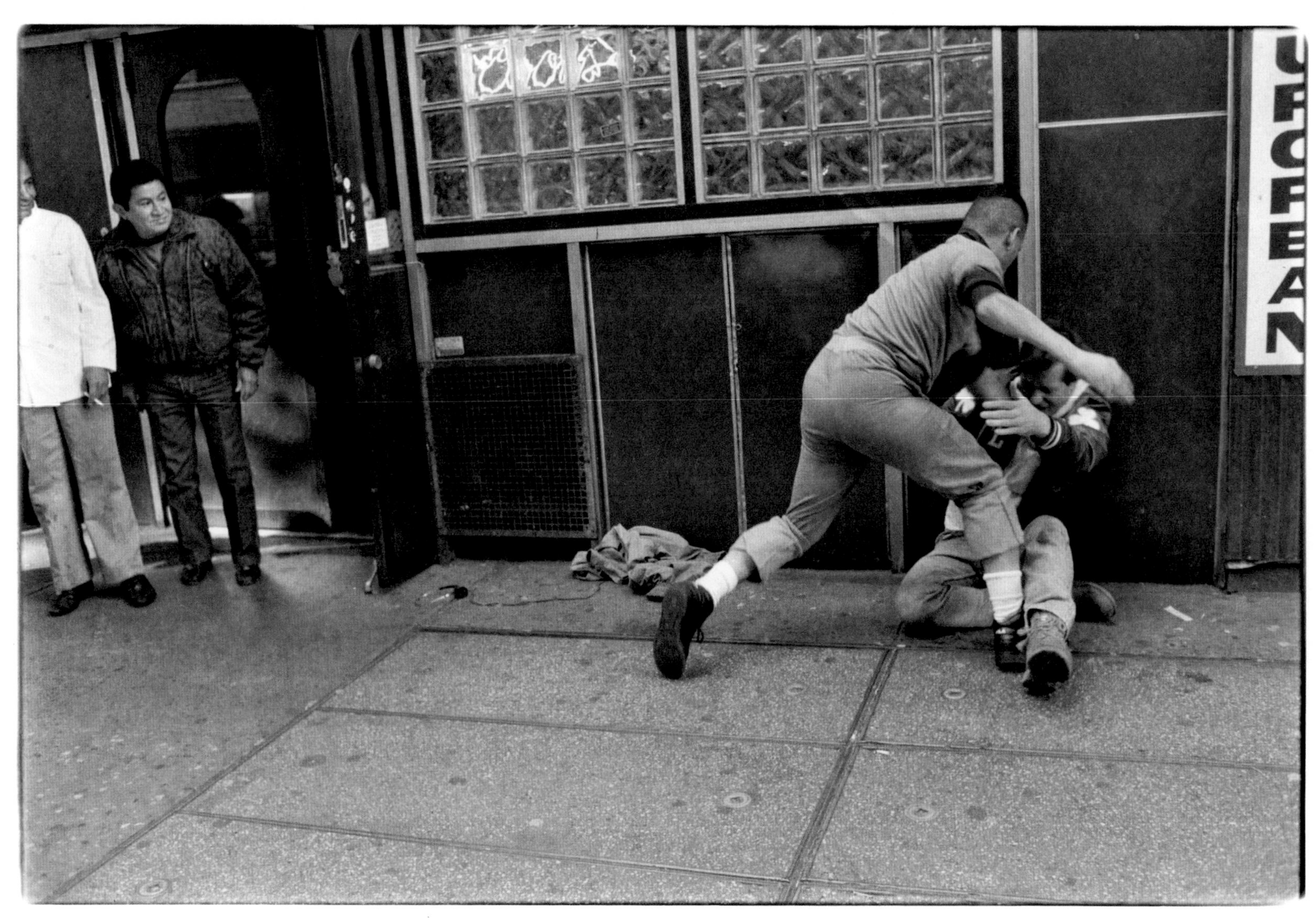

MEN FIGHTING OUTSIDE BAR — W. 43 ST.

1992

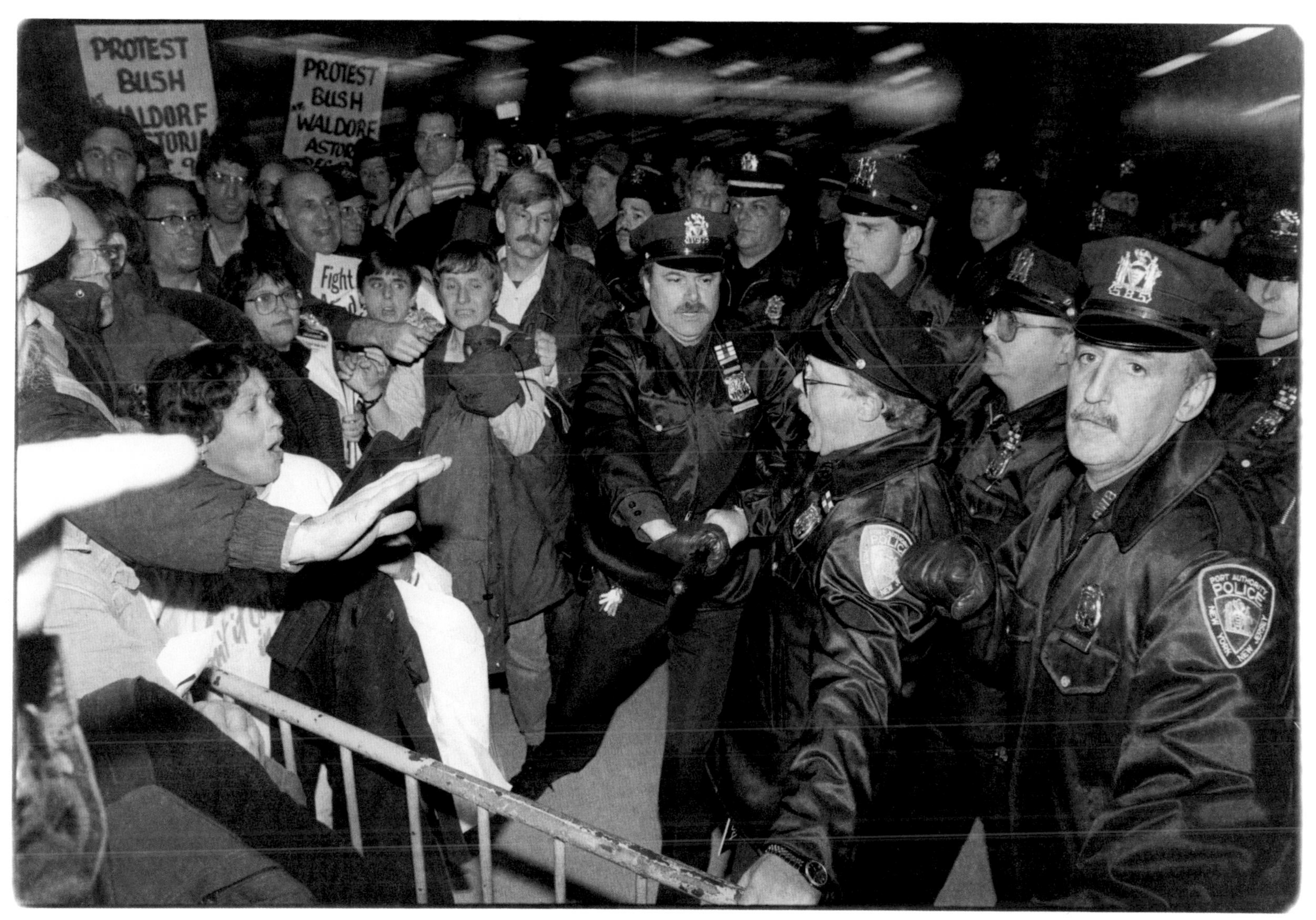

COP BECOMES UPSET WITH DEMONSTRATORS.

1990

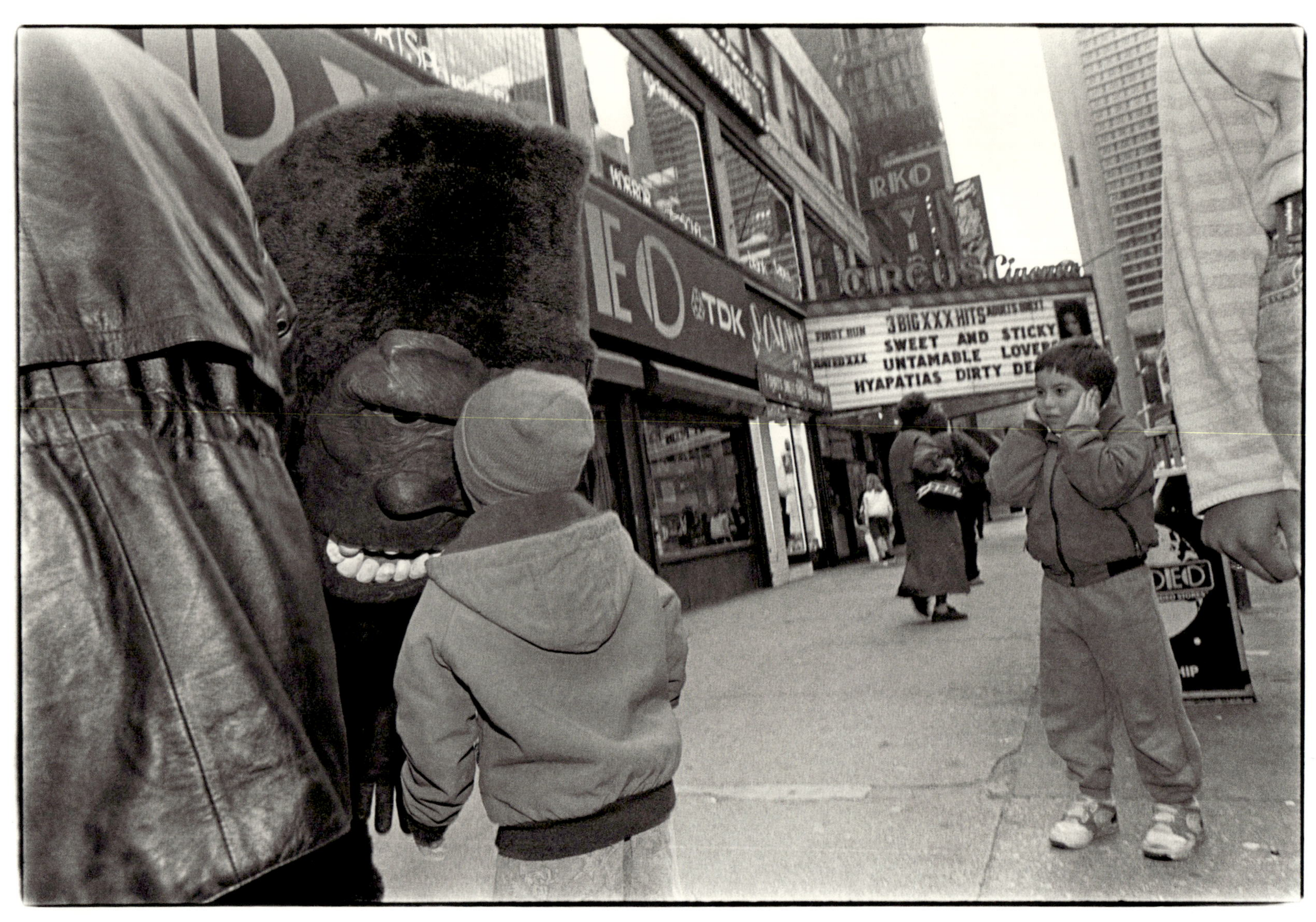

BOYS ENCOUNTER RECORD STORE PROMOTION.

1992

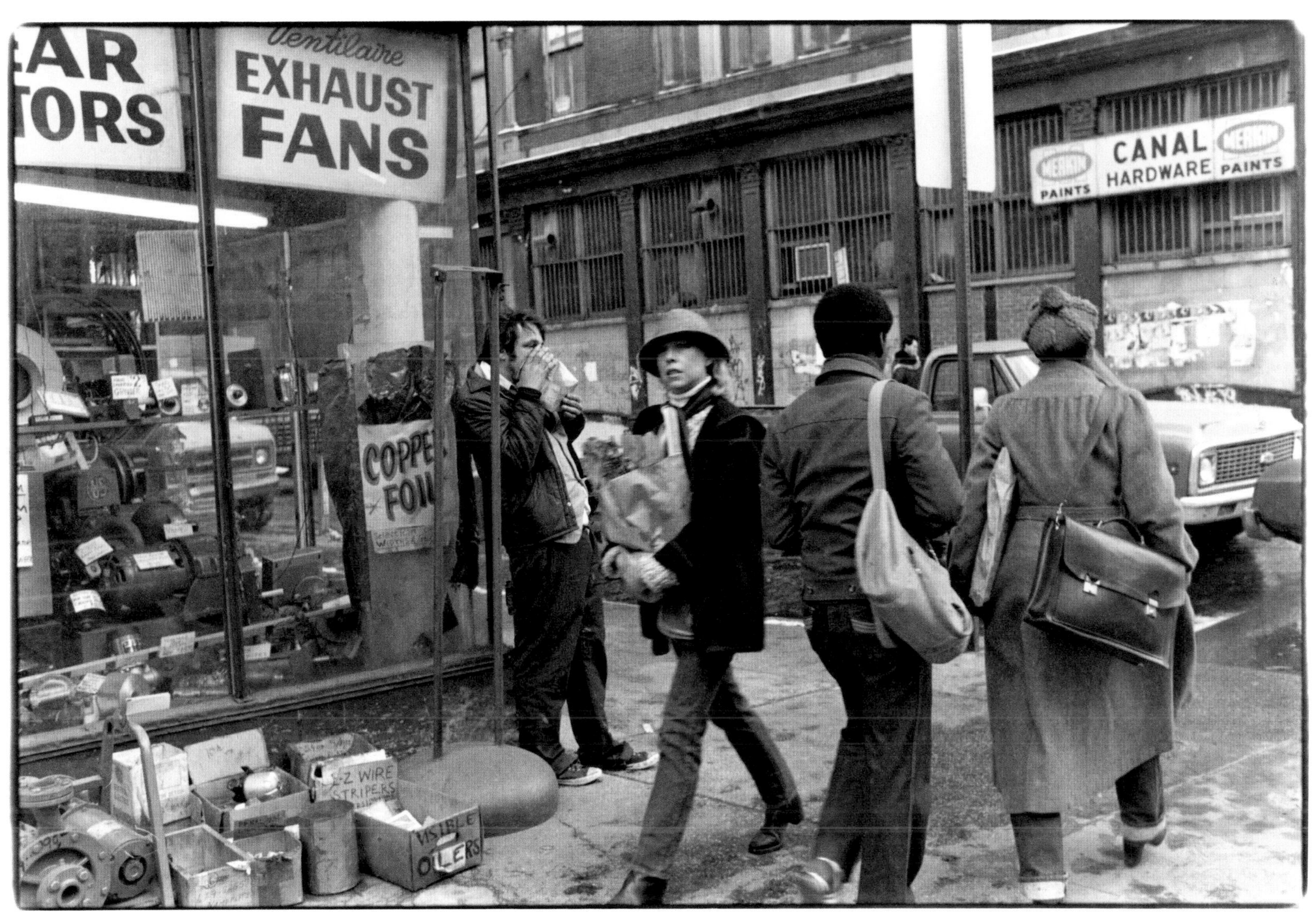

MAN SNIFFING GLUE FROM PAPER BAG.

1980

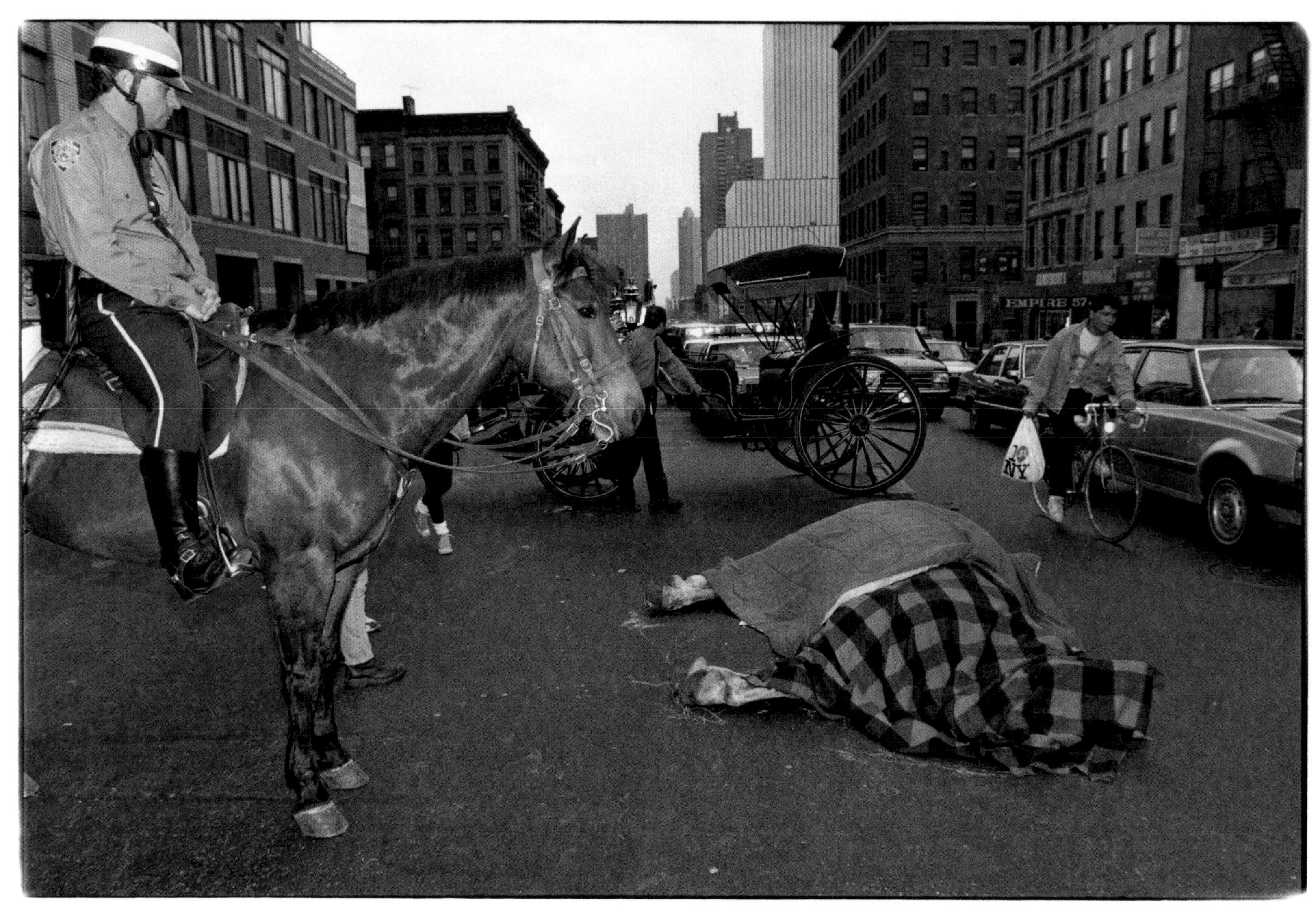

CARRIAGE HORSE COLLIDES WITH CITY BUS.

1980

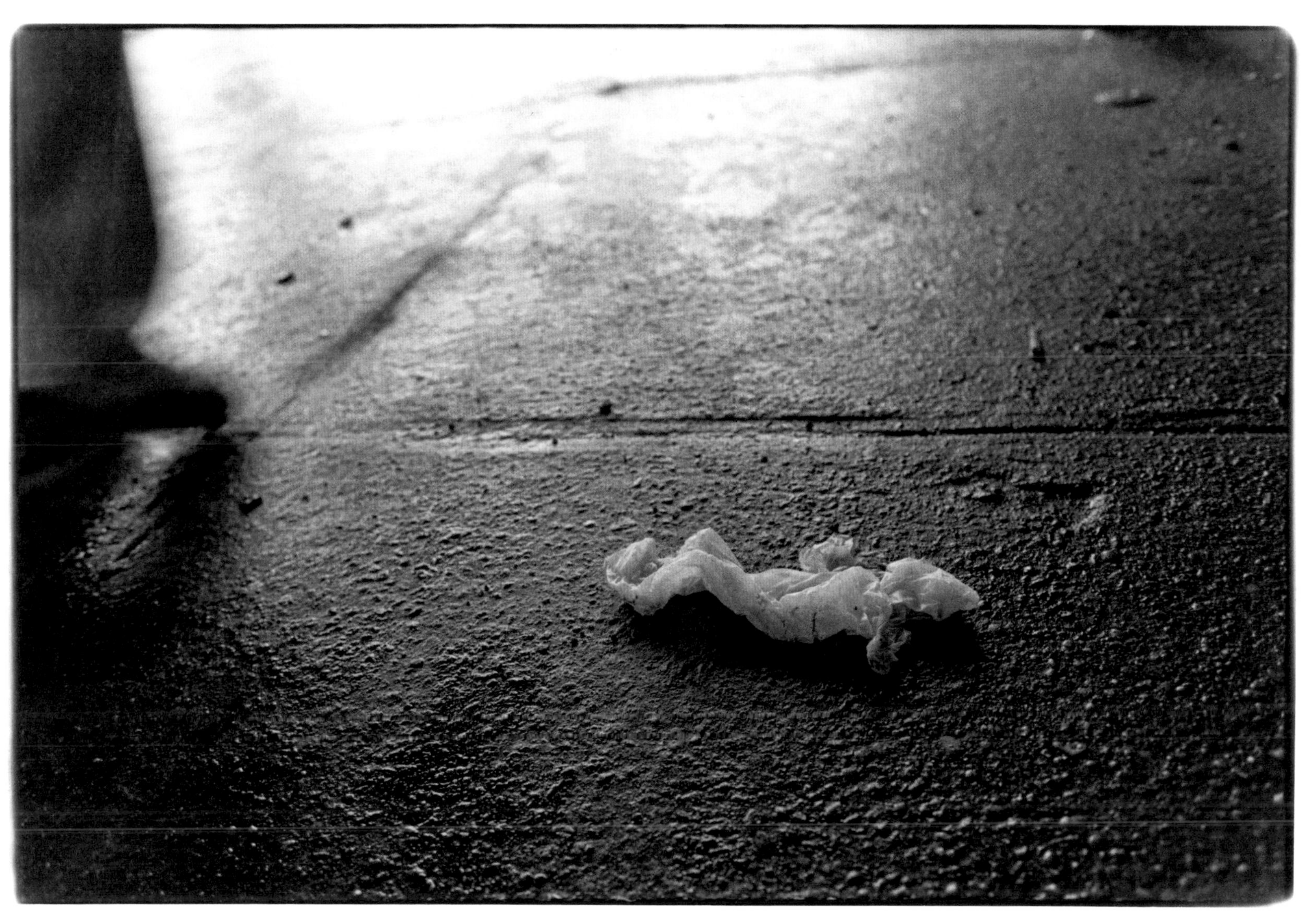

MAN WALKING PAST PAPER BAG.

1982

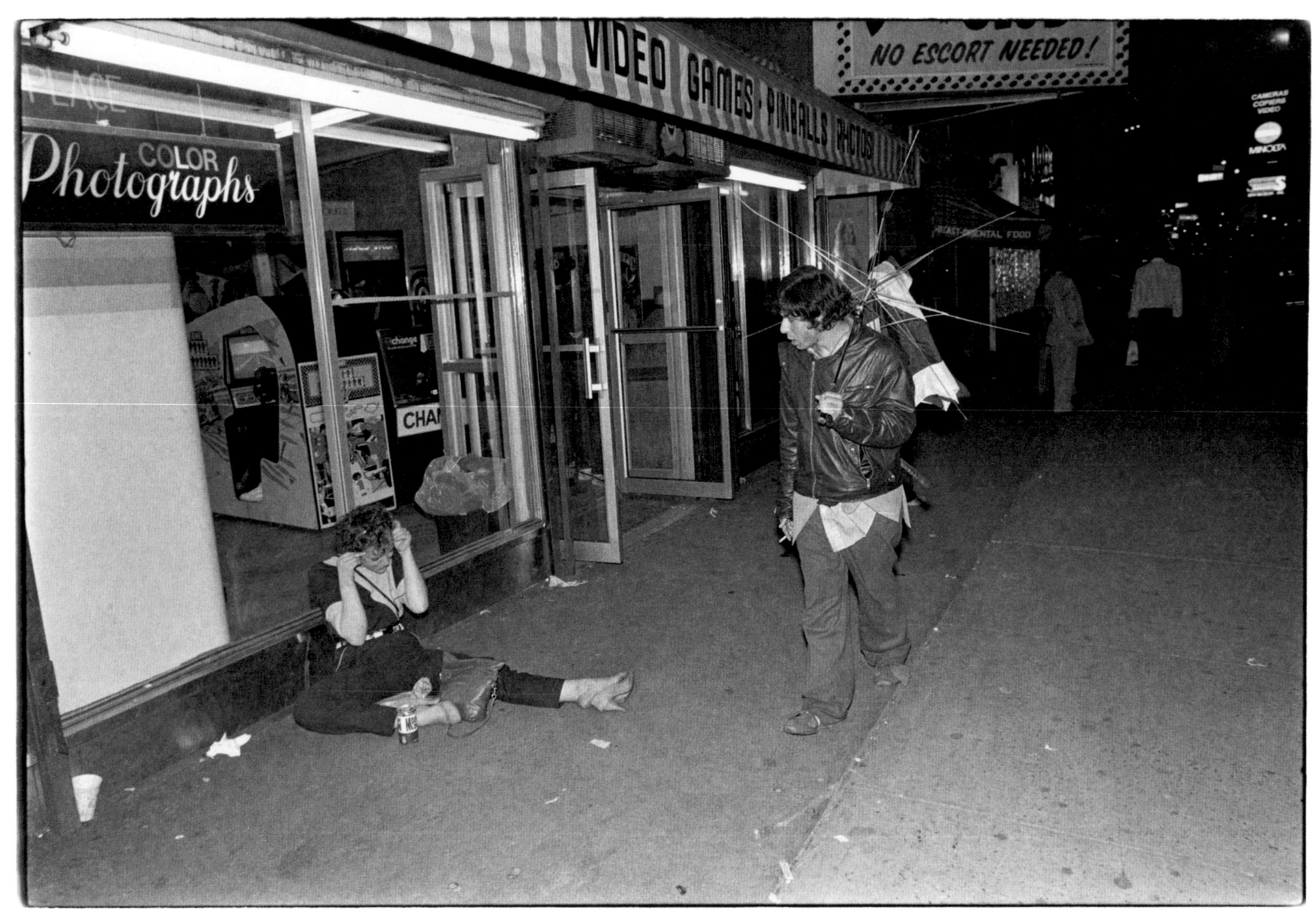

MAN WALKING PAST WOMAN LISTENING TO MUSIC OUTSIDE PLAYLAND.

1988

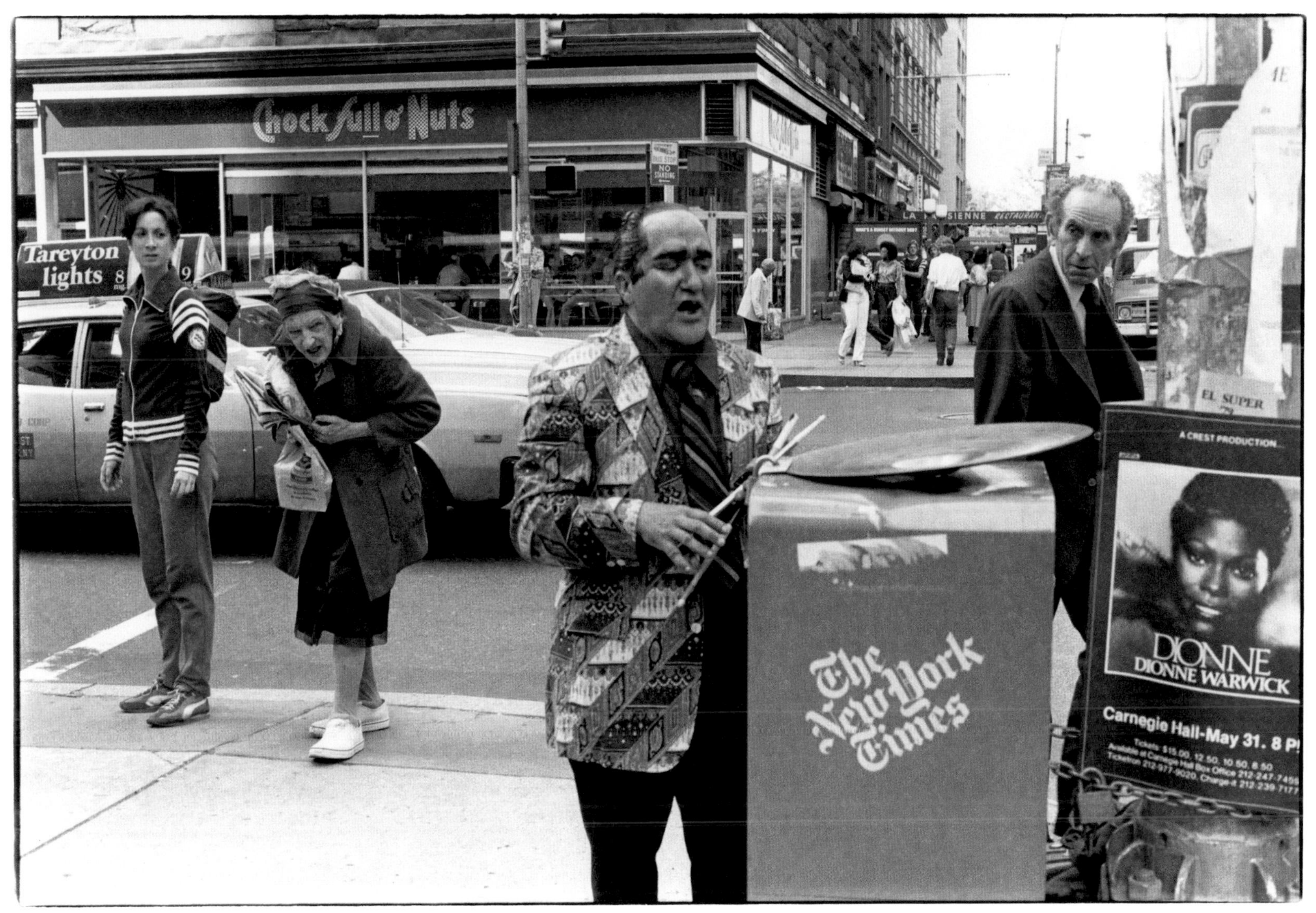

DRUMMER INTRODUCING HIS ACT.

1984

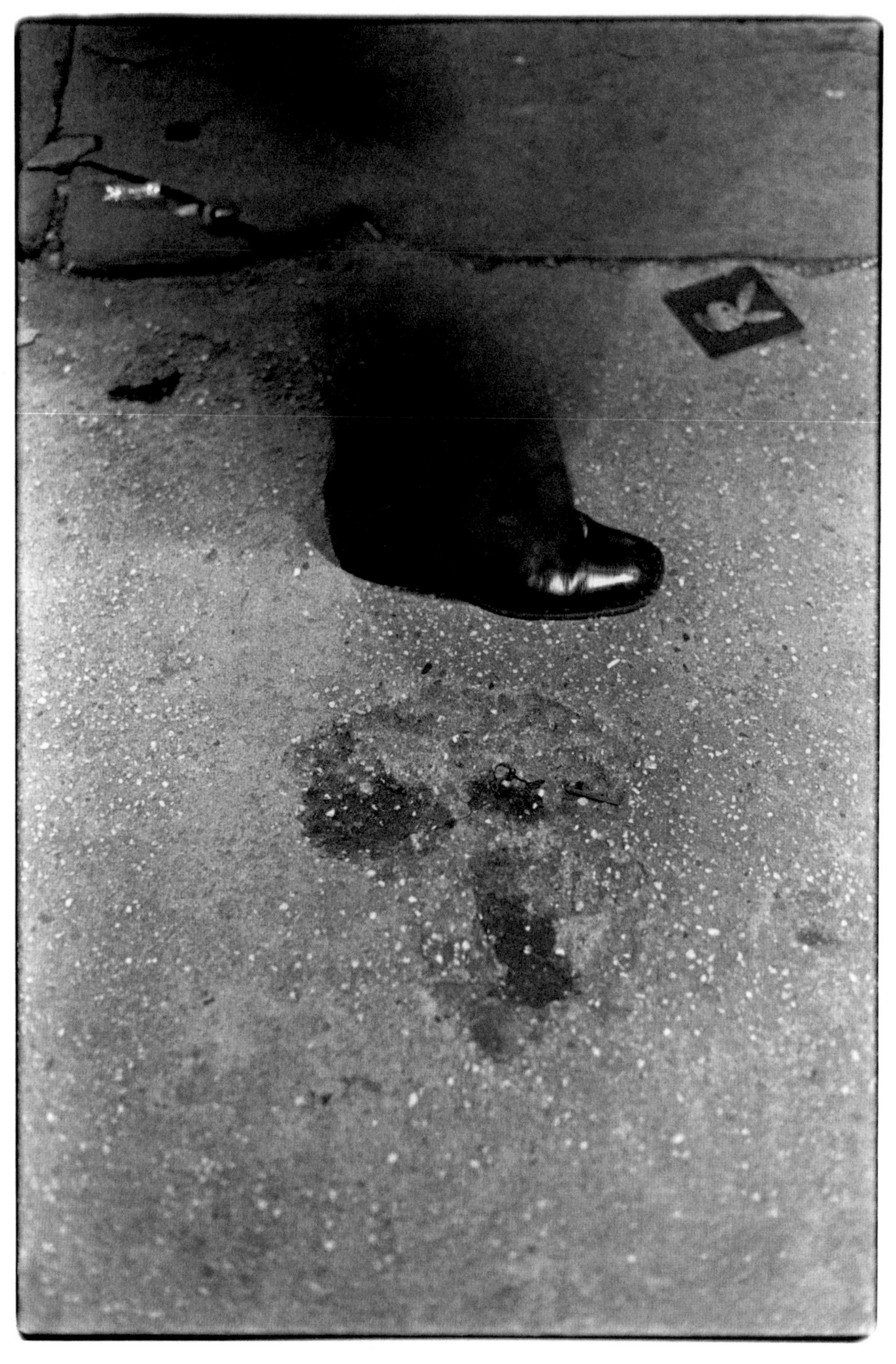

MAN WALKING PAST FACE IN SIDEWALK. 1980

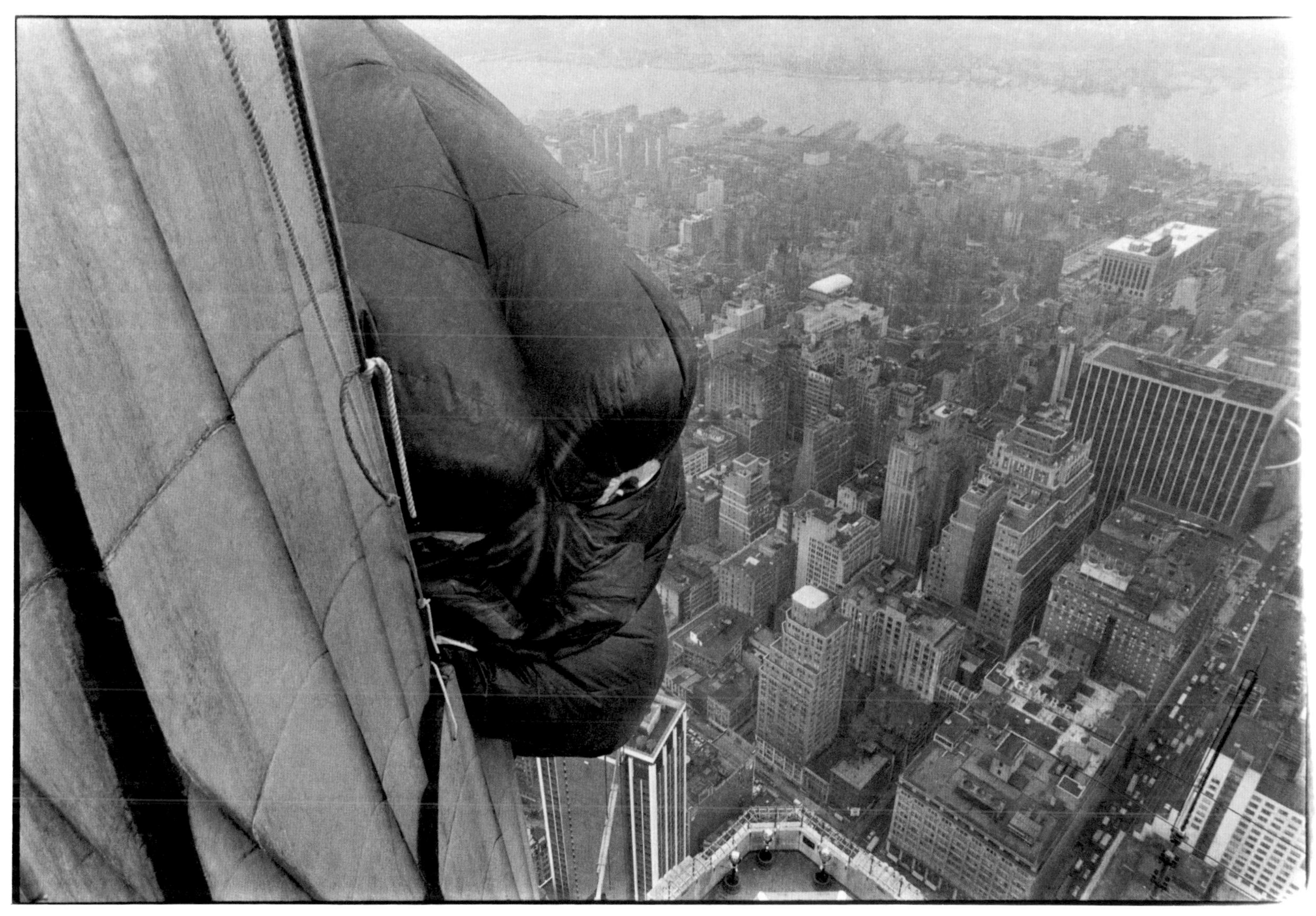

80 FT. KING KONG – INSTALLED AT TOP OF EMPIRE STATE BLDG. – SPRINGS A LEAK AND BEGINS TO DEFLATE.

1983

PASSENGERS

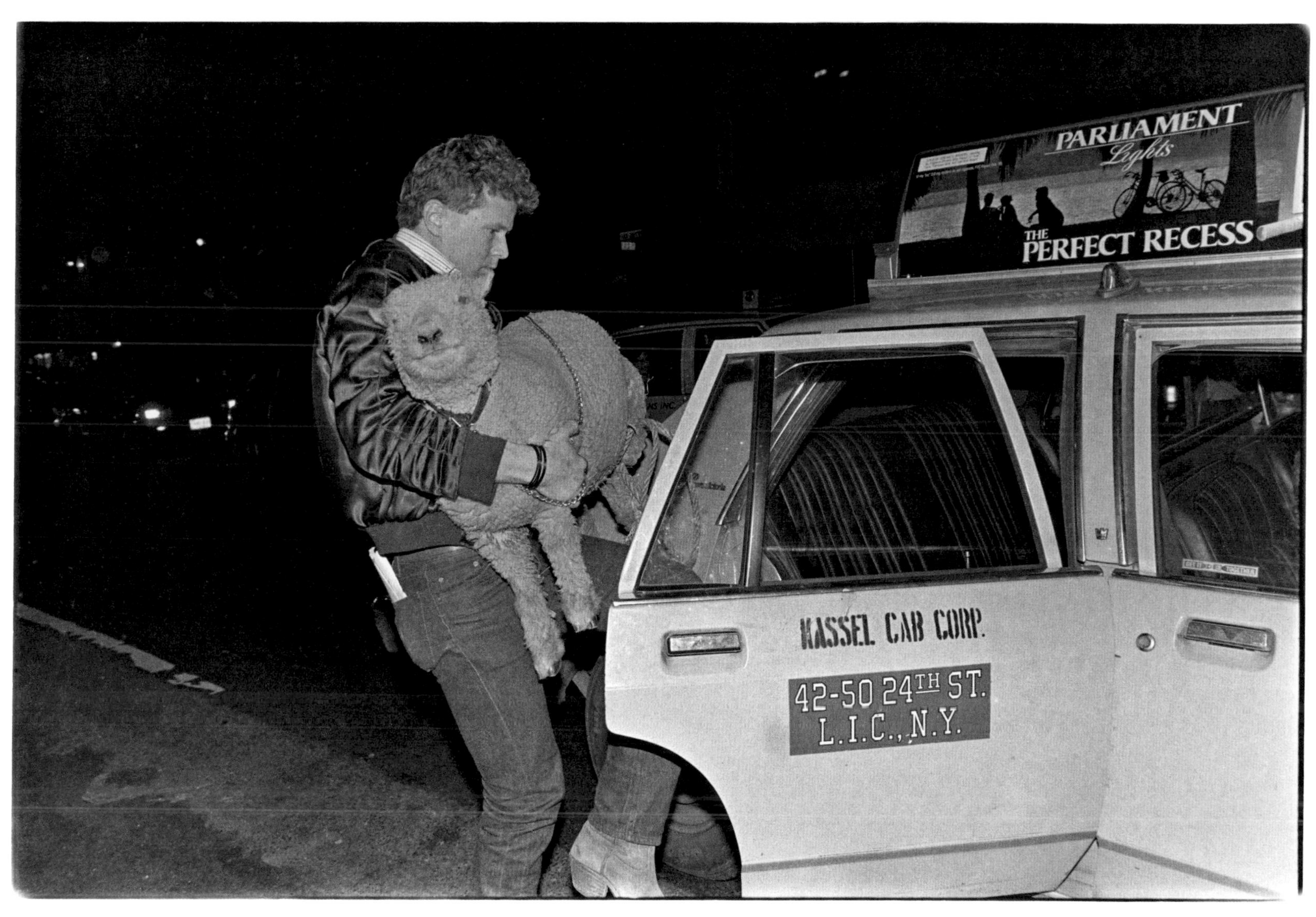

MAN PUTTING SHEEP INTO TAXI.

1986

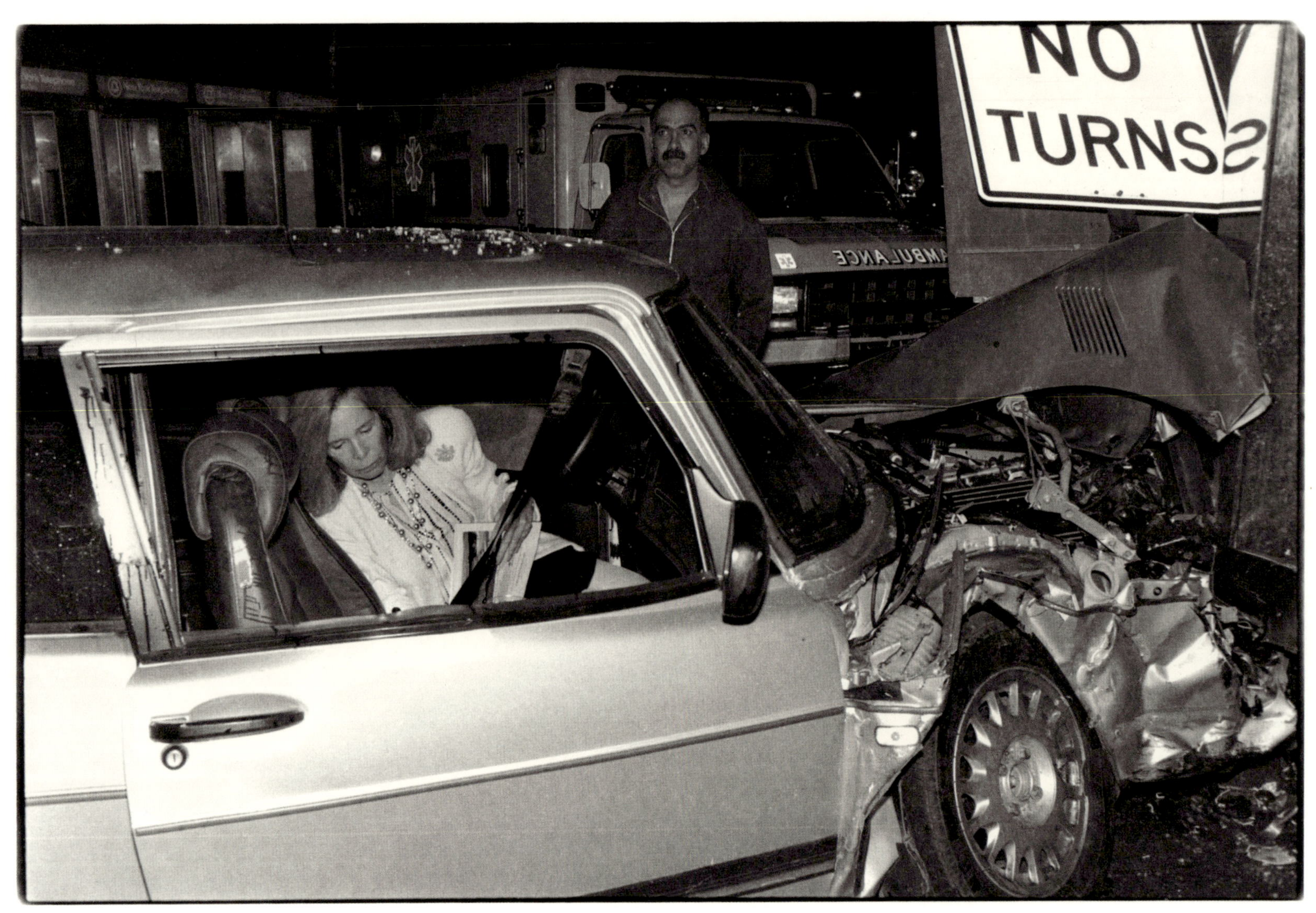

WOMAN READING MAGAZINE AFTER DRIVING INTO BUILDING.

1989

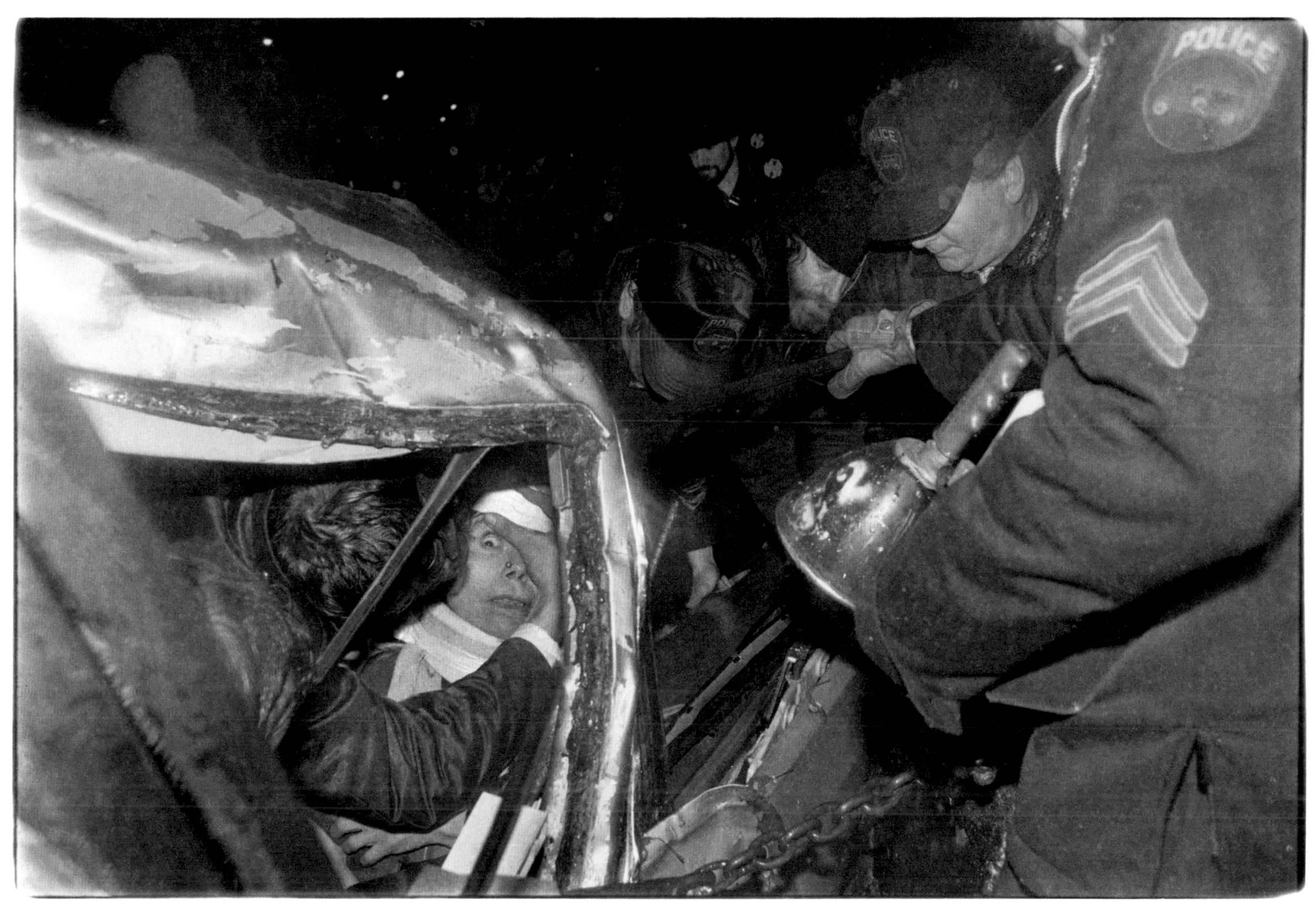

DRIVER TRAPPED IN CAR WRECK.

1985

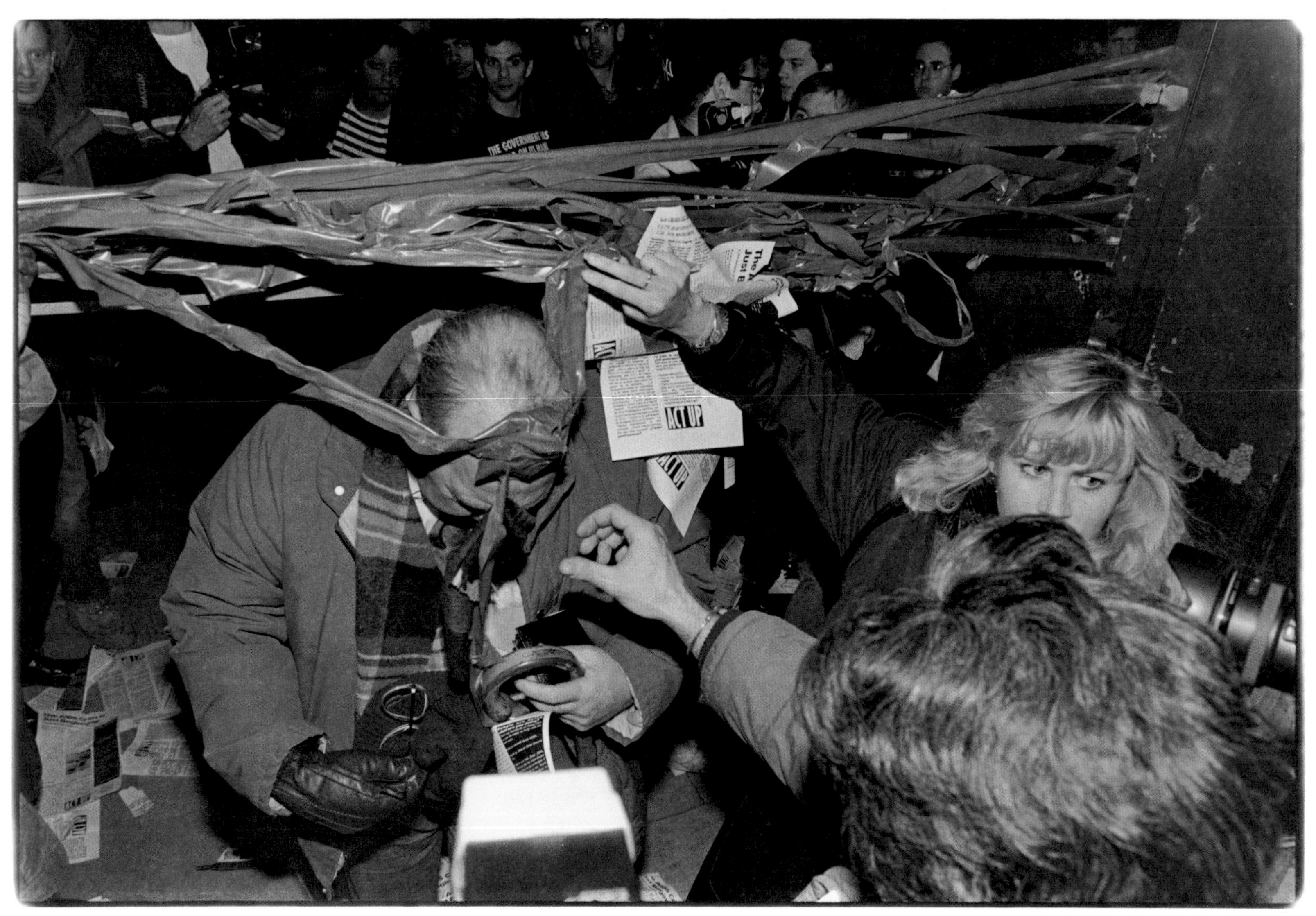

DEMONSTRATORS TRY TO PREVENT PASSENGERS FROM BOARDING COMMUTER TRAINS.

1991

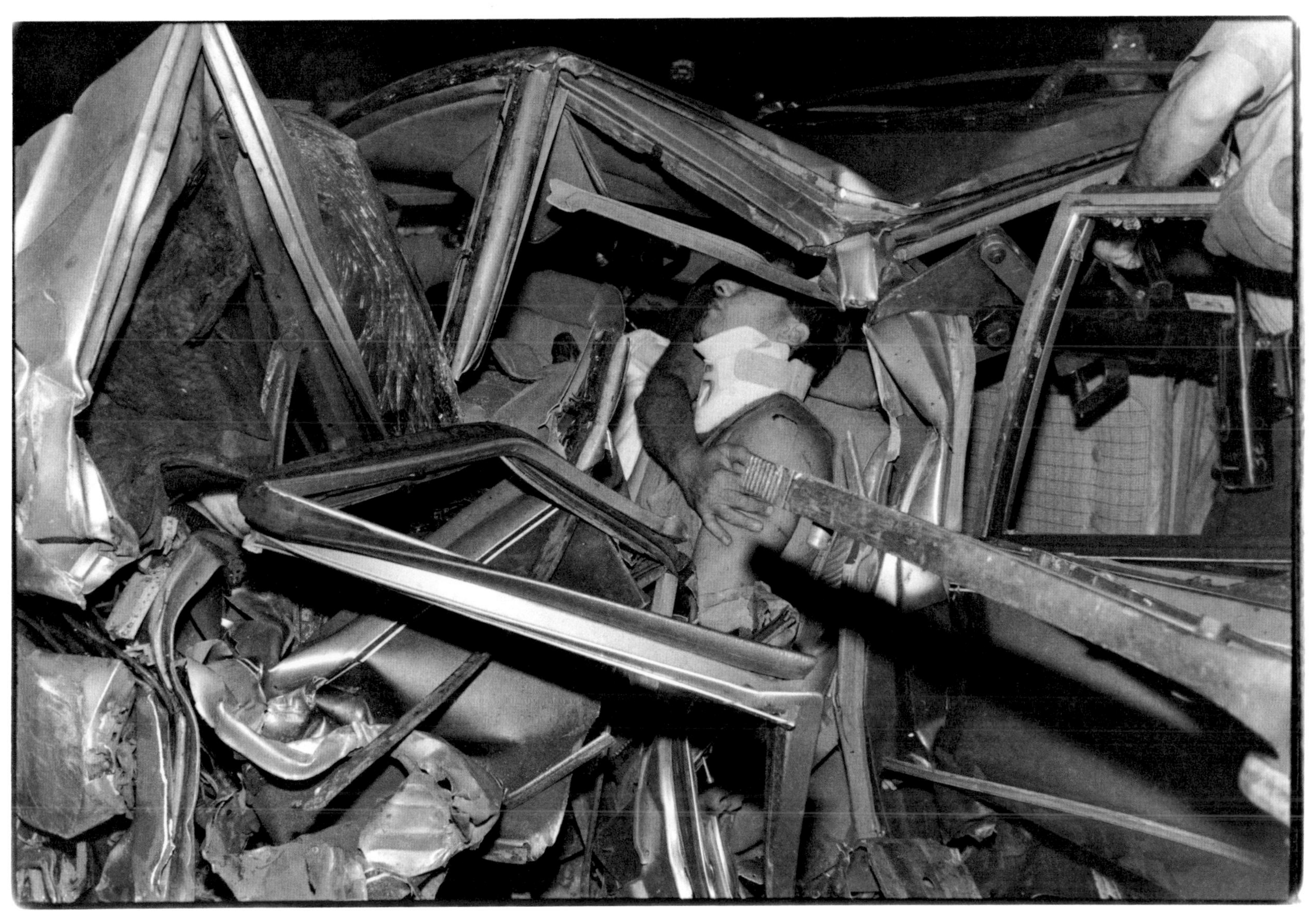

DRIVER TRAPPED IN CAR WRECK.

1989

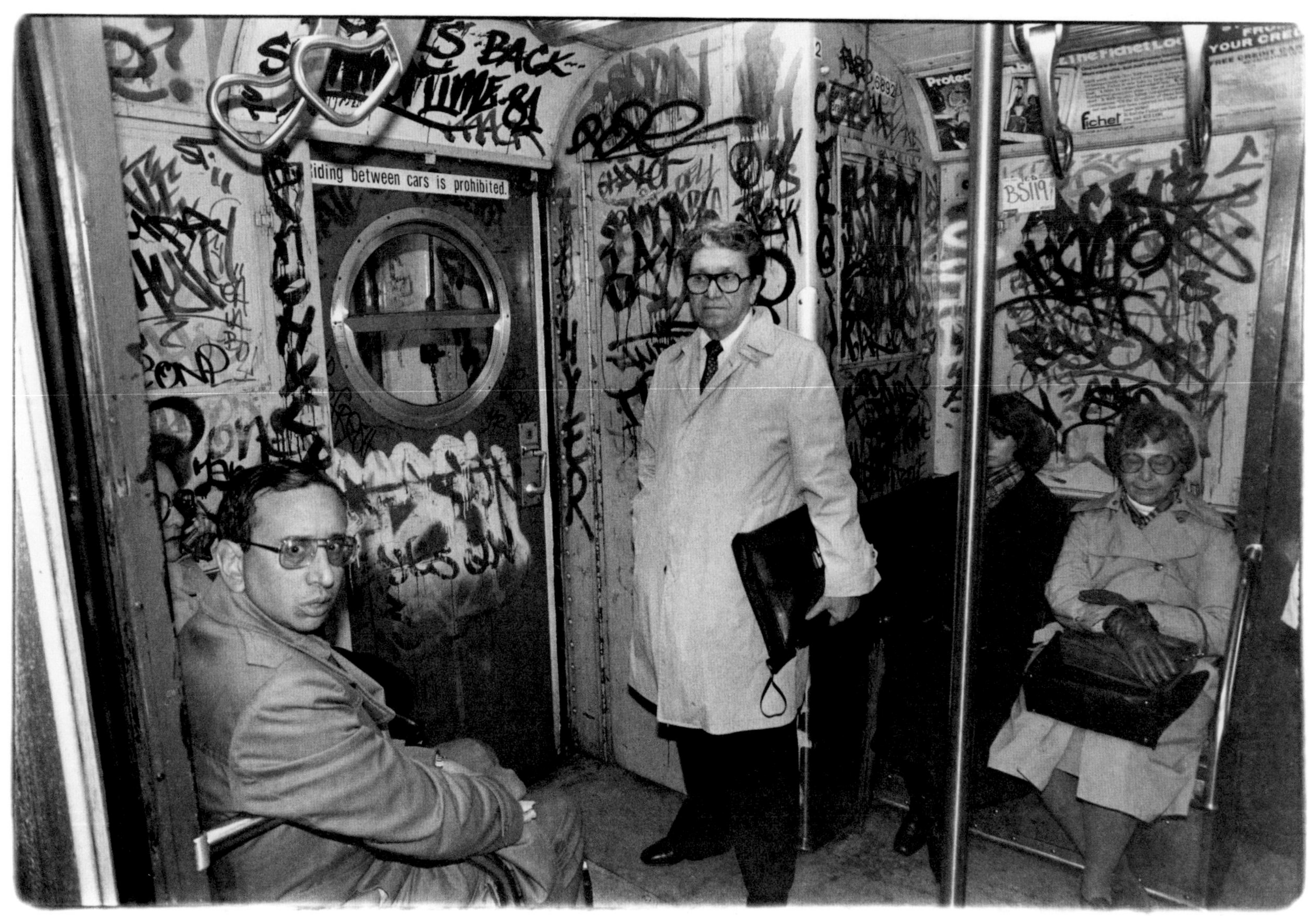

METRO NORTH TRAIN STRIKE FORCES COMMUTERS TO RIDE THE SUBWAY THROUGH THE BRONX INTO MANHATTAN.

1982

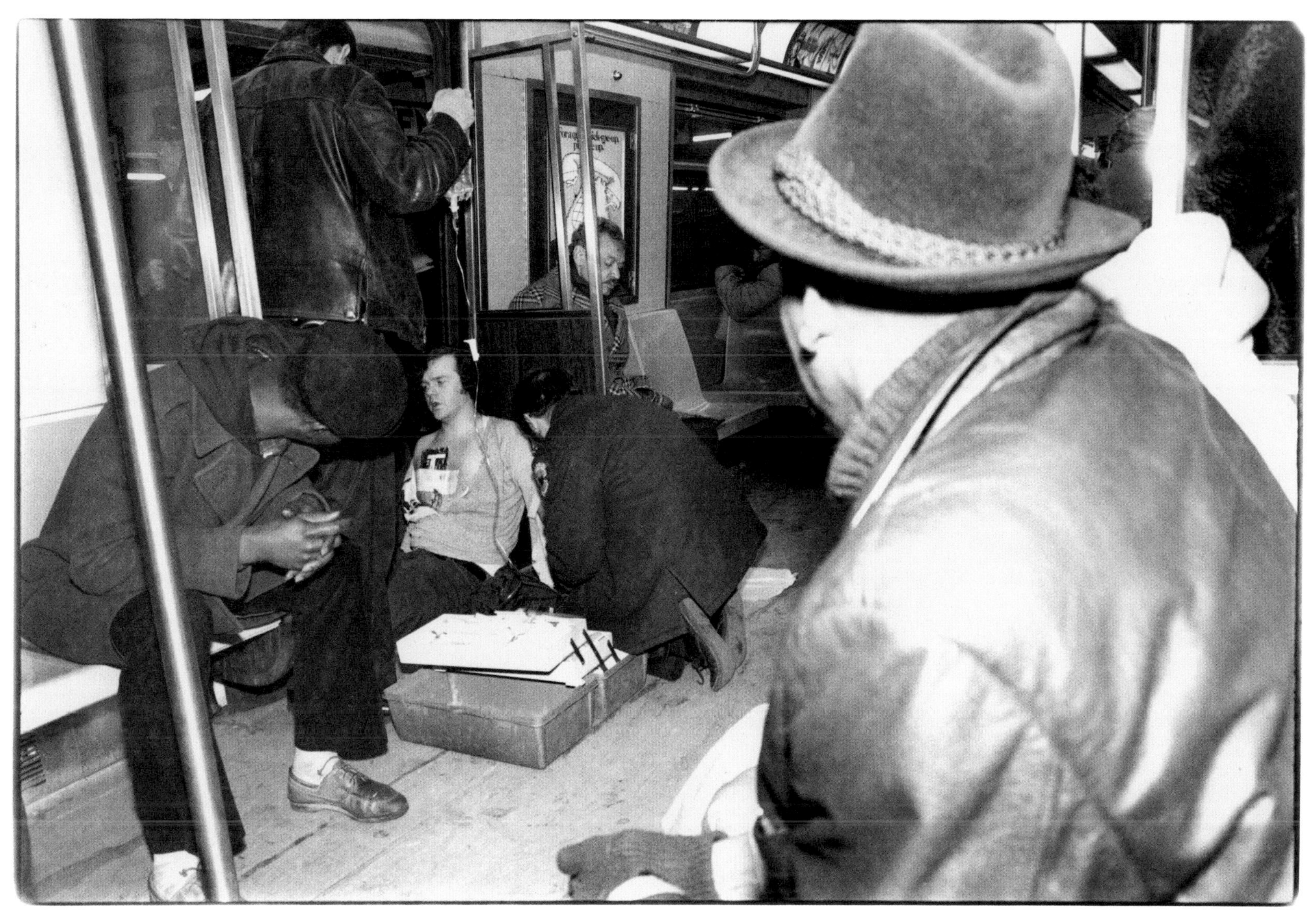

MAN STABBED IN CHEST AFTER WARNING KIDS NOT TO CLIMB ON SUBWAY GIRDERS.

1982

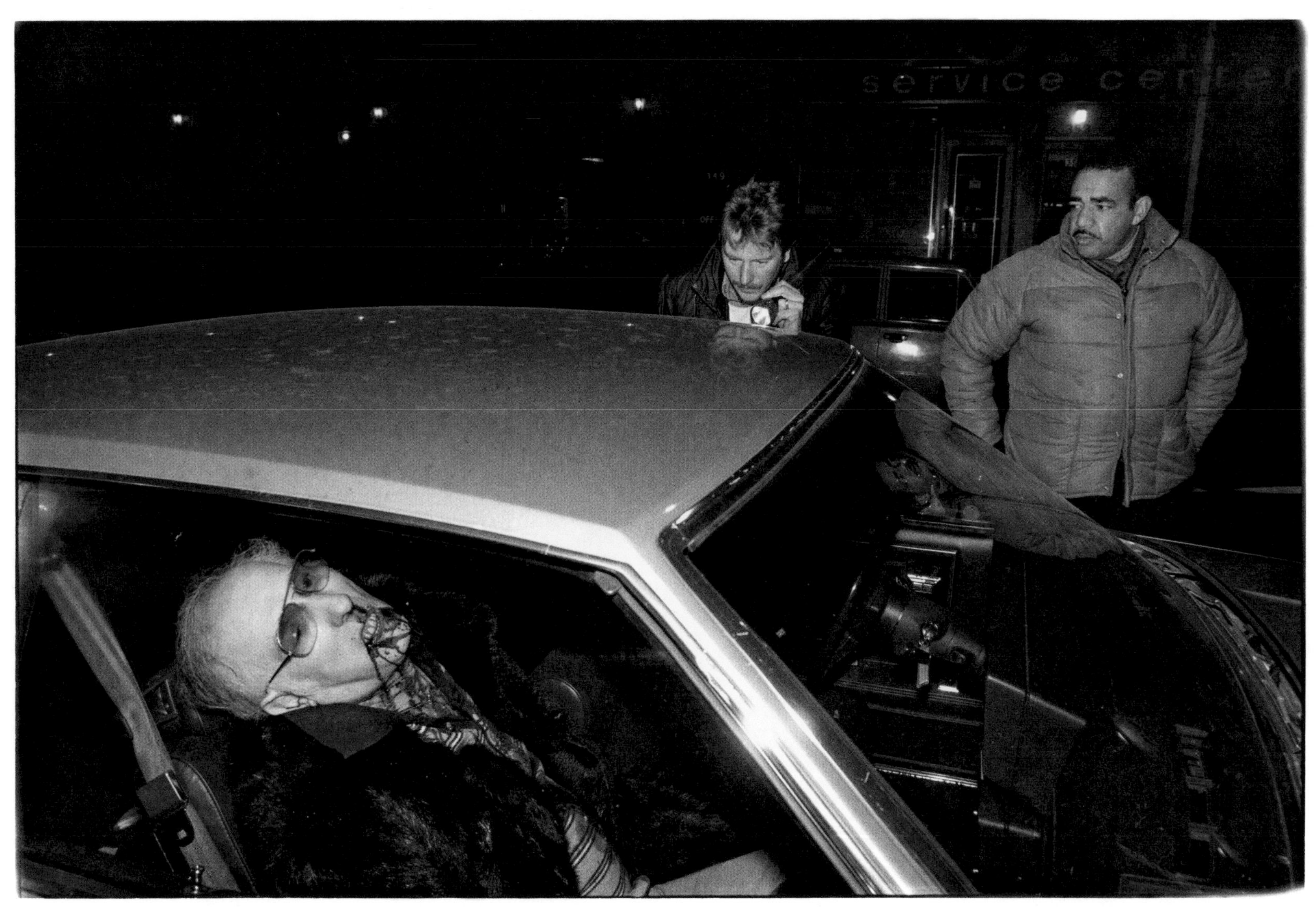

HOMICIDE INSIDE LOCKED CAR.

1984

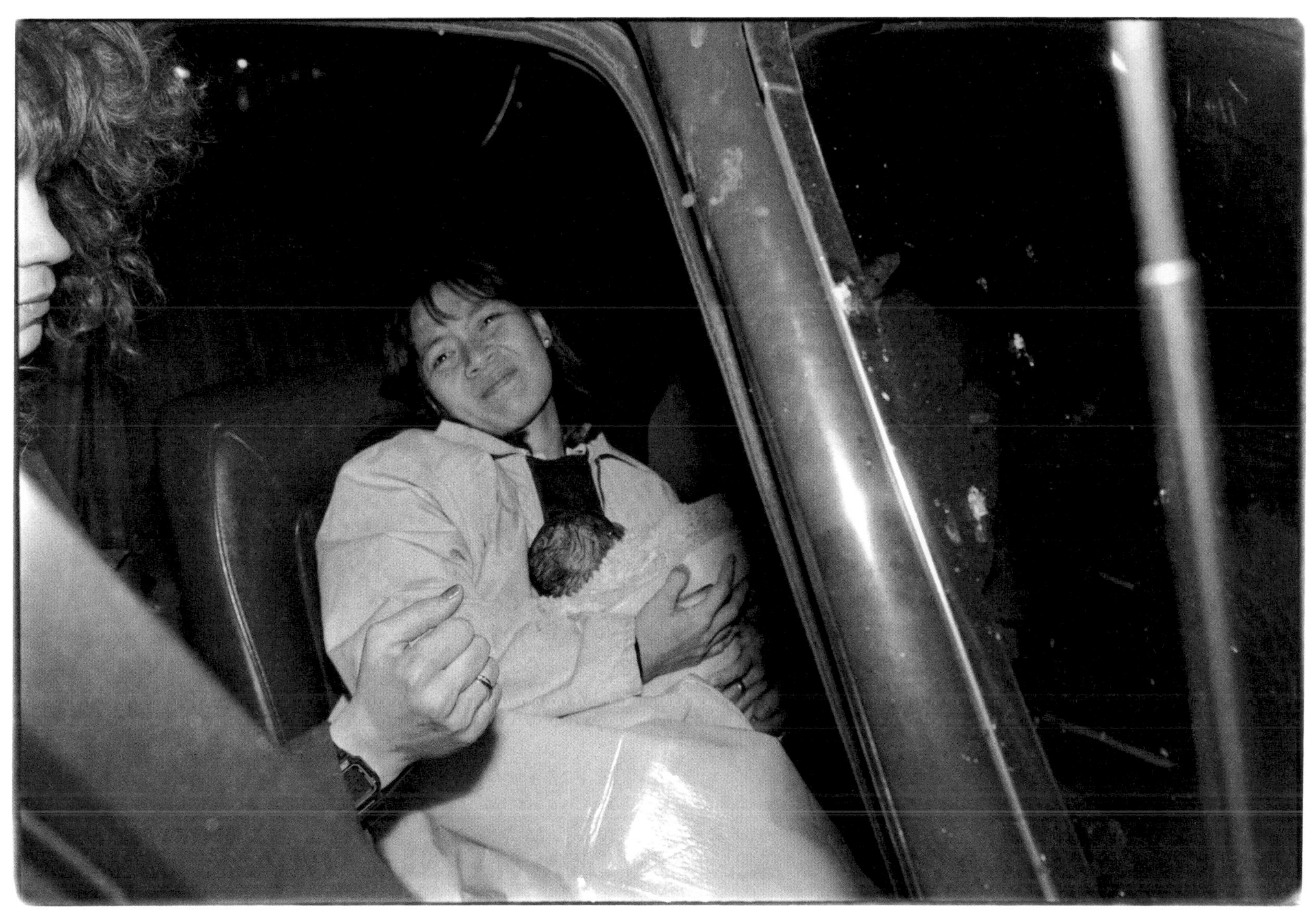

WOMAN HAS BABY IN SMAll TRUCK.

1988

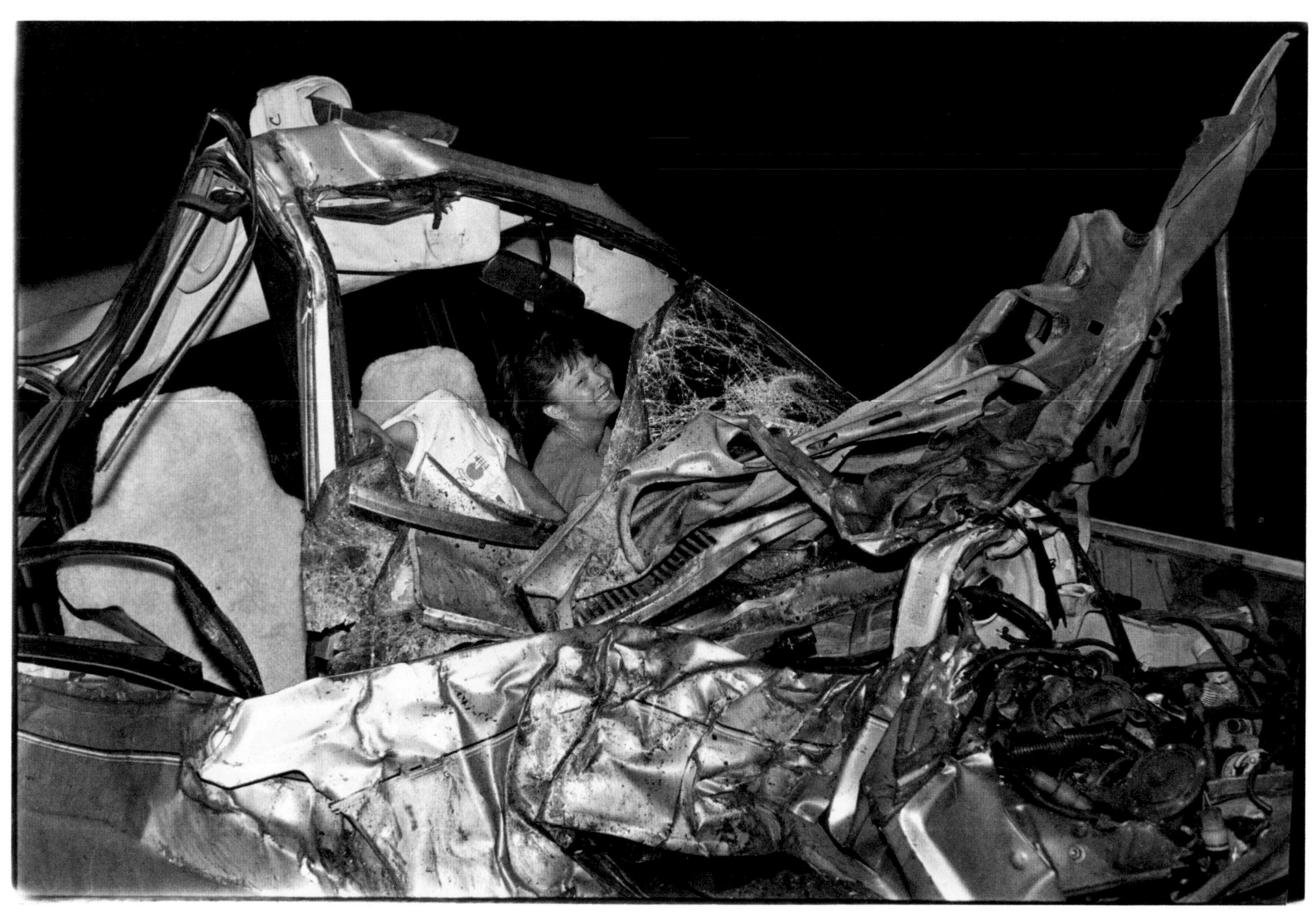

WOMAN LAUGHING AFTER CAR WRECK.

1989

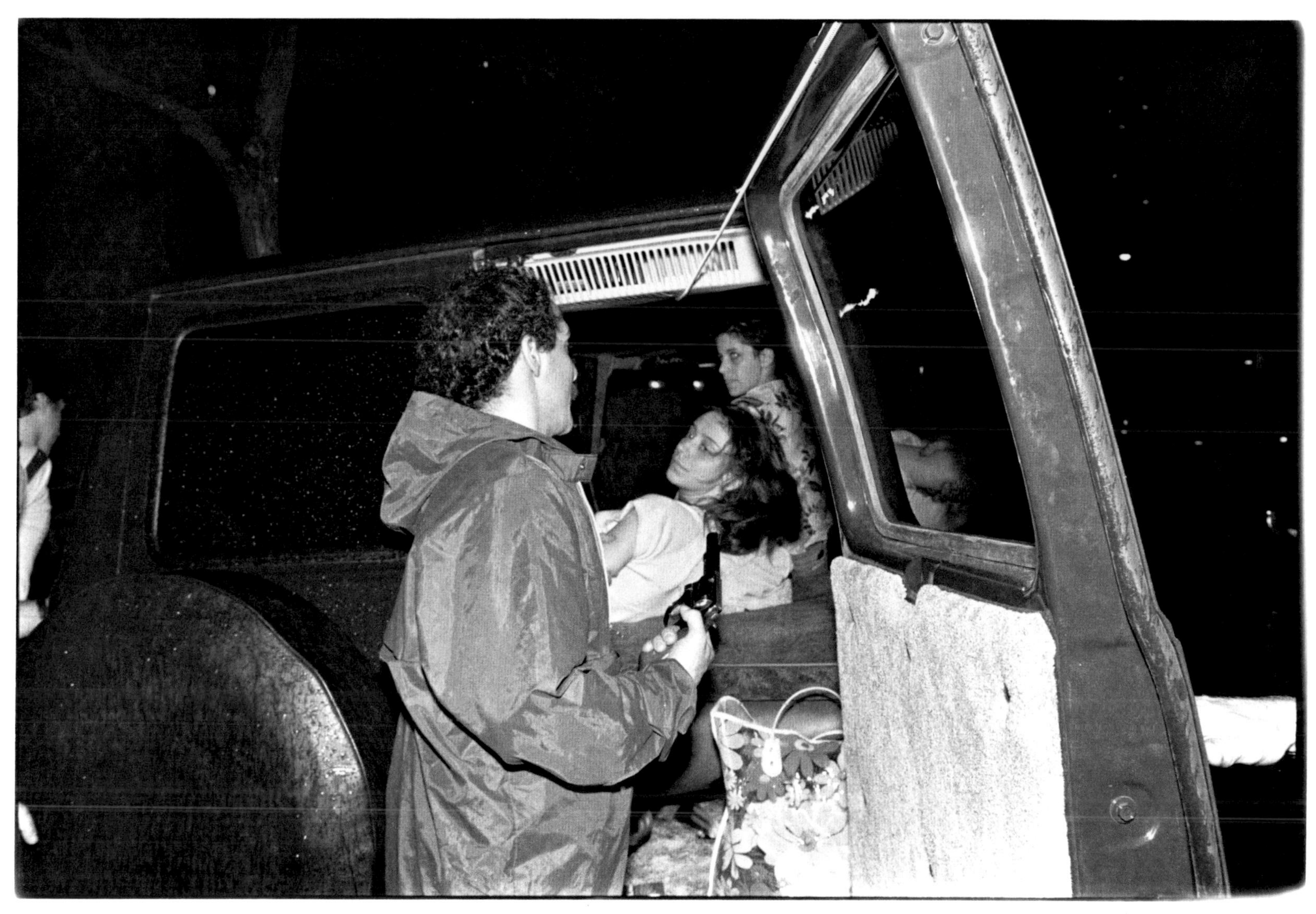

UNDERCOVER COP WAKING PEOPLE SLEEPING IN STOLEN VAN.

1987

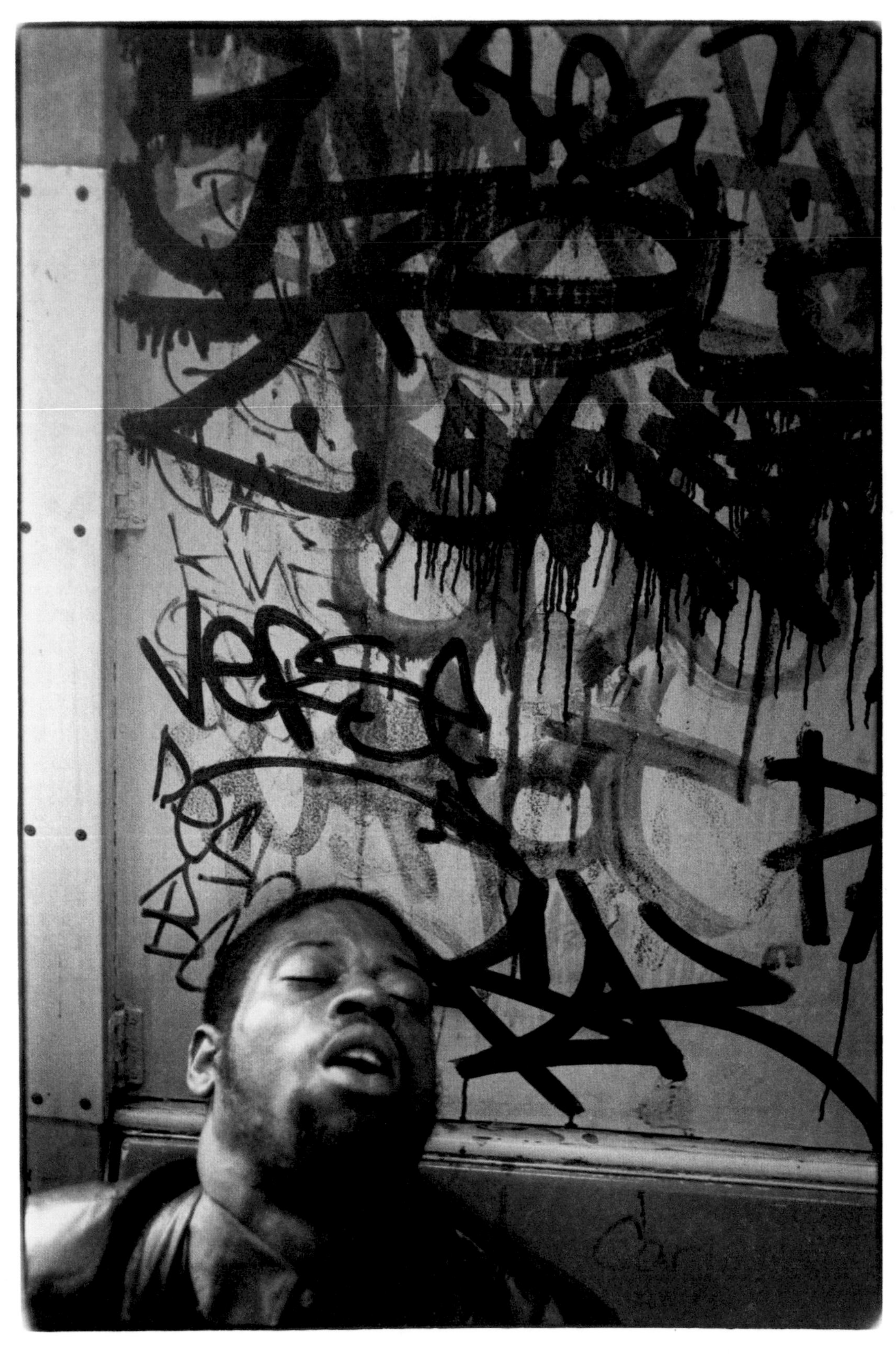

MAN sleeping in SUBWAY CAR. 1987

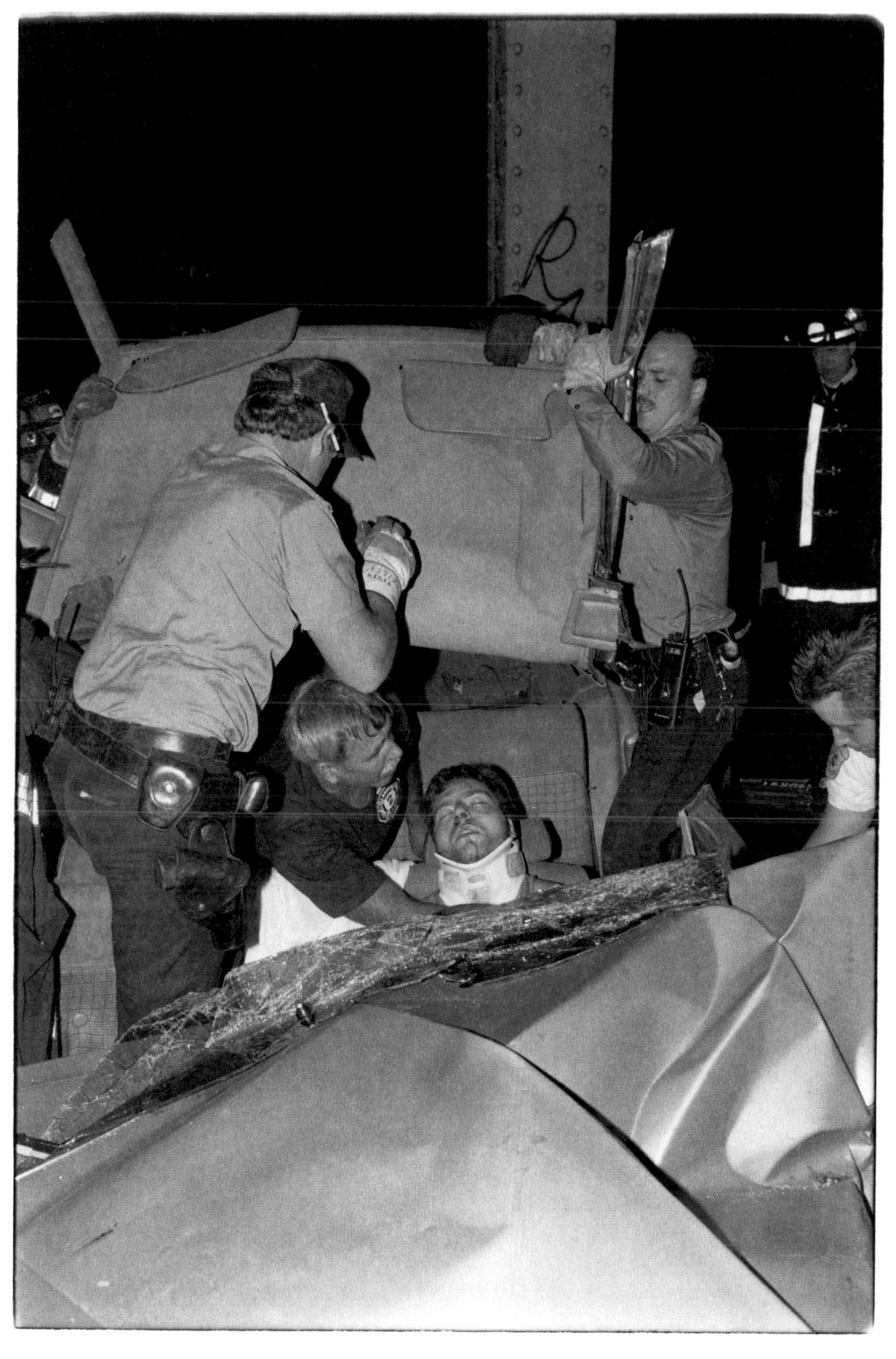

DRIVER TRAPPED IN CAR WRECK. 1989

WORKERS AND SWELLS

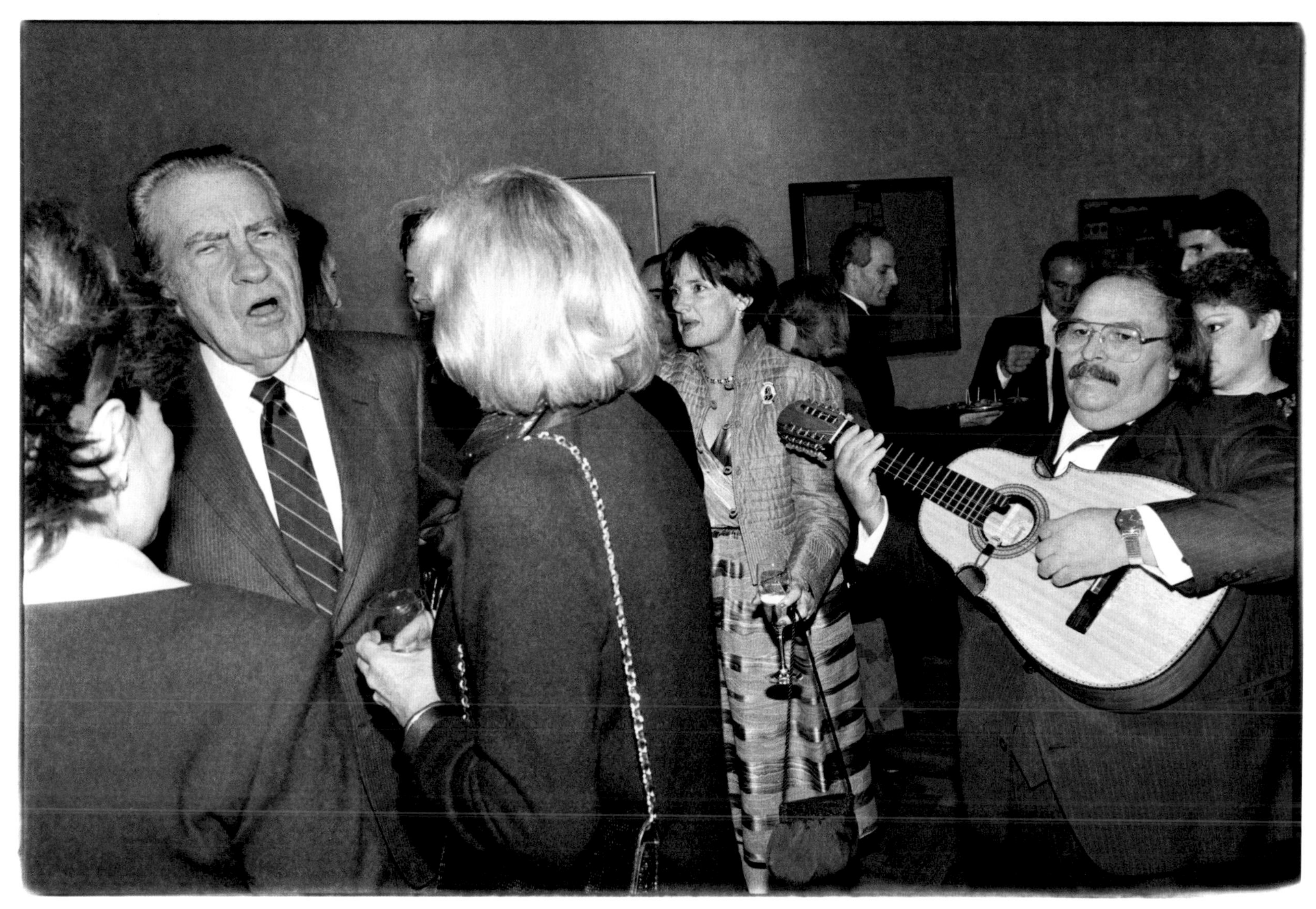

MAN ENTERTAINING SOCIETY BENEFIT FOR COLUMBIAN EARTHQUAKE VICTIMS.

1986

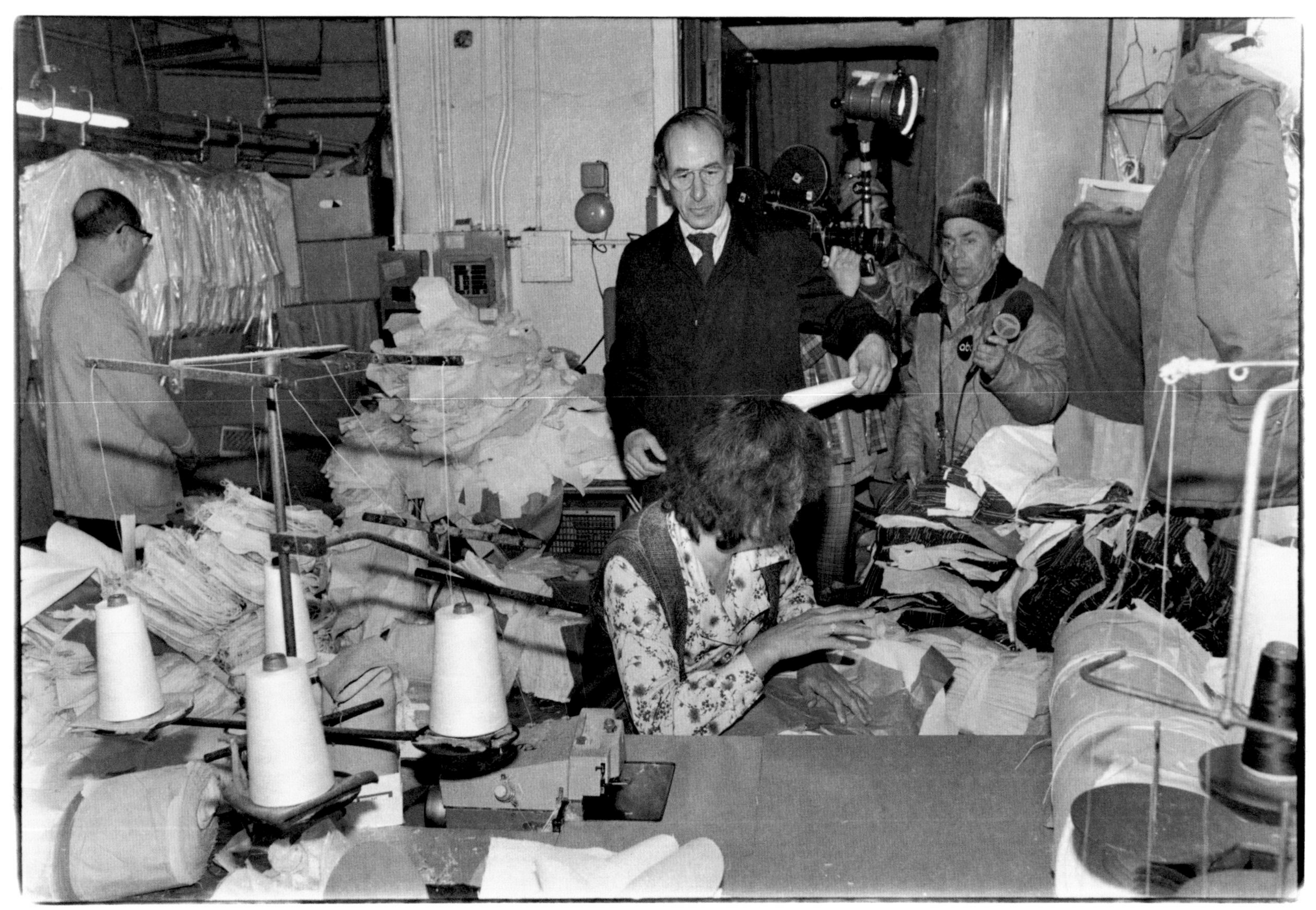

SWEATSHOP WORKER STARTLED BY INVESTIGATING STATE SENATOR WITH FILM CREW.

1981

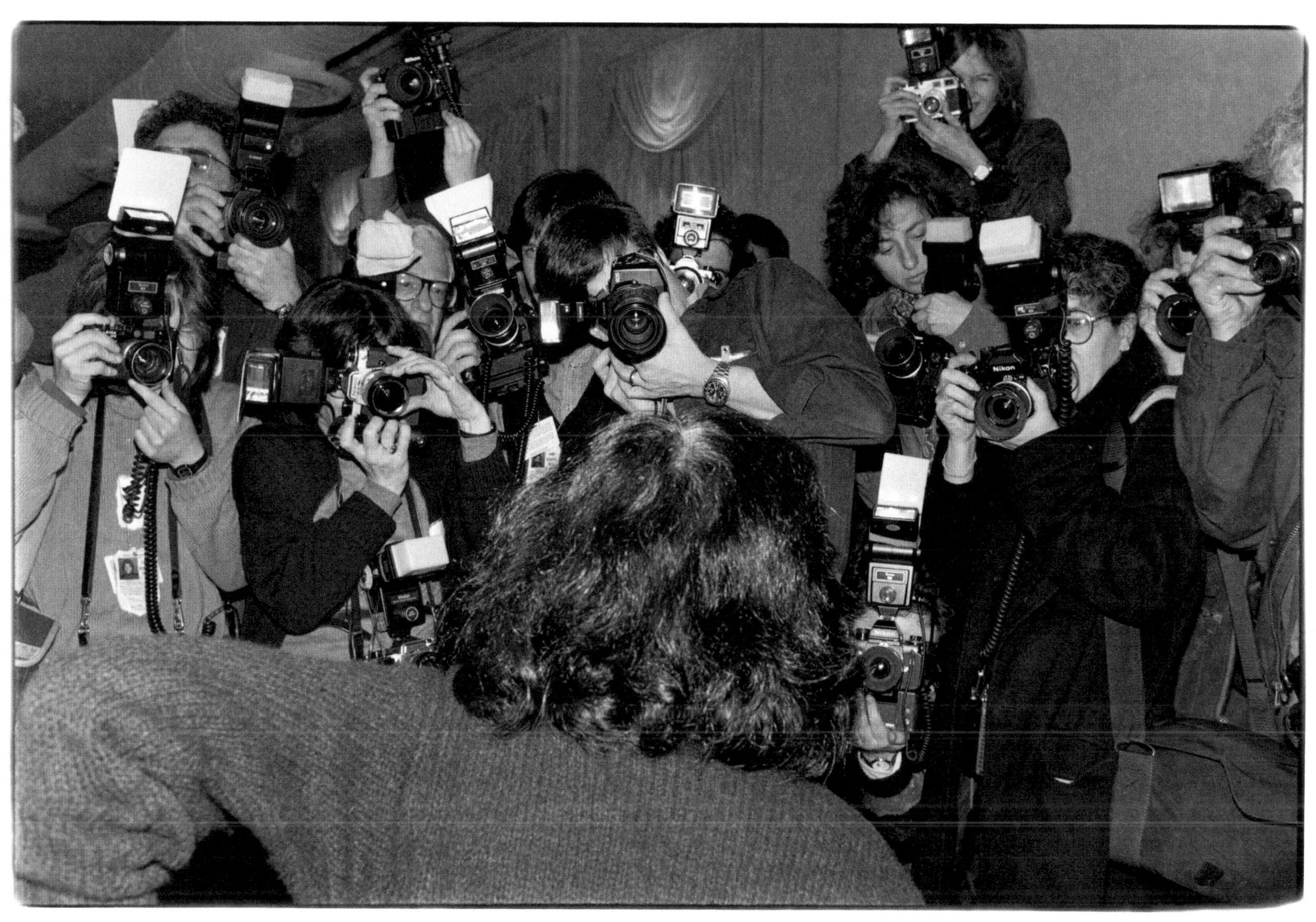

INTELLECTUAL ATTENDS PUBLIC READING OF "SATANIC VERSES".

1992

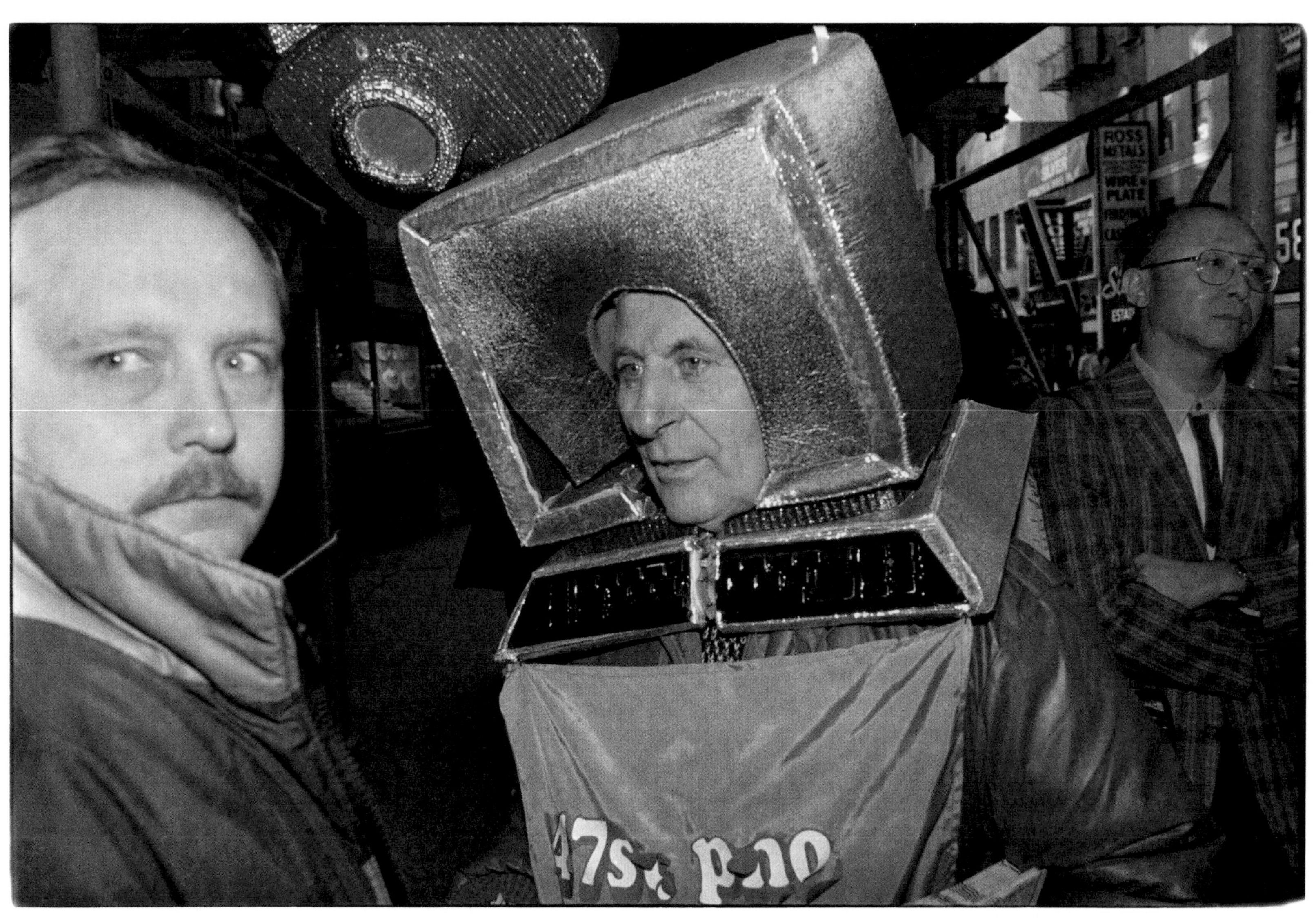

FRIENDS HAVING A CONVERSATION.

1987

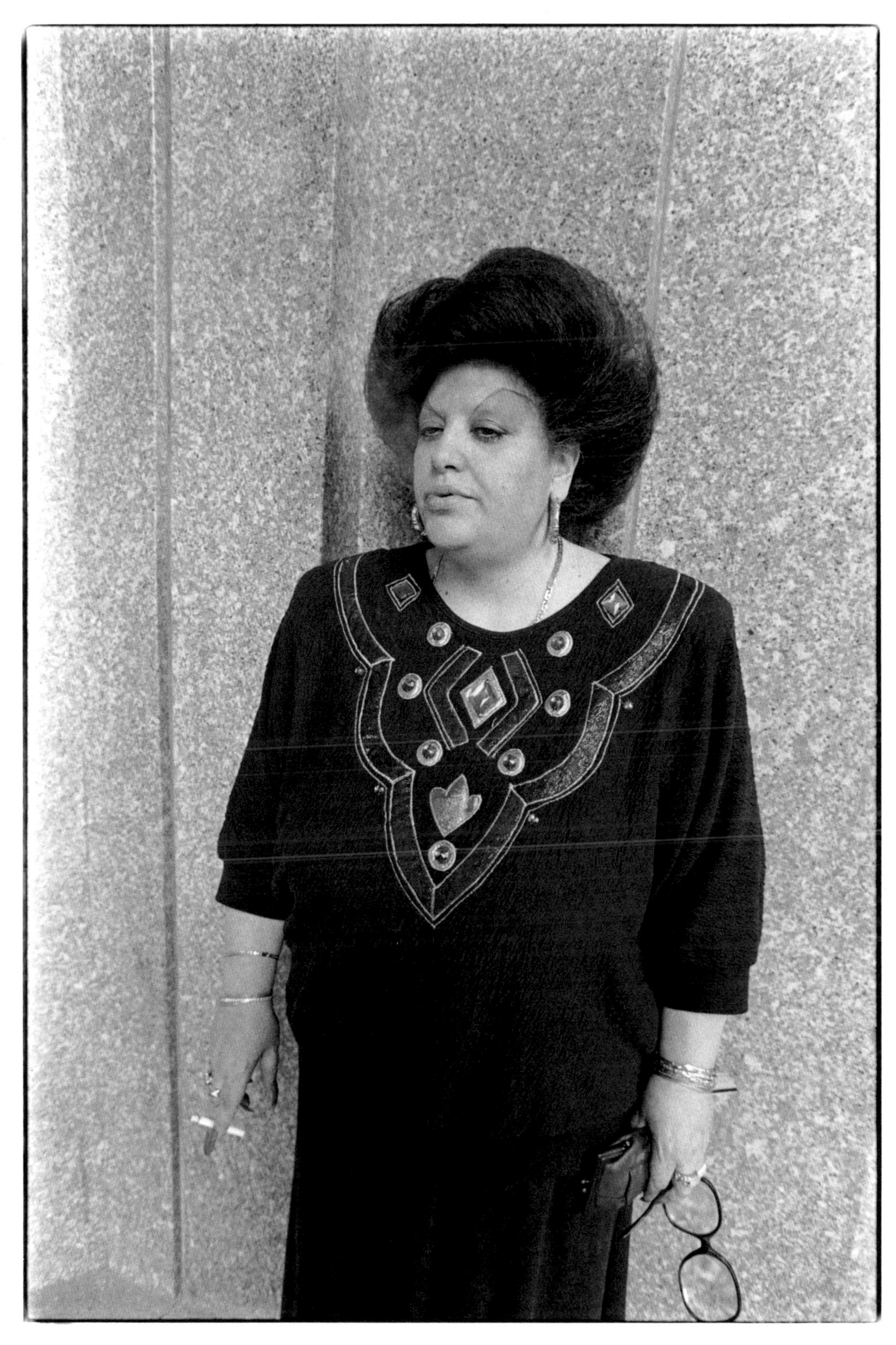

OFFICE WORKER TAKING A BREAK. 1991

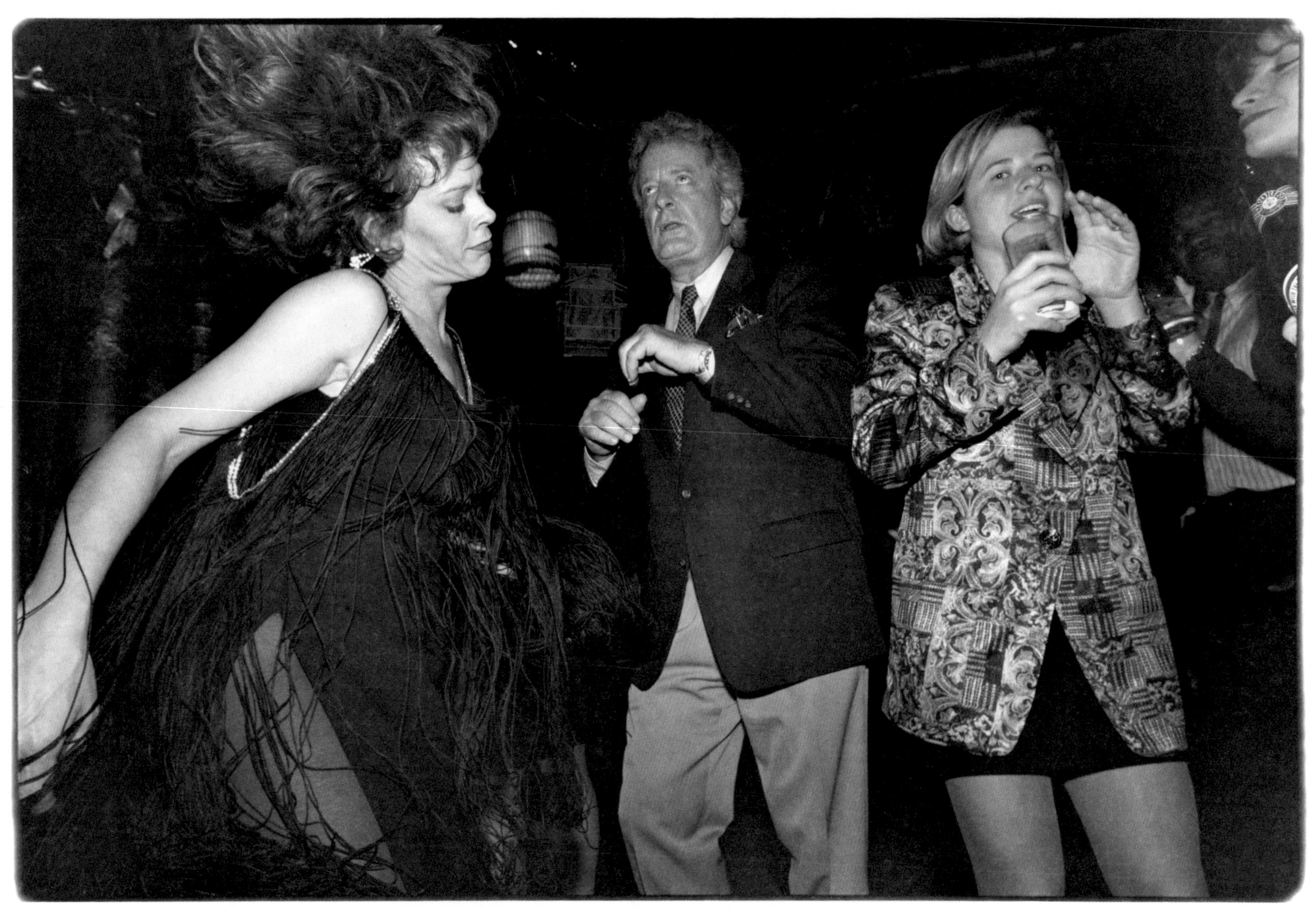

PARTY FOR SOAP OPERA STARS.

1994

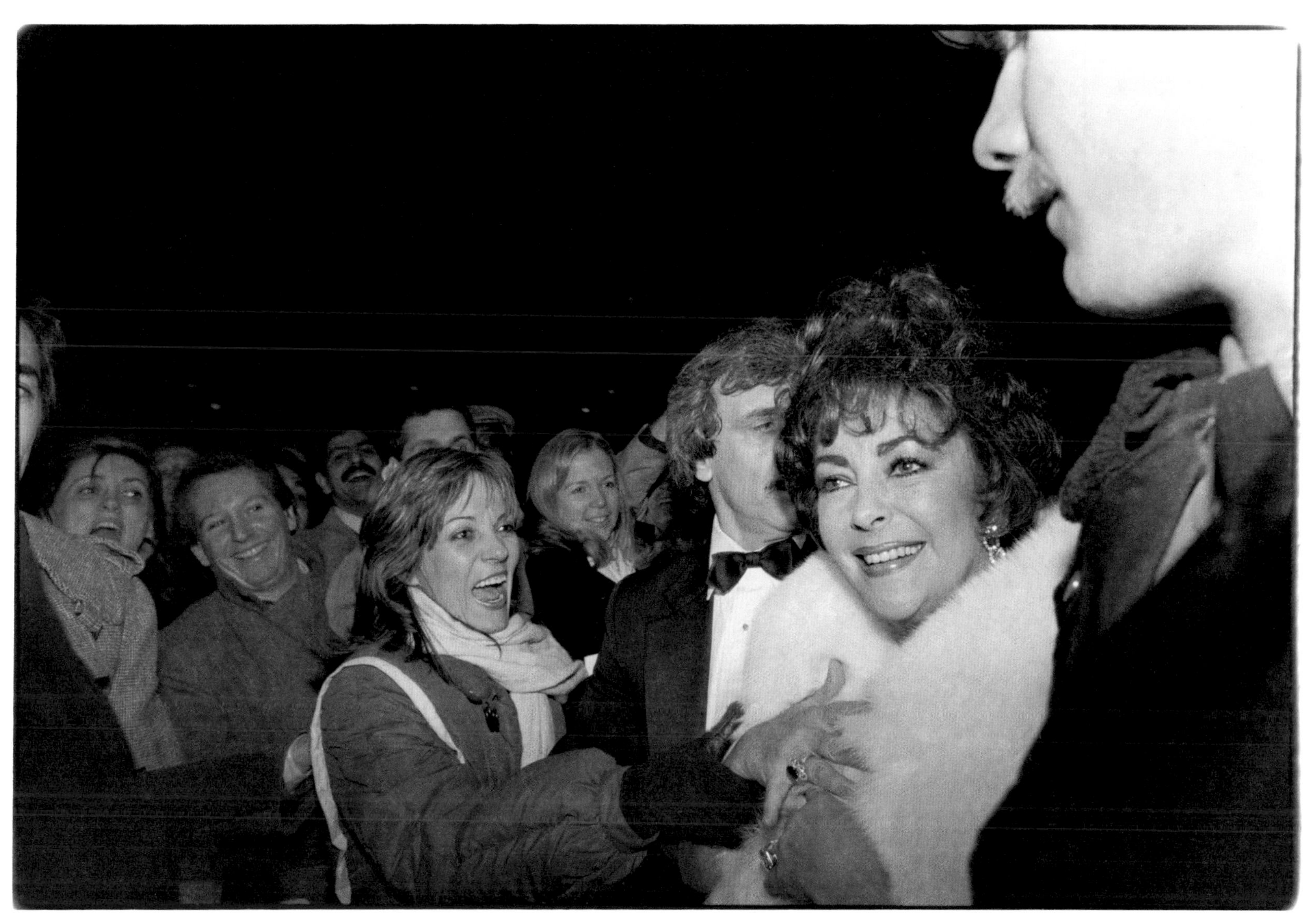

WOMAN TOUCHING MOVIE STAR.

1982

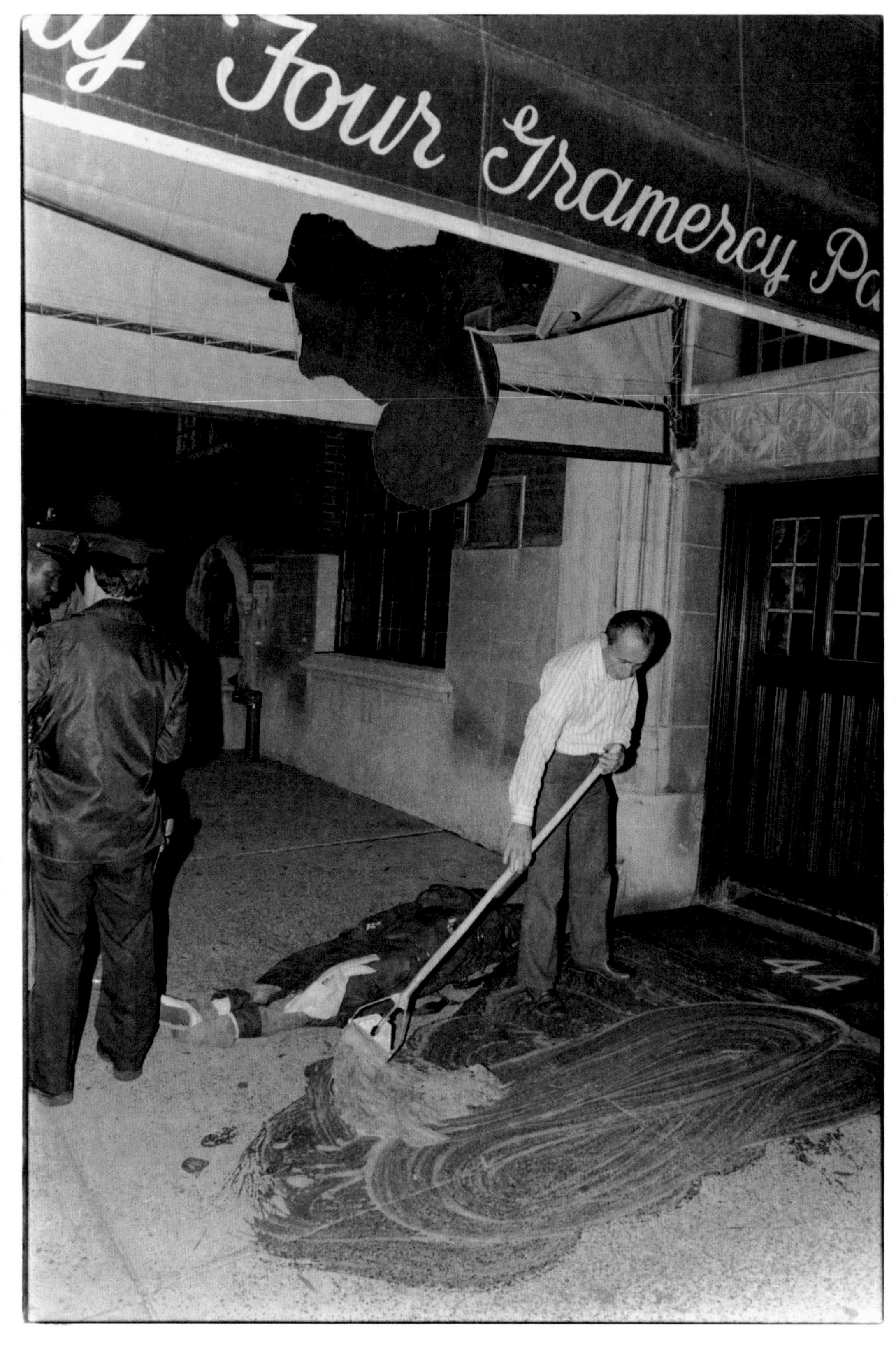

DOORMAN CLEANING UP AFTER SUICIDE. **1986**

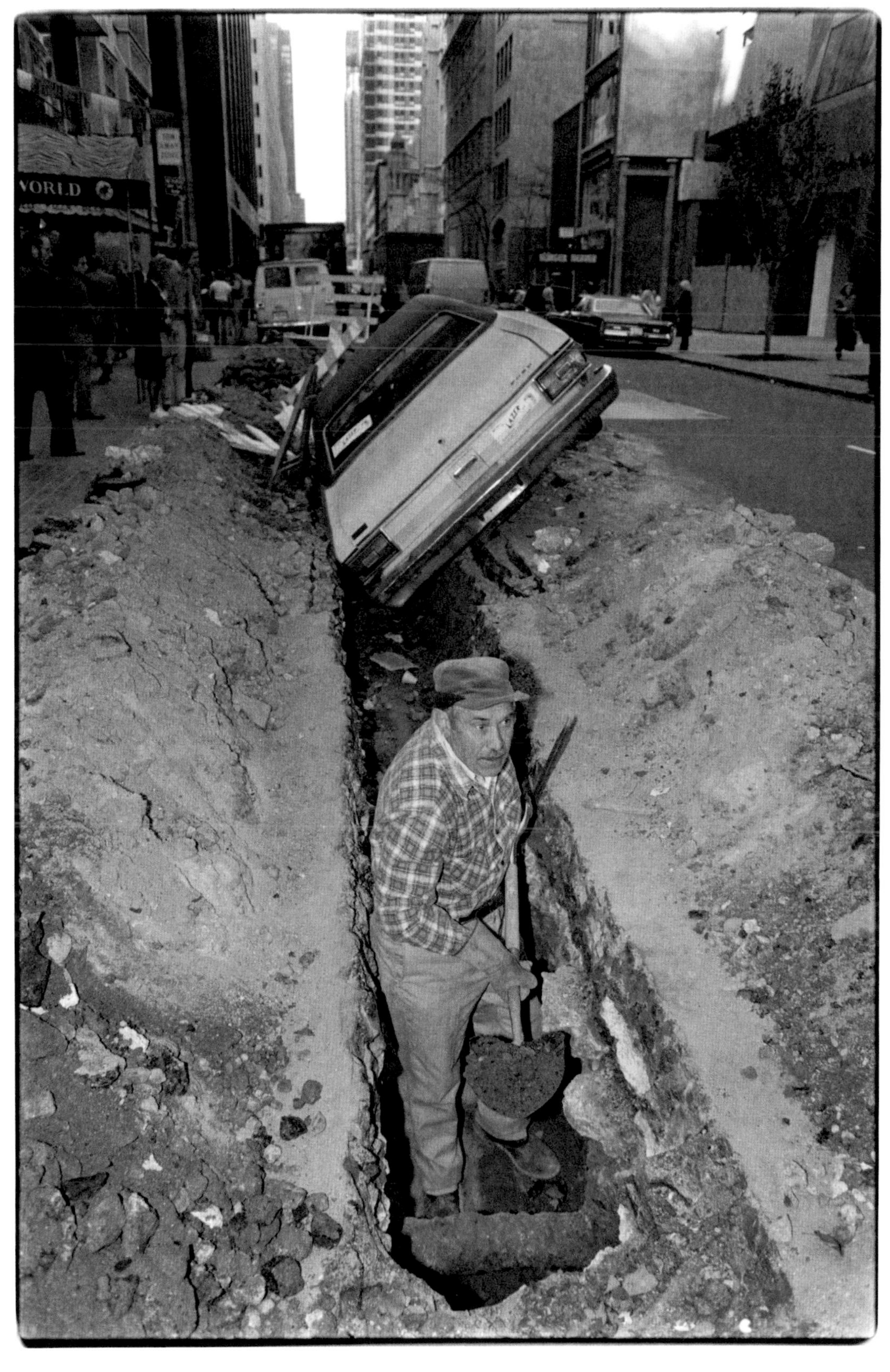

MAN DIGGING DITCH WITH CAR IN DITCH.

1982

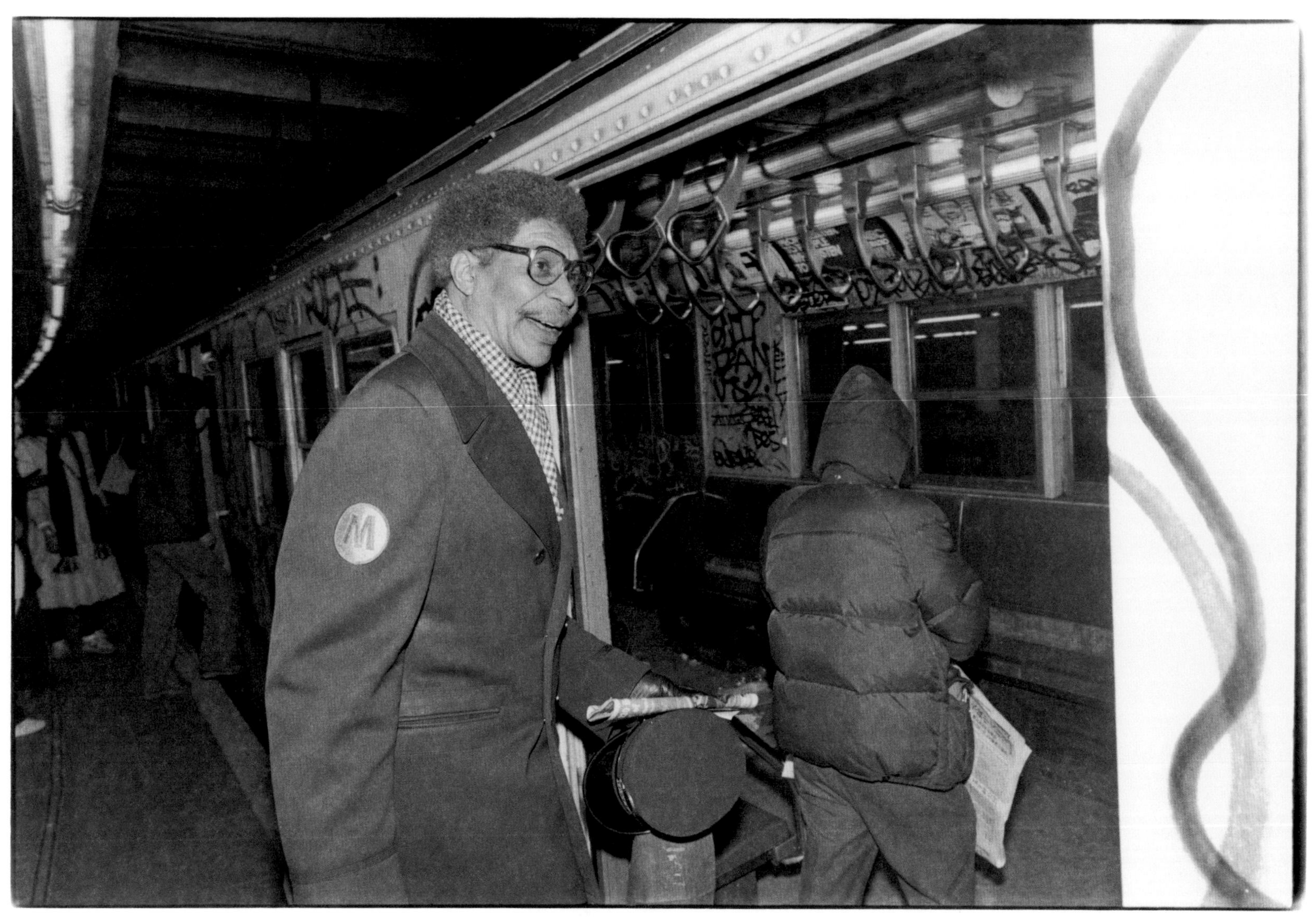

MOTORMAN GOING HOME AFTER WOMAN WAS PUSHED IN FRONT OF HIS TRAIN.

1984

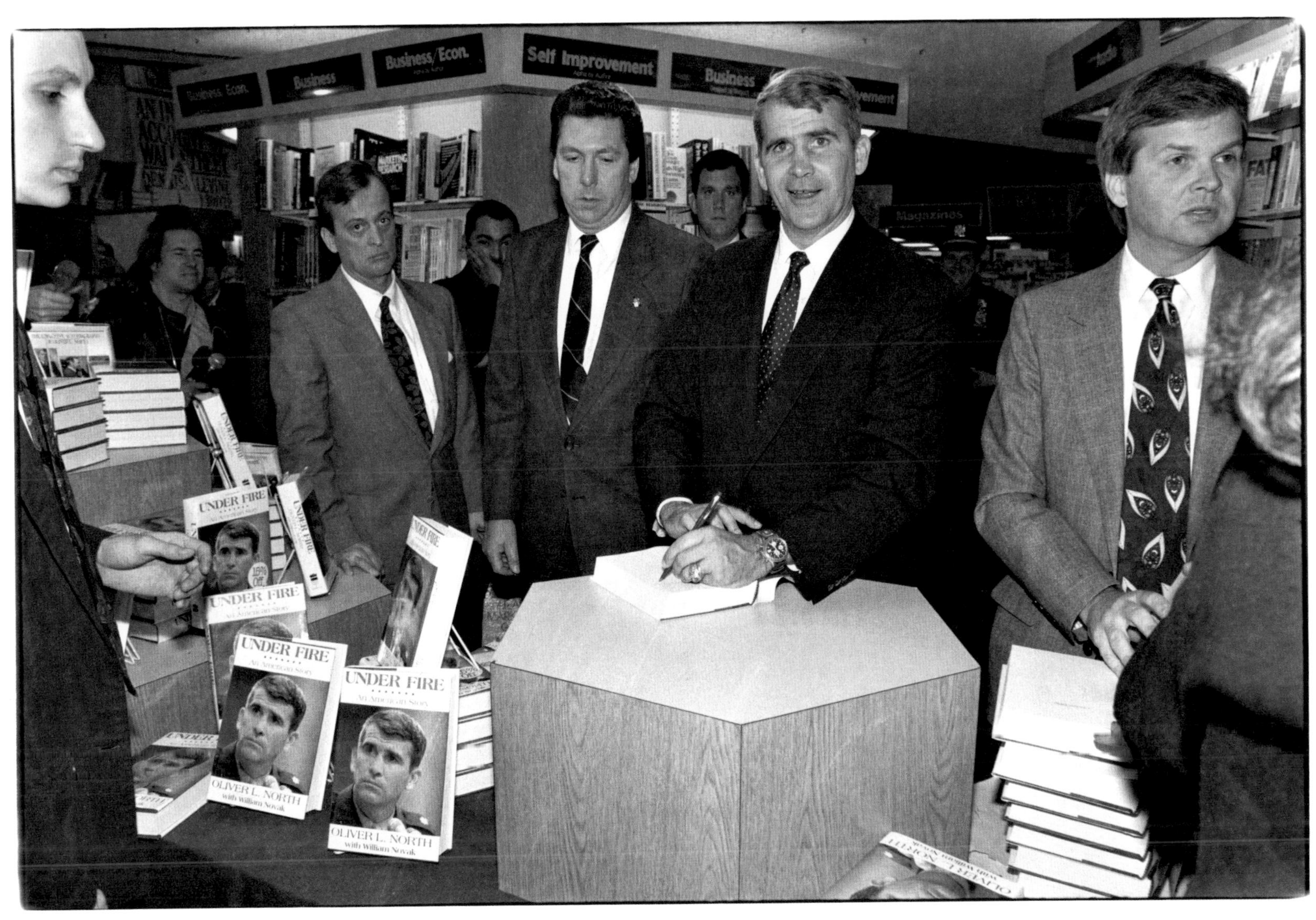

AUTHOR AT BOOK SIGNING PROMOTION.

1980

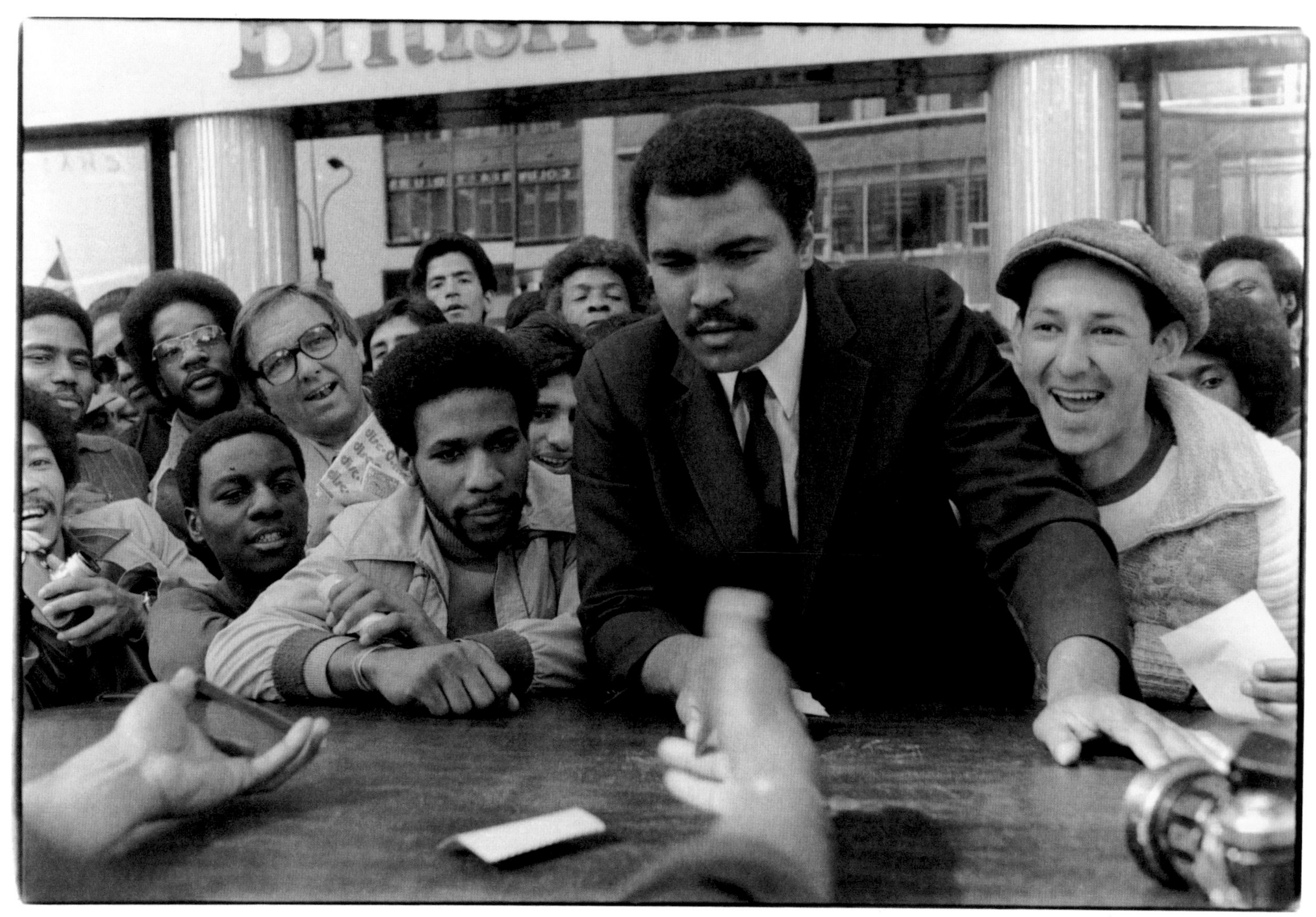

BOXING CHAMP WATCHES MAN DEAL THREE CARD MONTE ON ROOF OF HIS LIMO.

1980

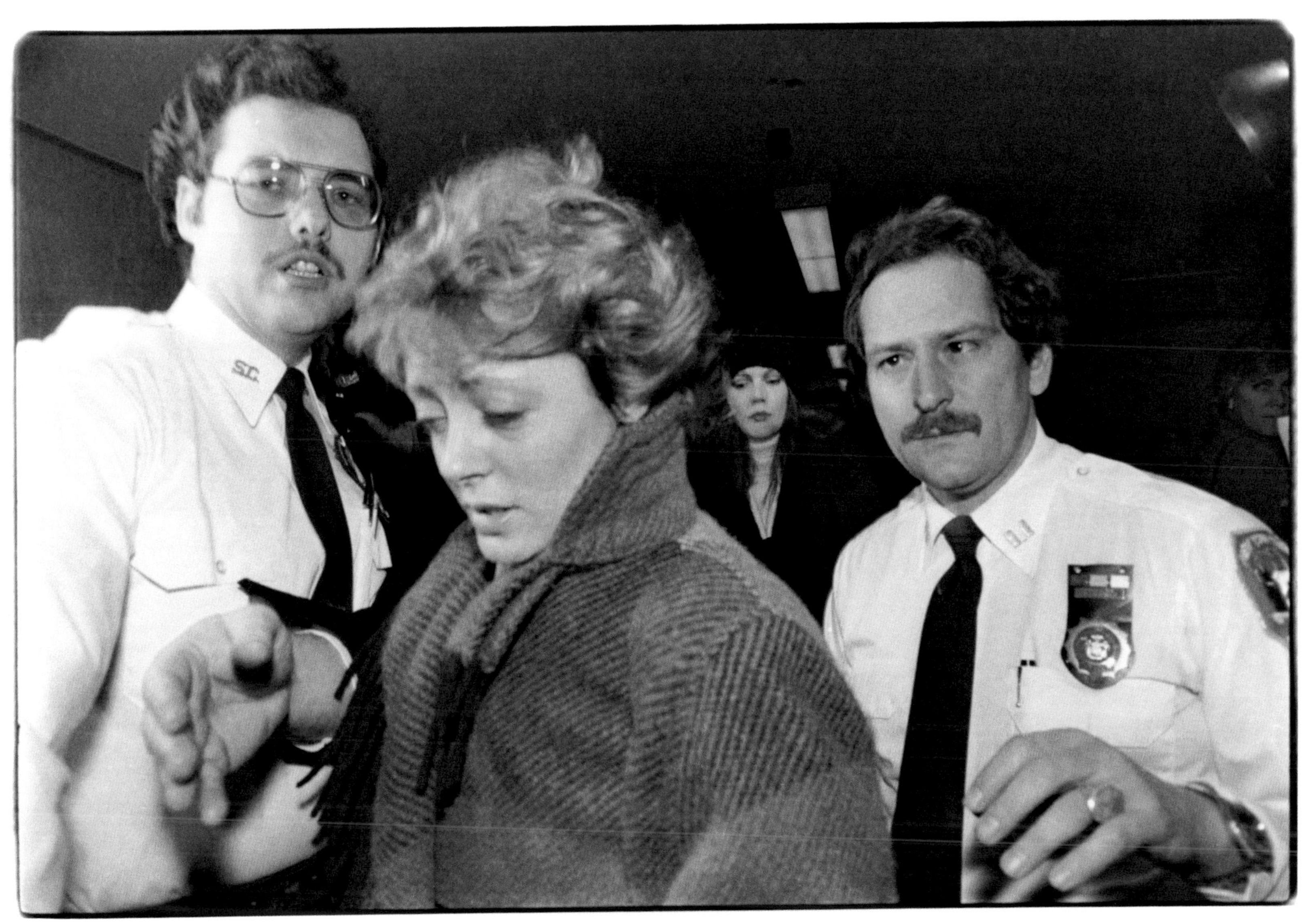

ACTRESS LEAVES COURTROOM AFTER OBSERVING JACK ABBOTT MURDER TRIAL.

1982

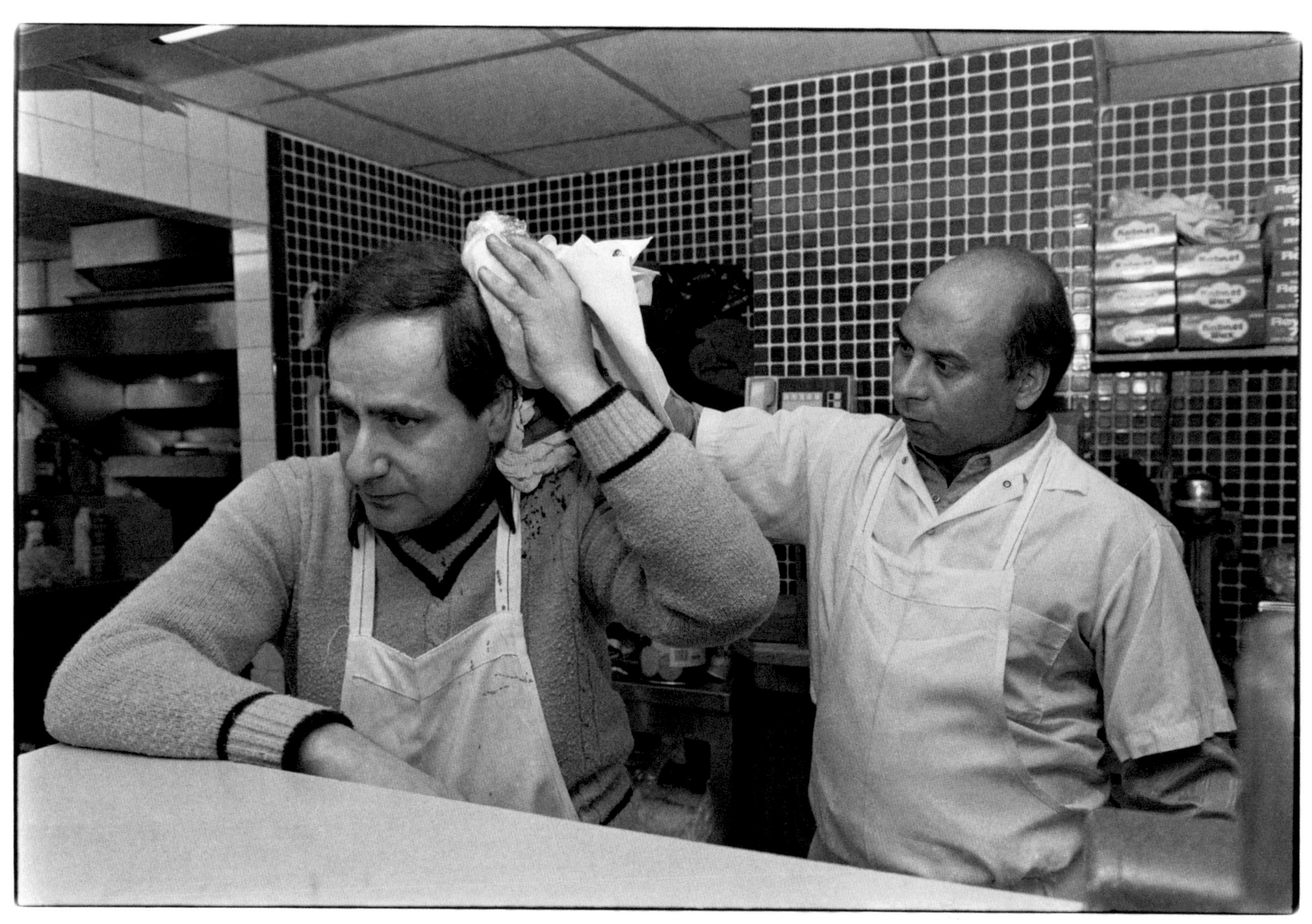

DELI CLERK AFTER CONFRONTING SHOPLIFTERS.

1989

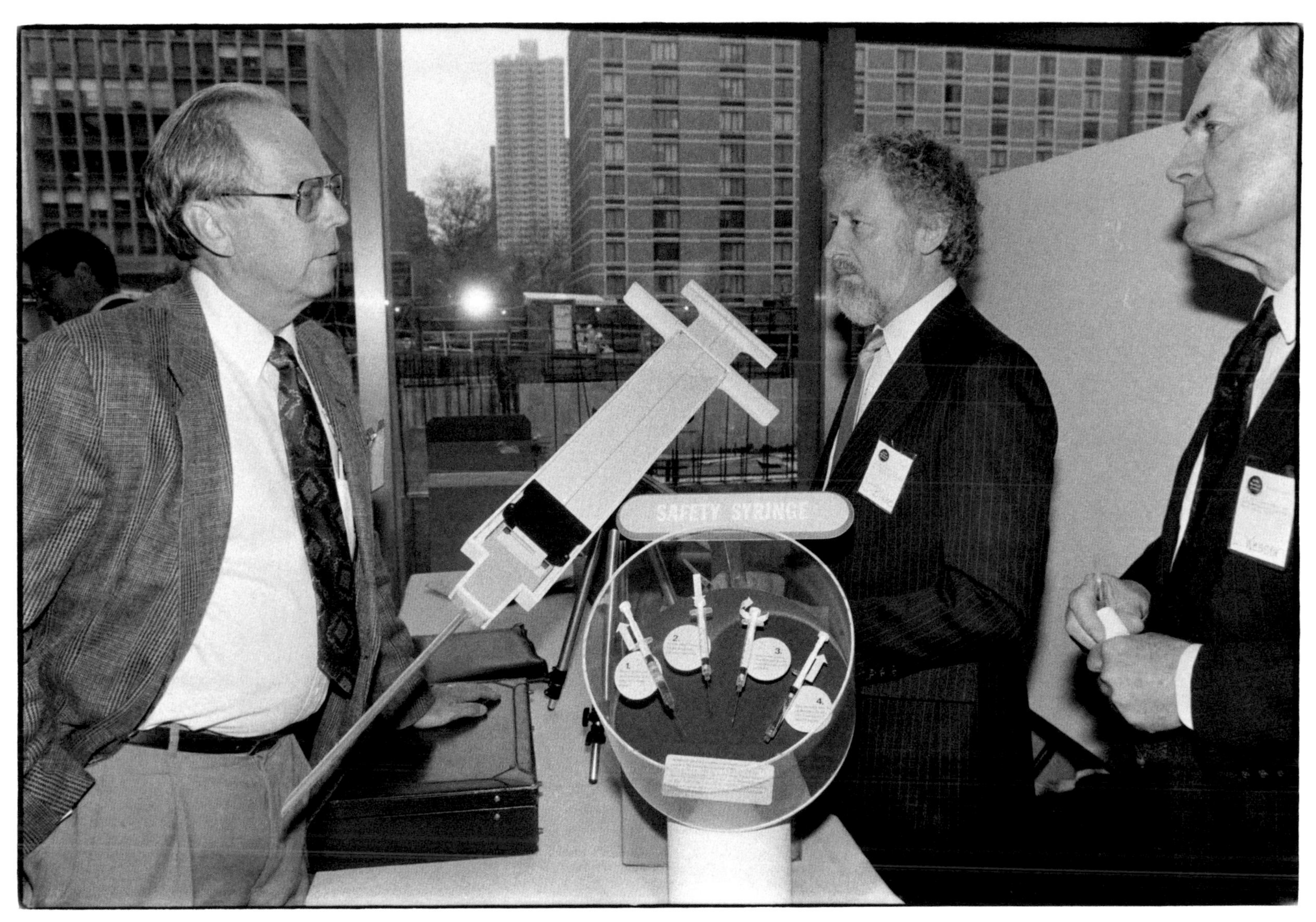

SAFETY SYRINGE SALESMEN.

1987

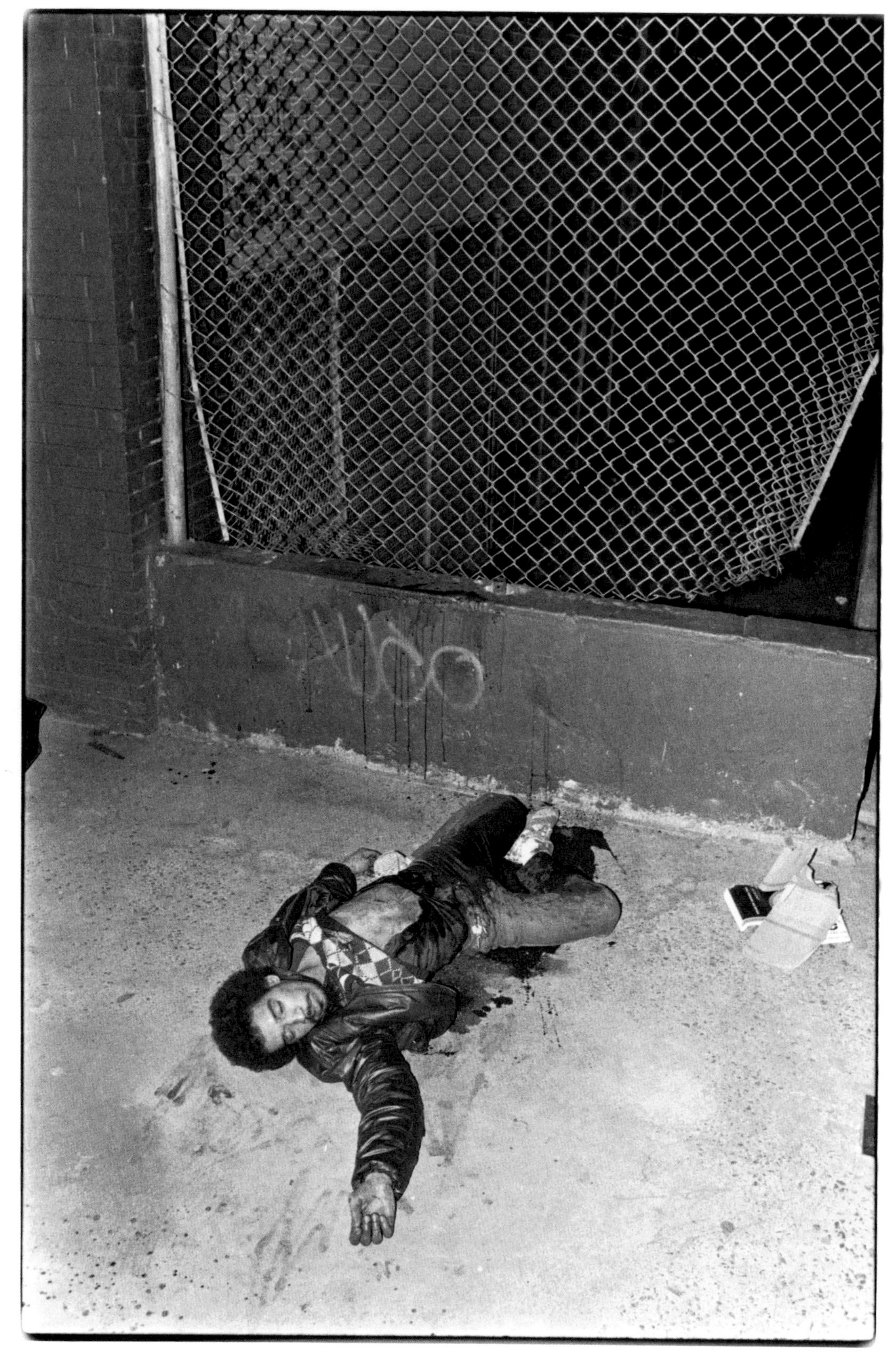

PROJECT STABBING — SPANISH HARLEM. 1983

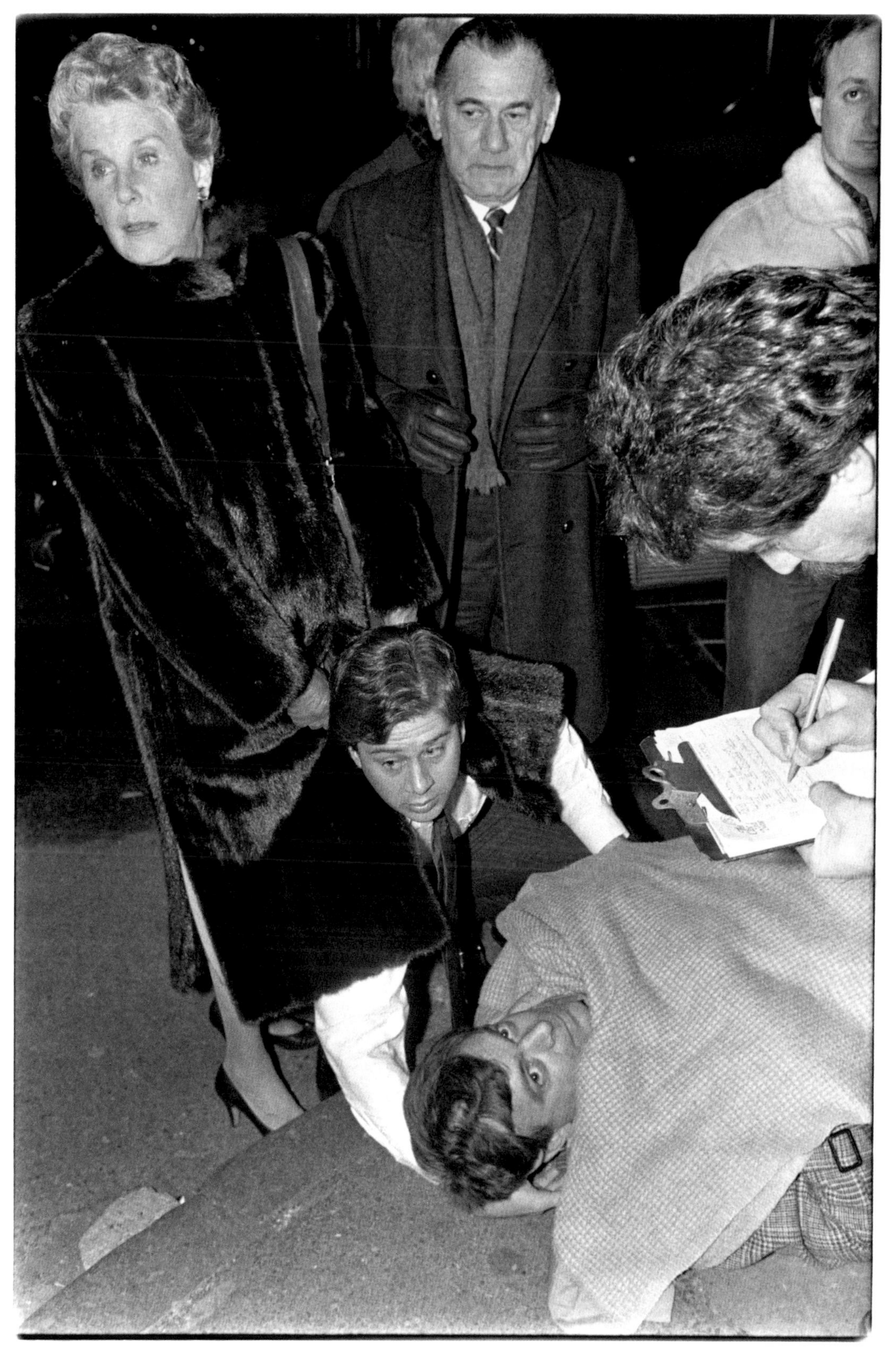

MAN SLIPS ON ICE IN FRONT OF THE WALDORF ASTORIA. 1984

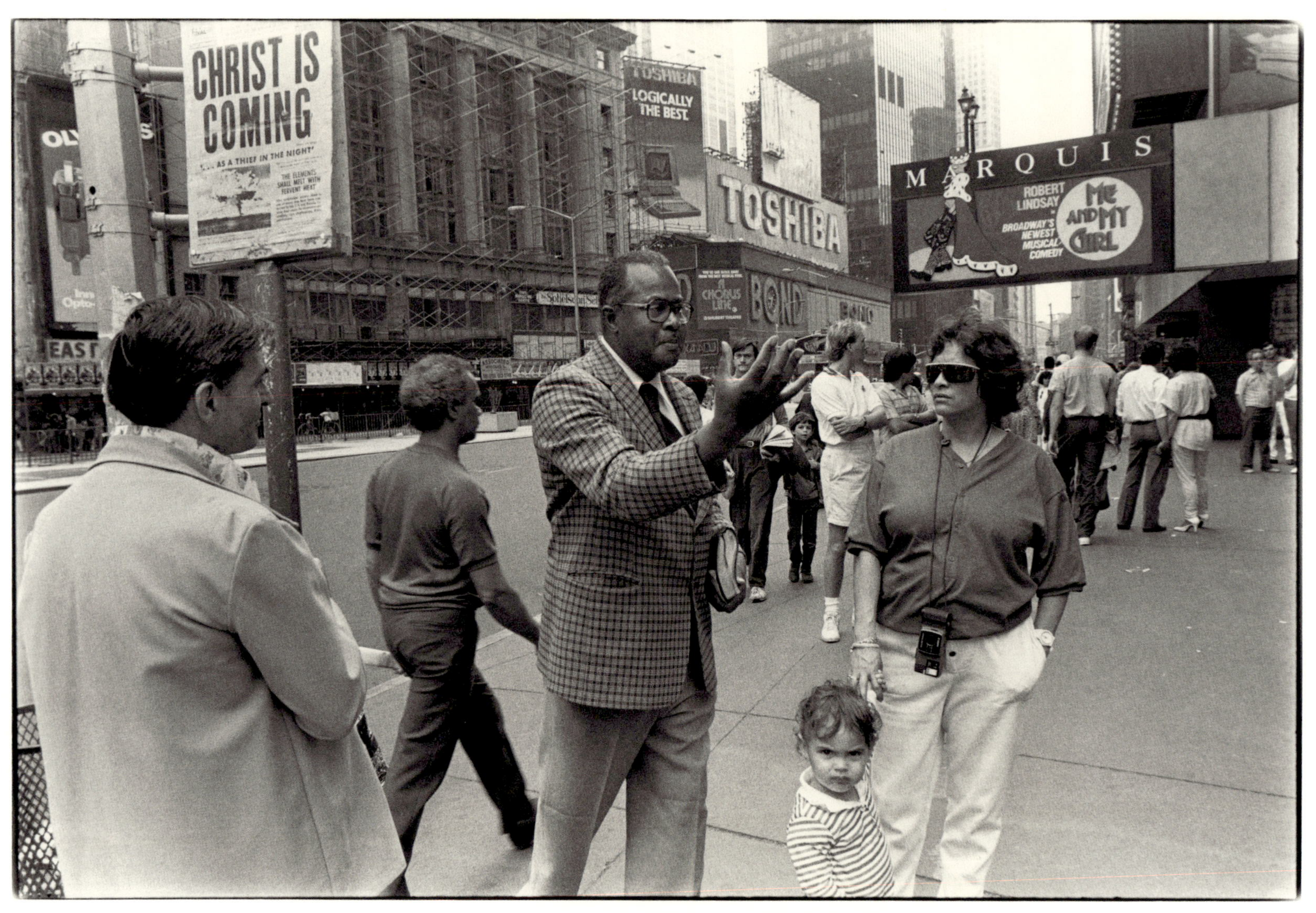

SIDEWALK PREACHER WITH PEDESTRIANS — TIMES SQ.

1987

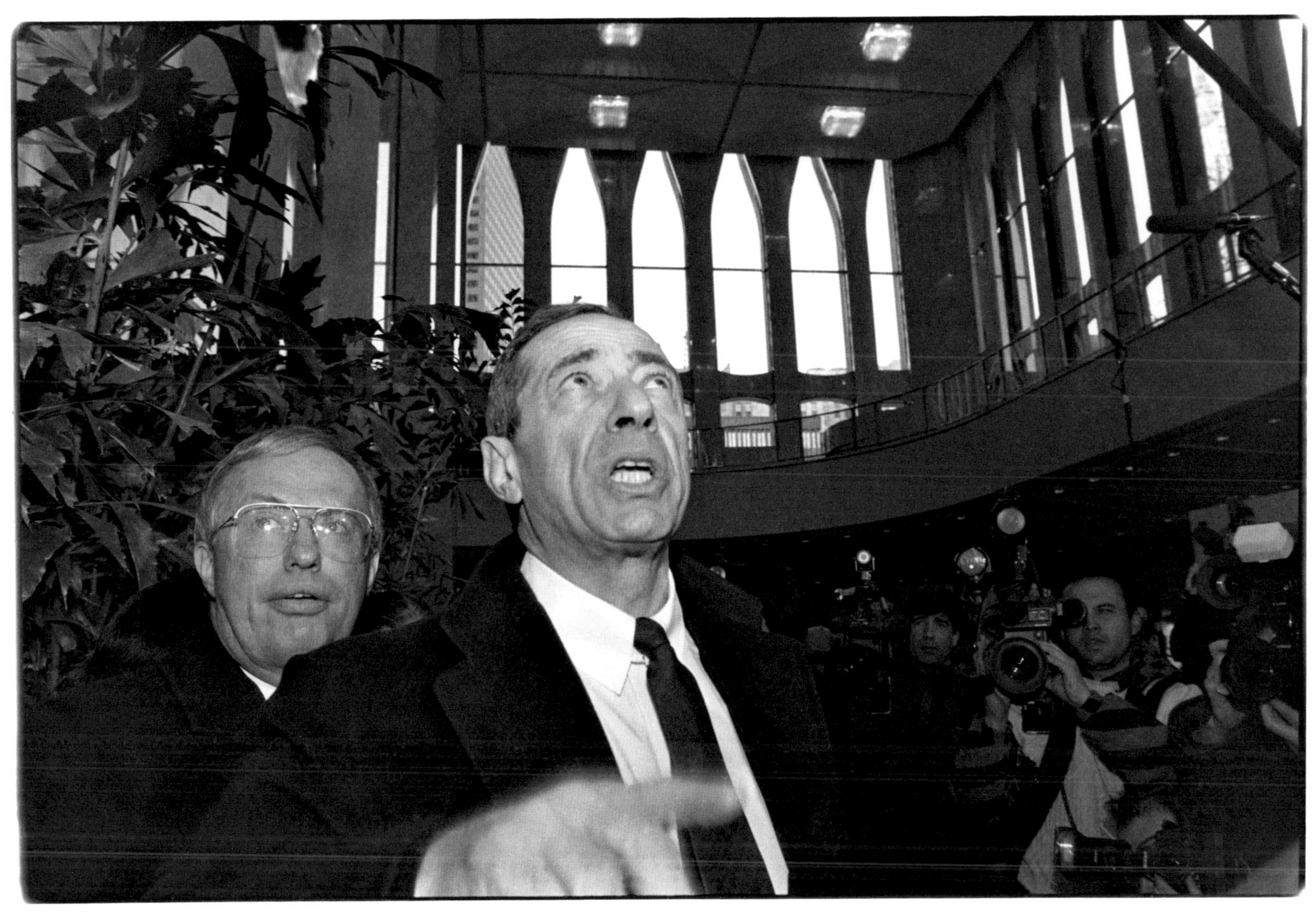

POLITICIAN DURING REOPENNING OF WORLD TRADE CENTER AFTER TERRORIST BOMBING KILLED 6 PEOPLE.

1993

BRENDAN BERNHARD

DRIVE FAST, THINK FAST, SHOOT FAST: IN TIMES SQUARE WITH ANDREW SAVULICH

For over fifteen years, Andrew Savulich parked his battered '67 Dodge Coronet on the edge of New York's Times Square, waiting for something to happen – preferably something disastrous. As anyone familiar with his work can tell you, he has not waited in vain.

A street photographer, Savulich is also a practitioner of what is known in the trade as "spot news" – capturing the daily dose of real-life madness, murder, mayhem, and sheer weirdness that sells newspapers and fuels a growing number of tabloid television shows.

In his singular way, Savulich is a part of this phenomenon. "Taxi Driver Explaining how an Argument With His Passenger Caused Him to Drive into The Restaurant" reads the caption to one of his funniest photographs – surely the ultimate image of someone trying to talk his way out of trouble in a foreign language without a chance of succeeding. "Stolen from a Brooklyn Church at Christmas – Saint Bernadette was Found Dumped Near the Belt Parkway" reads the title of another. The photograph shows a detective draping a blanket over a statue, as if it were a corpse. Does he do this out of respect for the Church, or merely out of habit? It's hard to tell, but Saint Bernadette, with her hands folded in prayer and eyes raised ardently to heaven, seems an apt symbol of crime victims everywhere: "Heaven help us!"

Then there are the two police officers looking on as the blanket is laid over the statue of Bernadette. In the impassive faces of men who have seen it all, one discerns an uncharacteristic trace of wonder: this is something new for them. As is the case with so many of Savulich's photographs, it is for us too.

On a brisk Saturday afternoon in the autumn of 1994, I join Savulich at his usual spot on the corner of 46th Street and Broadway. It is here that he took one of his favorite photographs, "Tourists Passing Sax Player and Woman on Drugs," a memorable depiction of midtown Manhattan at its seamiest.

But this is another day, with new photographs to take. Savulich, who is 44 at the time, listens to the cryptic messages coming in over his police scanner ("Box 6046, we have a 1030 EMS"), waiting for the particular one of interest that will send him racing across the city. Wryly, he points out the "Death Clock" across the street, on which the annual number of homicides in the U.S. is recorded. As for the last homicide he recorded, he can't remember when it was. "It could have been last week," he says with a shrug and a smile. "After a while it all gets mixed up."

About an hour later, a hot-dog vendor arrives with his cart. Savulich smiles and waves to him. Although they have seen each other on this corner for years, he is not sure if the vendor knows what he does. "A lot of people think I'm an undercover cop," he says. "Especially if I've got the window open and they hear the scanner."

Not that Savulich looks like an undercover cop. Rail-thin, his shock of grey hair set off by a black turtleneck and jeans, he could as easily be an undercover priest out to save wayward souls. Everything about him speaks of his sympathy for social outcasts – the poor, unlucky, addicted, insane, and just plain weird.

In material comfort, Savulich seems to have no interest whatsoever, as anyone spending five minutes inside the chaotic mess of his car would attest. From the outside, it's an interesting antique, the kind passersby like to point out ("Hey, that's a '67 Dodge Coronet!"). Inside, however, it feels like an antique, and an uncomfortable one at that. Junk covers everything, the seats are excruciating, the windows begrimed or impossible to open. The all-important police scanner is propped up on planks of wood; the glove compartment is held shut with a paper clip.

After waiting two hours for something unusual to happen, something finally does. Although the incident begins 28 blocks uptown, it ends up almost right in front of Savulich's car. On 74th Street and Columbus Avenue, a drunk has stolen a Con Edison truck belonging to the city and raced off downtown. By the time he barrels into Times Square, police sirens are wailing and Savulich is already out of his seat. Camera in hand, he races across the avenue, dodging vehicles and pedestrians as the truck screeches to a halt after being blocked off by police. A crowd of spectators gathers, impatient to learn the meaning of what they've just witnessed.

Savulich wants to know, too, but instead of asking the person next to him he dives into the fray and takes pictures. Inside the Con Edison truck, the police are giving the driver a good working-over. Savulich tries to get a picture of this but the police manage to keep him from doing so. At one point he gets knocked to the ground and gashes his knee. Whether the man stole the truck as a prank, or was so drunk he thought he was stealing an ordinary truck, no one knows. But the humorous possibilities make for typical Savulich material.

Nonetheless, even before he has had a chance to develop the photographs, he is dissatisfied with his performance. He knows he didn't get the shot he wanted. "If I'd been on the other side of the truck I could have had pictures of the cops arresting him," he says, visibly annoyed. "But by the time I realized what was happening, it was too late."

In the end, though, Savulich may have got something better. One picture, taken after the beating, shows the cops shoving the truck-thief into a car, his face cut and bruised. Whatever they did to him, it must have been painful. As if to underline the fact, a rental car ad in the background of the photo flashes a perfect visual pun: EXACTLY LIKE HERTZ.

Seeing Savulich at work like this, one realizes why he tends to shy away from discussions about his "art." It's not just a question of modesty (although he is modest), but because he feels such discussions miss the point.

To be a "spot news" photographer of Savulich's quality involves much more than a good eye and an original sensibility, even if those are what ultimately set him apart. For one thing, you need to know how to sit in a car as patiently as a gumshoe, sometimes for hours on end, waiting and listening to the cacophony of voices on the police scanner without dying of irritation or boredom. Then, once an interesting tidbit finally comes over the scanner – word of a fire or bank heist, or of a man threatening to leap off a building on God's personal instructions – you have to note down the address, decide on the quickest route, and arrive at your destination before the action is over. In short, you need to be able to drive fast, think fast, and shoot fast – usually in that order.

Once on the scene, events usually move too rapidly for Savulich to go on anything but instinct. Often he doesn't have time even to look through the camera lens. Instead, he just points and shoots, improvising composition on the spot, trusting that the sensibility he brings to the moment will show up on film.

Remarkably, time and again it does. Somehow, out of the sensationalist tabloid material saturating the media, Savulich has fashioned what is unmistakably his own edgy, unnerving vision. The first clue to this is laughter, which in front of many of his compositions is impossible to suppress. But the laughter, which at first seems heartless, is not misplaced. It surprises you into feeling. And when you are confronted by photographs before which it would be impossible to muster a chuckle, such as the gruesome "Driver trapped in Car Wreck," you feel the other side of laughter – terror – in a sharper, heightened way.

Savulich has sometimes been dubbed "the new Weegee." Although it's a label he finds embarrassing, it is to "Weegee" – nickname of Ascher Fellig, the legendary New York press photographer who worked the crime beat in the 1930s and 40s – that his work is frequently compared. Savulich likes Weegee but dislikes the comparisons. "It's not like I'm in competition with the guy," he says in some exasperation

Point taken. Nonetheless, the comparison with Weegee can be revealing. Weegee's gangsters, formally dressed as they were in dark suits, hats, and ties, at least occasionally had style and grandeur, even after being shot dead on the sidewalk. But the people in Savulich's photographs, belonging as they do to a less aesthetically coherent time, seem to have no style whatsoever. Everything about them appears as haphazard as the horrific deaths and freak accidents that befall them. Even when they're simply doing a job, as in the photograph "Man Delivering Bird Seed to Sex Shop," everything about the world they inhabit seems horribly, terribly wrong.

Savulich does feel comfortable talking about the economics of his vocation. He points out that it has been easier to place his photographs in museums such as the Metropolitan Museum of Art, and in magazines such as Artforum and Spy, than it has been to find a steady job taking pictures. He repeats an old photographer's joke: "The best way to make money with a camera is to sell it." After years of supporting himself by doing construction work, however, he did finally land a position as a staff photographer for the New York Daily News. Like most freelancers coming in from the cold, he is extremely grateful to have it.

Despite his reluctance to talk about his art, when pressed, Savulich does concede that "to some extent my pictures are about society and what's happening at this point in time." He mentions the work of August Sander, whose methodically encyclopedic portraits of post-World War I German society are a touchstone for him, and sees a similar documentary compulsion underlying his own work.

I ask Savulich if what he photographs ever gives him nightmares. He says it doesn't, but confesses to occasional insomnia and an inability to fall asleep "unless everything is perfect." Then he mentions the night he photographed a man who committed suicide by hanging himself from a tree in Riverside Park, which borders Manhattan's Upper West Side. The man was still dangling from the noose when he photographed him. "That was pretty heavy," he admits. "I needed a few drinks after that one." He titled the image, one of his most horrifying, "Man Hanging from Crab Tree." He didn't identify the man, but he did identify the tree.

As for the satirical streak that runs through so many of his photographs, Savulich refers to his ancestry. "There's a town in the Ukraine where they have an annual Black Humor Day. People play all these weird, sarcastic jokes on each other. Maybe I'm typically Ukrainian in that respect."

Maybe. But you suspect there is a little more to it than that.

BIOGRAPHY

1949	Born in Wilkes Barre, PA, on Sept 16
1971	BS Landscape Architecture, Rutgers University
1971-75	Lived in Boston/Cambridge, worked for firms as landscape architect, started interest in photography
1975-77	Lived in NYC and attended Hunter College, studied MFA (painting & sculpture), dropped out
1977-88	Traveled around the US
1979-93	Moved to NYC, became freelance photographer, worked as construction worker
since 1993	Staff photographer for the NY Daily News

SELECTED BIBLIOGRAPHY

Feb 90	*Art News*, Photographers and painters working in NYC
Aug 91	*Spy*, article about his work with photographs featured
Oc 91	*Photonews* (German), article about his work with photographs featured
Oct 91	*Tempo* (German), article about his work with photograhs featured
Jan 92	*The Independent* (British), article about his work with photographs featured
1991-93	*Spy*, photograph featured in each issue under title: "It's A Wonderful Town"
Winter 94	*Granta* (British), photographs featured in issue #46 "Crime"
Aug 94	*Das Magazin* (Swiss), article about his work with photographs featured
Fall 99	Reflections In a Glass Eye (Bullfinch), Anthology book of I.C.P. Collection
Sept 02	*City Of Chance* (Filigranes Editions) (French)

AWARDS

1986	N.E.A. Fellowship Grant in Photography
1992	Ernst Haas Photographer Work Grant

PERMANENT COLLECTIONS

1990	The Bayly Art Museum, University of Virgina
1992	The Metropolitan Museum of Art, NYC
1994	International Center of Photography, NYC

SELLECTED INDIVIDUAL EXIBITIONS

2002	Musée de la Photographie, Charleroi, Belgium
2001	Journées Photographies, Bienne, Switzerland
2000	Cas dos Crivos, Encontros da Imagen, Braga, Portugal
1995	Camerawork Gallery, San Francisco
1994	International Center of Photography, NYC
1990	Forum für aktuelle Fotografie Berlin e.V., Berlin
1989	Toronto Photographers Gallery, Toronto
1987	Fabrik-Fotoforum, Fabrik, Hamburg

First edition published in 2015 •

Book design: Andrew Savulich, Sarah Winter, Sabine Hahn • Scans and separations by Steidl, Achim Grohs, Reiner Motz • Production and printing: Steidl, Göttingen

Steidl • Düstere Str. 4 / 37073 Göttingen / Germany • Phone +49 551 49 60 60 • Fax +49 551 49 60 649 • mail@steidl.de • steidl.de

ISBN 978-3-86930-690-2 • Printed in Germany by Steidl